# LORD *of*
# PUBLISHING

*Cover image:* Working with Stan and Jan Berenstain involved constant growth. In the eighties, Stan began to dream of motion picture and/or television adaptations of the Berenstain Bears stories; he eagerly hoped a film or TV show would stimulate book sales. Eventually, we heard Nelvana, the Canadian animation studio, had a deal with PBS to provide an animated strip show and we began negotiating with them. The pile of pages in the cover photo represents that one deal alone. The resulting show premiered in 2003. Its half-hour-long episodes ran five days a week on PBS stations and have reached 92 percent of the US over the years.

# LORD *of* PUBLISHING
## by Sterling Lord

OPEN ROAD

INTEGRATED MEDIA

NEW YORK

*To each and every one of my writers*

# CONTENTS

# CHAPTER 1

# Kerouac and Me

He rang the bell and walked through the door of my office, a below-ground-level room I had liberated from being a one-room-plus-bath studio apartment just off Park Avenue. He was wearing a light-colored weather-resistant jacket with a lightweight checkered shirt underneath. He was striking looking—"diamond in the rough" was the phrase that came to mind.

Two weeks earlier, legendary literary editor Bob Giroux of Farrar, Straus and Giroux had called to alert me that Jack Kerouac would be coming by. Giroux was one of the first established editors I had met. He had called and introduced himself and then took me to lunch. Obviously he wanted to meet the new kid on the block, and in particular he had heard that my client Ralph G. Martin was working on a book that he—Giroux—might like to see. The Martin project never developed, but the Kerouac did. I'd heard of Kerouac but knew very little about him. Giroux had edited *The Town and the City*, Jack's first and only conventional novel. Jack had just been to see him—it was 1952—and he needed a literary agent. Giroux thought I would be the right man. I was two years older than Jack, and as a starting agent, I had a good deal of energy and time. He added that Jack had typed his new manuscript on a 120-foot scroll of architectural tracing paper. That would be *my* problem, Giroux said.

Jack had the manuscript wrapped in a newspaper, which he extracted from a weather-beaten rucksack. He called it *The Beat Generation*, and he had already taken Bob Giroux's advice and retyped it on regular typing paper. He was courteous and respectful, but we didn't talk at length. He was leaving the product of years of work (and three weeks of typing) in my hands. He told me Giroux had rejected it.

This is the agent that Jack Kerouac saw—the way I looked and the desk I used every day, while I was trying to get him in print—in the fifties and sixties. It took four years to find a publisher who would take *On the Road*. I wore a tie to work daily, but contrary to the dress habits in the early twenty-first century, almost every man in the agency business did wear a tie then. In that period, all male agents were called gentlemen. I wore a necktie because I was brought up to do so, and I had dressed that way previously in my magazine office in Paris. Jack did not mind. In fact, he told me he liked my wearing a necktie.

It was actually the first novel submitted to me in my agency work, and I read it carefully, carving out time from the demanding nonfiction projects on my calendar. I was really taken with it. I called Jack and told him how strongly I felt about the manuscript and that I was ready to go with it. I felt that his was a fresh, distinctive voice that should be heard.

As we started working together I came to respect him and he, me. That mutual respect prevailed over all the differences in our backgrounds. Jack had grown up in Lowell, Massachusetts, a mill town, and came from a working-class family. I'd grown up in a middle-class family in a primarily white, comfortable Midwestern city and had a nondramatic traditional upbringing (before World War II). I was impressed with Jack's commitment to serious writing at the expense of everything else in his life. At a time when the middle class was burgeoning with new homes, two-tone American cars, and black-and-white TVs, when American happiness was defined by upwardly mobile consumerism, Kerouac etched a different existence and he wrote in an original language.

Jack was handsome, and in a bar or a crowd I noticed women thought so, too. He had dark eyes and prominent eyebrows set off by ruddy skin. I don't recall his ever wearing a suit and tie into my office. He dressed in a slightly disheveled way, which was not an affectation; it was just Jack. In public, he bore an intense look, though when he was among family and friends he would offer enough of a smile so you knew when he was happy. He was articulate, careful in his speech. He did not talk the way he wrote.

Jack felt comfortable with me and with other friends, but I saw he was shy and did not do well in public. I think that was why, at least in part, he drank so much. When he drank he may have been a little less shy, but he was not obstreperous.

Book publishing was still very traditional then, and I was not totally surprised or discouraged with one rejection after the other. For four years I could not find an editor or publisher who shared my enthusiasm for *On the Road*.

The most striking rejection was from Joe Fox at Knopf, a publishing house known for the high quality of its books and for which Joe was one of the very best young literary editors at the time. Kerouac,

Joe said, "does have enormous talent of a very special kind. But this is not a well-made novel, nor a saleable one nor even, I think, a good one. His frenetic and scrambling prose perfectly expresses the feverish travels, geographically and mentally, of the Beat Generation. But is that enough? I don't think so."

Jack found the rejections too depressing. On June 28, 1955, disheartened by my lack of success, he wrote me that he wanted to "pull my manuscripts back and forget publishing." I noticed he was not saying he was discouraged about writing; it was publishing that discouraged him, and of course most of the male editors working at publishing houses at that time were from a very different generation. I thought I knew Jack well by then, so I ignored his request and continued submitting. Twelve days later he changed his mind and we went on as before. I still believed his work would eventually be published.

I had already begun to realize how subjective the publishers' decisions were and to rely on my own judgment. Jack told me he believed in me and my judgment, which helped.

After almost four years of trying to sell Jack's manuscript, I sold a piece of his to the *Paris Review* with the help of Tom Guinzburg, an editor at and soon-to-be president of Viking Press, and a board member of the *Paris Review*. He had read Kerouac and already believed in Jack. A few months later, I sold one, then another piece from the manuscript to *New World Writing*, a literary magazine in pocketbook format, published then by New American Library. Shortly after the second story appeared, I had a call from Keith Jennison, a young Viking editor. He, Malcolm Cowley—a distinguished literary critic and associate editor at Viking—and Tom Guinzburg were the strong Kerouac fans at Viking.

"Dammit, Sterling," Keith said, "we can't let that manuscript go unpublished any longer." He made me an offer of $900 against royalties. I said no, got him up to $1,000, and closed the deal. Jack took the good news in stride. He had come to believe the book would eventually be published, and its happening now was merely a confirmation of his belief.

Shortly after the contract was signed, Helen Taylor, an experienced senior editor, whose first love was music, began working with Jack to edit the manuscript, while the lawyers expressed their concerns about the names and likenesses of some of the book's characters. She and Jack had an initial struggle over style. Her editing was extremely sensitive. She made cuts and very minor changes without in any way impeding the flow of Jack's prose, although that wasn't how Jack felt. The two came to an understanding. Jack's understanding.

In an extraordinary letter to Helen—extraordinary because Kerouac had not yet become *the* Jack Kerouac—he wrote in almost defiant language what he demanded of his editor and publisher. He left no doubt who was in charge. And for any skeptic who might have thought his book was only the underdeveloped essays of a free spirit and not the thoughtful writing of an exacting writer, this letter alone would dispel the myth:

> Dear Helen,
> Here are the galleys exactly as I want them published. I want to be called in to see the final galley and check it again against my original scroll, since I'm paying for this and my reputation depends on it . . . Just leave the secrets of syntax and narrative to me.

He then went comma by comma, explaining why he'd done what he'd done. For example, he wrote:

> My "goodbye" (the spelling of it) is based on the philological theory and my own belief that it means "God be with ye" which is lost in the machine-like "good-by."

He advised her that he'd written "I was seeing the white light everywhere everything," not "the white light everywhere, everything."

He was not averse to having an editor. Jack acknowledged that in an entire manuscript he might have ten or twelve "mistakes or serious problems."

In a friendly tone, Jack suggested that on his next manuscript, they could thrash it out together, but, he warned, "no more irresponsible copy-editing of my Mark Twain Huckleberry Finn prose."

By then, he and Helen had an understanding, and so he concluded:

With freedom in mind I can write a book for every October.
See you soon, and mucho thanks.

Jack

I sold a subsequent book of Jack's, *The Subterraneans*, to another publisher, whose initial editing was totally insensitive. Fortunately, we caught it before publication. *On the Road* became the only manuscript of Jack's that was ever edited. Jack had become such an important literary figure that he could and did demand complete control over his words. At Jack's request, I would include in each contract the following clause: "The publisher may not change a word of the manuscript nor alter the punctuation," or some variation thereof.

But in preparing *On the Road* for publication, both Jack and Viking wavered on the title. It was to be either *The Beat Generation* or *On the Road*. John Clellon Holmes, who was Jack's friend and my friend and client, had used the term Beat Generation in a popular publication first. His article, "This Is the Beat Generation," appeared in the *New York Times Sunday Magazine* on November 16, 1952. In the end, *On the Road* won out. In my humble opinion there was never any contest. *On the Road* is a much more descriptive, seductive title. "Beat Generation," I am convinced, would have limited the life of this book.

A year after Keith Jennison's call, during July and August 1957—the book had not yet been published—I began to feel the swelling wave of enthusiasm and excitement for it. Half a dozen times in the early afternoon, I had calls from one publishing person after another, all expressing the same sentiment: "Sterling, I just had lunch with so-and-so of Viking, and all he (or she) could talk about was the Kerouac novel." It didn't make any difference which Viking editor they had lunched with, the conversation was the same. This was the book they were all excited about. At a publishing house like Viking, in those days the enthusiasm was genuine, not a conscious, staged production. It was very effective.

On September 5, 1957, *On the Road* was launched with an electrifying *New York Times* review by Gilbert Millstein. An extremely perceptive and talented writer himself and a man of great integrity, Millstein, who was well connected with the current culture, was filling in for the regular *New York Times* reviewer, Orville Prescott, who was on vacation. It was serendipity: No one at the *Times* could have done it better. Prescott was of a different generation, and his reviews tended not to be as colorful or dramatic as Millstein's turned out to be. Millstein called the novel "a historic occasion . . . an authentic work of art," adding that it was "the most beautifully executed, the clearest and most important utterance yet made by the generation Kerouac himself named years ago as 'beat,' and whose principal avatar he is." Millstein likened the importance of *On the Road* to Hemingway's *The Sun Also Rises*, and he called the writing "almost breathtaking."

One striking reaction was that of the excellent young literary editor at Lippincott, Corlies "Cork" Smith, who had been reading the Millstein review on the train en route from Philadelphia to his office in Manhattan. He was so affected that he did something rather extraordinary in publishing: Instead of going to his office—where he could have phoned a fellow editor at Viking for a complimentary copy, as was the usual practice—he hurried to the closest bookstore and actually *bought* a copy himself.

At the same time, *Esquire* magazine, known for publishing new and interesting writers, had been sitting on a story by Jack Kerouac for months without making an offer for it. I couldn't get a decision from them. But the day after the Millstein review appeared, they called and made me an offer for "Ronnie on the Mound," a portrait of a pitcher and an interesting piece, but not Jack's best work. So much for *Esquire's* good taste.

The review made a very strong impression, and the press wanted Jack in New York immediately. I reached him in Florida and left word. He called back shortly after, asking if he could borrow $25— this was 1957, remember—for a bus ticket to New York. I had previously loaned him $40 so he could buy a Christmas present for his mother. Years later I learned he had also borrowed money from his mother and written his friend Joyce Glassman asking for $30. At that time, Joyce's apartment—although I didn't know where it was in the city—was Jack's personal headquarters when he came to New York. And using our money, he managed to get to the city without delay.

Once Jack arrived, he was taken in hand by Pat McManus, Viking's very experienced head publicist, but shortly thereafter, around 11:15 one morning, Viking phoned: Where was Jack? He was about to miss publicity appointments. I thought I knew where he was. I had heard it from Jack the day before. I hailed a taxi to take me to 65 West Sixty-Fifth Street, Joyce's apartment. When I arrived, Jack was lying on his back on the living-room floor. He was already overwhelmed, shocked by the swift change from obscurity to smothering adulation. But he pulled himself together and made the appointment on time.

From that day on, writers, all of whom had read the Millstein review, and most of whom had actually read Jack's book, began phoning, mailing, and drifting into my office from all over the country. I remember a would-be author who had driven nonstop from Denver in his battered Ford with a cardboard patch over a broken window. He was not alone. There were a number of other young men who wrote about or acted out copycat cross-country trips like those described in *On the Road*. The manuscript of the Denver writer, as you might guess, was totally unpublishable, as were most of the others. Almost all were superficially imitative of Jack's writing on his subject, but without his talent.

The displays of curiosity, admiration, even hero worship continued for months. One night after Jack had spent a tiring day in New York City, he took the train back to Northport, Long Island, arriving shortly before midnight. He had to walk across a couple of fields to get home to Gilbert Street, where he was living with his mother, whom he called Mémère. When he arrived, his front porch was crowded with young people—none of whom Jack knew—who had been waiting for hours to party with him. It was almost dawn when he climbed into bed.

Benzedrine was a part of Jack's creative life. Before he told me that in letters, I was reading a manuscript of his and noticed the tempo and pacing of his prose changed around page 40. When I called him he explained he'd been drinking a lot of coffee. (He had written *On the Road* on "after dinner black coffee," explaining that he was younger then.) I interpreted that to mean that as he aged, he needed stronger stimuli. Early in 1960 he planned to write a novel called *Beat Traveler*, but was waiting for his supply of the amphetamines to arrive so he could start.

Jack never actually spoke to me about using drugs. I think he looked on me as rather a nonuser of any stimulant—I was a social drinker in those days, I never did drugs, and I hardly even smoked cigarettes or cigars. For a while, in my thirties, I smoked one pack of cigarettes a week, though I never inhaled, and I stopped abruptly one evening when my wife said, "Sterling, you never used to cough like that when we first met." I never finished that cigarette. I'd played sports all my life, and it was important to me to stay in good physical shape.

What my writers did in this area was their business, not mine. I was concerned only if and when their indulgence negatively affected their creative talent, and even then there was not anything I could do about it. I remember one Southern writer, a fine talent, thought drinking was a part of being a successful writer. He eventually dried out, but that was an area of his life I wouldn't touch unless asked.

In my experience, Jack was extremely confident in himself and his own writing. But he was also somewhat psychologically reliant on me.

One by-product of his sudden fame was comments on his sexuality. He hung out with men and with his mother. Many readers of *On the Road* thought the relationship between Dean Moriarty and Sal Paradise had homosexual overtones. Jack was never seen escorting women. A historian wrote a play about him from the point of view of his alleged homosexuality. I had a different experience. One night when I was out on the town with Jack, at his suggestion we visited one and then another woman he knew, and there was nothing in Jack's demeanor that indicated anything but attraction to the female sex. Subsequently, I spoke with Ed Adler, former professor of art at New York University and the author of *Departed Angels: Jack Kerouac, The Lost Paintings* (2004), who told me he had recently seen a list drawn up by Jack, and in the possession of John Sampas, one of the Kerouac heirs and a relative of Jack's wife Stella, of around forty women—names and locations—with whom he had had sexual relations. Jack may have been high at times, but he was also methodical.

Jack did not respond well to the sudden fame, and the long-term effects were devastating. I felt he was basically shy, and any time he came to New York City, which he considered not to be part of the real world, he had to fortify himself with alcohol. Jack was asking for help—he knew he was drinking too much—and I agreed to take him to a doctor who thought he could help. The doctor turned out to be totally ineffective. Eventually I began to accept the fact that, fond as I was of Jack, I was only his literary agent, not his life agent.

One positive, creative response to the publication of *On the Road* came from John Knowles, an editor at *Holiday* magazine, a glossy, high-end Curtis Publishing travel magazine. Knowles, who was also an author—*A Separate Peace* (1959)—assigned a number of articles he wanted Jack to write. The articles "New York Scenes," "Alone on a Mountaintop," and "The Vanishing American Hobo" were later published in Jack's book *Lonesome Traveler*, a collection of his short pieces about his travels through the United States, Mexico, Morocco, Paris, and London. They were written with the same intensity, stream of consciousness, sense of detail, and storytelling as his novels.

Even though Jack eventually stopped working for *Holiday*—there were editing problems—I was so taken with those pieces and with Jack's original point of view in general, I actually thought having Jack write about a Manhattan office building would make an interesting book. His whole point of view was so different and original to people of my background and, I think, to many traditional book buyers, that I thought he could write on almost any subject and it would be interesting. Jack declined. "I'm writing about my life, like Céline," he told me. That was the second time I had heard him mention Céline, and it was now obvious to me that Louis-Ferdinand Céline, author of what many consider to be one of the most brilliant and controversial novels of the last century, had been a strong influence on my client. Jack indicated to me that he had read *Journey to the End of the Night*, Céline's first and best-known work, which was published in French in 1934. It wasn't published in English until 1983 (New Directions), but I assumed he had read it in the original French since Jack was raised in a French-Canadian family and it is well known that his first language was French.

As original as Jack's prose is in the English language, it reflects that of Céline, who many years before wrote not in formal French but in bursts of innovative language of the street, which at the time was considered vulgar.

Critics and literary historians have speculated about the connection and some have suggested that not only Kurt Vonnegut Jr. (who in a 1981 collection of his writing acknowledges Céline's influence), but also Henry Miller, Charles Bukowski, Joseph Heller, William S. Burroughs, and Ken Kesey, in addition to Jack, were indebted to Céline, though the critics and literary historians questioned the connection because the English translation didn't occur until many years later. For Kerouac, the date of the English translation would have been irrelevant.

When he first lived in Northport, Jack invited me out to spend a weekend—or at least part of one—with him and his mother. This was before he married his third wife, Stella. He and Mémère were living in a rambling frame house at 34 Gilbert Street with a spacious front porch and a garage behind the house. They didn't own a car, but the garage supported a basketball backboard and basket at regulation height, and there was a flat dirt-and-gravel area where you could bounce the basketball and expect it to come back up almost as predictably as it would from a hardwood floor.

Jack thought of me as a deskbound shirt-and-tie man, far from athletic. But he had heard in passing that I was interested in tennis, one of the few sports he had never played. (He was a star football player in high school and promising as a freshman at Columbia University, until he broke his leg.) In honor of my appearance in Northport, Jack created a basketball game scored like a tennis match. I discovered later that he'd also been practicing all week before I arrived. I didn't tell him I had played basketball in junior high, high school, and college (as well as half a dozen other sports), and I beat him soundly. Jack was stunned. And he never forgot it. Years later—in fact, the last time I saw him before he died—he brought it up again, still astounded at the outcome. "I still can't believe it," he said.

Jack also had a nice, subtle sense of humor. Not boisterous or often apparent, but it was there. One day, impressed by a line I had heard in a television commercial, probably for an insurance agent, I started closing my letters to Jack, "Your friendly neighborhood literary agent," and then signing my name. A few weeks later I had the following letter from Jack:

> Dear Sterling: —
> Just a note to say "Hello" —
> From yr. friendly neighborhood writer —
>
> GIVE MY REGARDS TO BROADWAY
>
> As ever
> Jack

When he and his mother moved to Florida in May 1961, he wrote enthusiastically about the home, its screened porch and its backyard. It was a relatively simple wooden structure. It was, he said, like coming back to America. They had a guest room they named "Sterling's Room." Hoping to lure me down for a visit, Jack assured me there was a tennis court nearby. I did eventually go down, but without my tennis racket. (Although I was playing tennis several times a week in New York, I always preferred to choose my opponents myself—that's what a national ranking will do to you.) And when I was visiting a client, that's what I was there for—not tennis. Any time I spent with Jack and Mémère I was reminded—not told—that Jack had promised his father on the latter's deathbed that he would take care of his mother. In general, I think he did.

Since then people have asked me how it felt for me, being a small-town Iowan, spending time with a cultural icon. Before this question came up, I hadn't thought about it. Jack was just Jack, and I treated him the same way I treated the boy who lived next door to me as I was growing up. His name was also Jack—Jack Birkenstock, who wanted to be a Major League pitcher but didn't make it. Kerouac was an interesting man, and I always felt comfortable with him.

The last night I spent with Jack was a sad one. I was in Tampa to lecture at the University of South Florida at the request of Professor Ed Hirshberg, brother of my longtime client Al Hirshberg, the well-known Boston sports columnist. I had one free evening to spend with

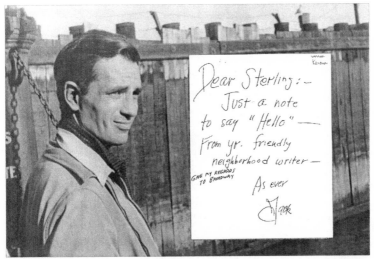

Photo of Jack Kerouac courtesy of the Allen Ginsberg Trust

Sometime in the early 1960s, I noticed newspaper ads for an insurance company, the name of which I don't remember, which referred to their friendly neighborhood agents. I didn't know any friendly neighborhood insurance men myself, and it seemed a little ridiculous, but it was a catchy phrase, so I started signing my letters to Jack Kerouac, "Your friendly neighborhood literary agent." Jack did have a sense of humor. It wasn't evident very often, but one sunny day I got this letter (above), which not only copied my friendly neighborhood reference, but gave his regards to Broadway. In all our years together, it was the only letter I received from him that was so openly humorous.

Jack in St. Petersburg. At our first stop, I ordered a beer, and Jack ordered a double scotch with a bottle of beer as a chaser. By the time I finished one-third of my beer, Jack had consumed both scotches and his entire bottle of beer.

At the second bar, just a few streets away, the same thing happened. As we moved on to a third, luxury bar, I noted that Jack was still pretty steady on his feet. At that bar a pool game was in progress, and you could get in the game for twenty-five cents. Jack did, but I looked around at the other players and outside at their trucks, and after chatting briefly with one of the players, I realized this was no ordinary pickup game. These players were mainly truck drivers en route from Chicago to Miami (or vice versa) who had by prearrangement all shown up to play. Fortunately, the player in charge realized Jack was a little shaky and gently eased him out of the game before he could rip the felt, and we, soberly and drunkenly, went back to Jack's house.

Two weeks later, when I had returned to New York, Jack more or less repeated his tour of the St. Petersburg bars. This time he was alone, and the men he confronted were not gentle. This time they broke his arm.

On October 21, 1969, at 4:30 in the morning, I was sound asleep in my New York City apartment when the phone rang. The call was from Stella, Jack's wife. She was choked with emotion as she told me that Jack had just died. He was forty-seven years old and died of alcohol-related problems. It had been almost twelve years since *On the Road* was published; I was shocked and expressed my sorrow. I had the presence of mind to tell her I was in the process that very week of negotiating a film sale of *On the Road* to JGL Productions at Warner Brothers. She had been dreaming of such a sale, but it was too much for her to address. With a short gasp she hung up. Despite her sorrow, she also called a St. Petersburg bank officer, the trustee of Jack's estate. By the time I reached my office at 9:30 that morning, the trustee was on the phone assuring me of my right to continue functioning as Jack's agent. And I, in turn, told the bank that Jack had on his own initiative on March 4, 1958, signed a note appointing me his literary executor.

A few days later, I was on a plane to Boston en route to the funeral in Lowell, Massachusetts, the old mill town where Jack had grown up. It was a Friday morning, and I went directly to the church where the service was under way. Then on to the cemetery for the funeral.

I can still see the scene around the grave: the sunlight filtering through the trees, the leaves brown after losing their fall colors. And there at the gravesite were Beat author and close friend John Clellon Holmes; Allen Ginsberg, full of sadness; Jack's first wife, Edie Parker; members of his wife's family, the Sampases; and a group of the working press. At the wake at the Sampas home I was told that Jack had done nothing but drink—no food—the last few days of his life. A knowledgeable friend told me that's impossible—you have to eat something, usually around ten to eleven in the morning. It turned out my friend was right: Jack had been taking bennies.

Decades later, near the end of the twentieth century, I was in Lowell, Massachusetts, for the annual Lowell Celebrates Kerouac Festival, and on my last day there—a Sunday—I visited Kerouac Park, so that I would have a quiet moment to reflect on Jack. The sun was bright and the sky was a delicate blue with a few scattered clouds. Surrounded by old mills and buildings of another time, the park is an extraordinary tribute, which seems to promote reflection and tranquility. On a patch of green, eight triangular columns of carnelian granite stand with carved quotations from Jack's books. On one side of one column are Jack's name and dates, on the other are quotes from *On the Road* including the final words. I thought how poignant and beautiful. It was Jack at his best:

> So in America when the sun goes down and I sit on the old broken-down river pier watching the long, long skies over New Jersey and sense all that raw land that rolls in one unbelievable huge bulge over to the West Coast, and all that road going, and all the people dreaming in the immensity of it, and in Iowa I know by now the children must be crying in the land where they let the children cry, and tonight the stars'll be out, and don't you know that God is Pooh Bear? The evening star must be drooping and shedding her sparkler dims on the prairie, which is just before the coming of complete night that blesses the earth, darkens all the rivers, cups the peaks and folds the final shore in, and nobody, nobody knows what's going to happen to anybody besides the forlorn rags of growing old, I think of Dean Moriarty, I even think of Old Dean Moriarty the father we never found, I think of Dean Moriarty.

The park is a work of beauty and, like Jack, it embraces America: The granite was quarried in South Dakota and cut in Minnesota, the graphic design was done in Virginia, and the sculptor, Ben Woitena, a Texan, studied in California.

This was the last day of my appearance at the festival, and there was no one in the park at that hour—no one except me and a friend. I had been forty-two years old when I met Jack, and had made a few little-known writers famous, but none had risen from obscurity to such worldwide acclaim as Kerouac. As I stood there reading the inscription devoted to *On the Road*, I couldn't help but reflect upon Jack's enduring impact on my life and the lives of many others.

My thoughts returned to the present when I noticed a man waving at me from across the street. I vaguely recognized him from the crowded hall where I had spoken with him the day before. He came striding across the street toward me, thirty-five-millimeter camera in hand. He asked if he could take my picture as I stood in front of the monolith containing the inscription from *On the Road*. I agreed, of course, and after he had snapped three photos and thanked me, he said, "You know, Sterling, none of this would have happened without you." Although that was more than a slight exaggeration, I thanked him.

In the years after *On the Road* was published, Ed Adler interviewed a number of prominent artists about influences that had shaped their work. He talked with Robert Rauschenberg, who worked in mixed media with found objects such as stuffed hens, tennis balls, and tires, and who bridged the worlds of abstract expressionism and pop art; Roy Lichtenstein, who painted eye-popping, primary-color comic-strip-type characters on canvas; Jim Rosenquist, a pop artist who painted disconnected objects in a billboard genre; and Tom Wesselmann, who painted nudes in bold colors with pop art's advertising aesthetic. Adler interviewed many others, and they all told him that their greatest literary influence was Jack Kerouac and particularly *On the Road*.

In 1999, at the funeral service for Gilbert Millstein at Frank E. Campbell Funeral Chapel on East Eighty-First Street in Manhattan, among the many laudatory remarks on Millstein's life, the one specific event mentioned was his review on September 5, 1957, of *On the Road*. Millstein's greatest contribution to our culture may have been his ode to a once-obscure author.

Years later, as I was starting work on this book, I called Bob Giroux, then retired, to ask him about his relationship with Jack and his encounter with Jack's 120-foot manuscript. "I did not reject *On the Road*," Bob told me. "I never read it. I merely told him, 'Jack, don't you realize that the way authors present manuscripts now is on eight-and-a-half-by-eleven-inch white paper?'" Bob had rolled up the scroll and handed it back to Jack. He didn't say so, but I'm sure that despite his list of very prestigious authors, he regretted losing Jack. A few years after publication of *On the Road*, he came to my office to look at the original manuscript, there in my safe.

Bob, a remarkably gifted and clever editor, suspected that the scrolled version of *On the Road* was appreciably different from the edited version published by Viking, but his reading told him that there was not enough difference to allow for a separate publication, which defeated his imaginative idea. (Interestingly enough, in 2007 Viking published the scrolled version of *On the Road*.)

In 2009, more than fifty years after its original publication, *On the Road* was selling 100,000 copies each year in the United States and Canada. It is read, taught, and assigned in high schools and colleges all over the United States and has also been published in twenty-four foreign countries. In some Greenwich Village bookstores, paperback editions are kept under lock and key to avoid pilferage.

## CHAPTER 2

# From Iowa to New York City—via Paris

The free-swinging and energetic world of Jack Kerouac and Allen Ginsberg and the atmosphere of the Beat Generation were light-years apart from the pleasant, orderly Iowa town where I grew up. In some ways, Burlington, Iowa, represented the life the Beats were trampling on in the fifties and sixties.

Burlington was a modest and prosperous town on the west bank of the Mississippi River, which at that junction was a mile wide. Any young man who swam across it was honored with his name in a two-inch story on page two of the *Hawk-Eye Gazette*.

From the spacious Victorian homes of friends of mine on the bluff in the south part of town, I could look down at the railroad track along the river and then look eastward across twenty miles of flatland to the hills beyond. The legend was that through the centuries, the river had moved west to where it is now.

On sweltering summer days, I could see static fishermen lazing on the bank with a rod and line, waiting for fish to mosey by. On the bridge across the Mississippi was a sign facing drivers entering Iowa from Illinois that read:

WELCOME TO BURLINGTON
30,000 FRIENDLY PEOPLE AWAIT YOU

That always bothered me as a young boy because I knew it was inaccurate; there were only 26,000.

Burlington was known as the shopping center of southeastern Iowa and western Illinois. On Jefferson Street, the main street of the city, the Schram Brothers owned the big department store, which hired me at an early age to stand at the door and count the people who came in the last weekend before Christmas.

Burlington, like Rome, was built on seven hills—all of which, by the time I arrived in the autumn of 1920, were dotted with houses. The city stood at the confluence of rail lines and the Mississippi River. It was home to the Burlington Route, formerly the Chicago, Burlington and Quincy Railroad. With the arrival of the Burlington Zephyr in April 1934, local businessmen were able to board the train for Chicago early in the morning for a day's worth of business and return that night—and many did.

Timber from the forests of Minnesota was floated down the Mississippi to Burlington, which became a center for furniture manufacturers. My father was general manager of one of four furniture factories in town and every day—until we moved to the edge of town, when I entered the third grade—he walked to work.

We led a simple, orderly life in a town with few social or political divisions.

Burlington was an almost all-white town whose citizens were Protestant and Republican. When the first African American minister moved in, my father immediately befriended him at a time in history when my father's friends would not have dreamed of doing such a thing. But at the same time, they all had such respect for my father, they would never judge him for doing it. Along Main Street, near where the Burlington Route passed the tracks of a north-south railroad called the Burlington & Northern, is where the few African American families lived. There was little interaction between the races. In a bluff farther south paralleling that railroad was a cave that years before had been occupied by the Black Hawk Indians. On weekends, my father and I would climb up and explore inside.

My parents were such private people that they never told me how they voted. They were conscientious citizens but they weren't particularly political, and given how accommodating they were, I'm sure they voted for the same candidate so as not to cancel out the other's vote. The only Democrat I knew in town was Ray Baxter, our outspoken postmaster. I knew he was a Democrat because Franklin Delano Roosevelt was president, and postmaster was a political appointment.

Burlington was not a culturally rich city, and few creative spirits were nurtured there. When I grew up, Catholics were considered an outside group. Sammy Goldberg, two years younger than I, played on my high-school tennis team, but at the time I didn't know he was Jewish or what being Jewish meant. I liked him.

Half a block off Jefferson Street was Gnahn's bookstore, which was highly regarded but not large enough to hang out in. The Burlington Public Library, about three blocks up the hill, was operated by stern-looking older women and was forbidding to a young boy.

Long after I left Burlington, the library became the focal point of a controversy that was emblematic of our small town. Whittlesey House, a division of McGraw-Hill, published *One Foot in Heaven* by Hartzell Spence, about life with his father, a Methodist minister who had preached in Burlington as well as other towns in the Midwest. It was a delightful book, very well reviewed, and the publisher had to go back to press at least eight times to keep up with reader demand. But a number of women in Burlington recognized their town and felt they had been depicted critically in the book without their permission. The town was called Riverton, which the author acknowledged was a pseudonym, describing it this way: "The city was notable chiefly for its insincerity and entrenched smugness." The women of the town pressured the local library not to order or stock the book. And the newspaper editors obliged, not running stories about the book, which is not unusual for life in a small town that considers itself under attack and where everyone knows everyone else, or at least their husbands do.

I was born Sterling Lord Jr.—my father was Sterling Lord—but I later dropped the "Junior." As a child I was close to my family and stood apart from my peers. Other kids, I believe, saw me as standoffish. I think my name, which separated me from the Bills, Dicks, and Toms of Burlington, was part of that. Everyone called me Ster. I didn't particularly like it, but I never thought of dumping it either. Sterling was a family name.

I grew up in a rented house only four blocks from Jefferson, the main business street, but when I was in the third grade, my parents bought a home on the edge of town, which further distanced me from my peers. When we moved into a two-and-one-half-story stucco house on Bittersweet Place, life changed. We were right next to the Burlington Golf Club, with its nine-hole course, a pond on the eighth fairway that was good for ice skating in winter, and two clay tennis courts.

Both my parents played tennis, and they had me out on the courts when I was five years old. I liked the game almost immediately and must have had an aptitude for it. Those early experiences and successes on the court (by the time I was thirteen, I could beat my mother) gave me self-confidence. And it would be tennis that in later years would give me confidence in dealing with other people.

We were a compatible family, in some ways a universe unto itself.

My mother was the quiet disciplinarian. She ruled with calm authority. She wasn't much of a cook, preferring to garden flowers and vegetables. Even while gardening, she wore cotton dresses that came down several inches below her knees, as women of that era did. She was a devoted wife, serious about her role. She was a beautiful woman with an open face, high cheekbones, and dimples when she smiled. She wore her long, dark hair pulled into a knot on the back of her head. She had expressive eyes and a lovely smile.

My father had a Roman nose and thinning brown hair and was clearly the man in charge, and yet he always retained an inhibiting shyness. When he was courting my mother on the family farm just outside Pittsfield, Massachusetts, he went to her house a few times in disguise, once as a fictitious representative of a foreign-language school in Boston and another time as a hobo. He was amused by the fact that no one recognized him. He had a sense of drama that I think was a way of dealing with his own shyness. In later years, he enjoyed playing charades.

My brother Tom, four years younger than I, was an emotional musician who attacked me with a knife once, when I was teasing him about a girlfriend. (I still carry the scars.) Dick, two years younger than Tom, was busy with projects like an electrically controlled lock for the door to his room. I admired his mechanical and scientific prowess and soon accepted the fact that he wanted to sleep late. When he was thirteen, he set up a toy train that could feed the chickens in the morning without his having to get out of bed. He'd look out the second-story window to see that the track was clear of leaves and then throw a switch, sending the two-car train through an opening in the fence and into the chicken coop. He'd have placed an impediment like a stick on the track. The car would flip over, causing the grain to spill on the ground where the chickens would gather to peck at the grain. It was ingenious! In the late afternoon, he'd load the car with grain and put it in a nearby doghouse, covering the freight car with a large piece of cardboard to ward off nibbling rats and squirrels overnight. The cardboard was wider than the door of the doghouse, so that it fell off as the train left to go into the chicken coop. It took the chickens a few days to get used to it, but it worked smoothly thereafter.

If Dick was our family inventor and scientist and Tom the artist, I was the student and the tennis player. Although I didn't study a lot (there wasn't as much homework then as grade-school and high-school students get today in New York City), I always received top grades. Also, as the eldest, I was closer to my parents than my brothers were. I never heard Tom or Dick complaining about it, but I knew they felt I was the favorite son. I didn't realize it at the time—in fact, I denied it—but in retrospect they may have been right.

My brothers and I formed our own team, although as the eldest, I sometimes had an unfair advantage.

Our parents hoped to interest my brothers in music. My father had played the flute in his younger years, and my mother's family had been interested in opera. We had an upright piano in the dining room, and my parents arranged for lessons for Tom and Dick, but neither one had any interest in practicing. One day over lunch my exasperated father said, "I'll pay five dollars to the first boy who learns to play 'Home on the Range.'" Before either brother took him up on the offer, I taught myself how to play the piece, even though I'd never had a piano lesson. When I demonstrated that I had learned "Home on the Range" for my father, I didn't expect him to pay me the princely sum, even though he had not limited the offer to only Tom and Dick. And he didn't.

My room was across the hall from Dick's room, which was often locked. Two of my three windows faced east, letting in the morning sun, which often woke me early, a habit that worked to my benefit later in life. After looking out over the golf course across the street I would pull down the shades in summer before going downstairs for breakfast. Lowering the shades was important to keep the house cool during the summer, as air conditioning had not yet invaded Burlington. In school, when I wore a short-sleeved shirt, papers on my desk stuck to my sweaty forearms.

On days when the white morning light didn't accost me, I was often awakened by the smell of burned toast, because my Dad, already up and dressed, was in the kitchen listening to the news on the radio and forgetting the bread in the toaster. That was followed by the sound of scraping, as he brushed off the burned part of the toast. As the first son up in the morning, I was assigned by Mother, who slept later, to inspect Dad before he left for the office. Dad, of course, wore a suit and tie every business day, and when he came home at night, he would take off the suit jacket and hang it in the downstairs closet next to the front door. In the morning, he wouldn't put on a suit coat until he was ready to go, and often he would finger the wrong jacket—one that didn't match the trousers. I was to stand at the front door to see that everything matched.

In my bedroom, I had a flat glass-enclosed box on one of the tables, filled with mounted butterflies. This was the era before TV and extravagant children's toys, when young people often were left to create their own entertainment. A number of my friends were collecting butterflies, and for a brief time there was a friendly competition—they would come over to look at mine and try to identify them, and I would go over to their houses and do the same. The butterflies were near the end of my animal-raising period, a common hobby in Burlington in those days, which included white mice, white rats, guinea pigs, chickens, and rabbits, in that order.

In my room I had my wooden tennis racket—a Wilson—and two single beds (one for me to sleep in, the other to throw my clothes on), and pasted to the closet door I had a newspaper clipping from the *Des Moines Register* Peach Sports Pages (yes, printed on peach-colored newsprint) about Buck Newsom, a very talented pitcher who had played on nine Major League baseball teams in his career, but in 1933 was with the St. Louis Browns. The clipping recorded the day Newsom was asked to pitch both games of a Browns doubleheader, and the headline read: "Hurler Batted Out In Nightcap." I had a vision of Newsom getting out of bed in the morning, forgetting to take off his nightcap, and subsequently pitching and losing the game. I was attracted to clever headlines.

When I started school, my father was elected to the local board of education and reelected many times, staying on until my youngest brother finished high school. Thinking we would be interested in it, Dad also became president of the Southeastern Iowa Area Council of Boy Scouts, but that didn't appeal to any of us. And every year he organized and managed a Labor Day weekend amateur tennis tournament—there were almost no tournaments for professional players in those days (the only pros were teaching or traveling pros)—that attracted players from Chicago, Omaha, Des Moines, St. Louis, Kansas City, Minneapolis, and many cities in between. It was truly amateur; the tournament never paid one penny of expenses for visiting players, who were all put up in local homes, thanks to the energy of my mother and her connections with the community.

My father worked to persuade the city to build the tennis courts next to our high-school stadium, which were named after him. And in part because of his success, I convinced the school to buy a ball-throwing machine, an important piece of equipment that allowed the school's tennis players to practice during the winter; we would stretch a net across the indoor basketball court and practice our strokes. It was our way of playing catch-up with California tennis players, who could play on courts year-round.

Although Dad was clearly the head of the family, it was our well-organized, conscientious mother who made everything work and took care of her four males. Mother strongly supported each boy in any activity she and Dad knew about. If the two of them ever had an argument, we never heard about it. It appeared to be a very happy marriage. Each had his or her role, and my mother never seemed to balk at her status as the official helper and caregiver, though I imagine that had she been born in another era, she might have become a serious painter.

While my mother spoke clearly, my father often had trouble explaining himself. I always believed it had something to do with his being ambidextrous. In those days, people who were born left-handed were taught in school to use their right hands. Dad played tennis left-handed and wrote right-handed. There was also his shyness, which I always suspected was the result of his father having gone bankrupt while Dad was at the Hill School, a prestigious prep school in Pottstown, Pennsylvania. As a result of the bankruptcy, Dad was pulled out abruptly, a shattering experience for an already-shy young man. As a teenager, he had to face a situation none of his well-educated brothers had known. At a young age, he had to start earning a living, and I think this experience made him cautious for the rest of his life.

As a young adult, Dad had a number of rather dismal experiences that he wouldn't talk about. One positive experience was his training at Elbert Hubbard's Roycroft Shops in East Aurora, New York. In 1895, Hubbard had been inspired to restore the tradition of the handcrafts in the United States, and Dad was very interested in—and later successful at—bookbinding by hand. My father taught us many subtle lessons: to work hard, respect others, and listen. He introduced me to many accomplished people within his circle of personal and business friends, and there often was a "What did you learn?" dialogue with me afterwards.

During my early years Dad taught bookbinding to Boy Scouts who wanted a merit badge for that activity.

Twenty-five years earlier, after graduating from Roycroft, he and a fellow Roycroft trainee, Peter Frank, opened up the Oakwood Bindery in Pittsfield, Massachusetts. But when World War I broke out, Dad and Peter, who had been born and raised in Munich, Germany, were so ideologically and politically opposed to one another that they parted ways. Dad was out of work and so, too, was the attractive young Oakwood designer, Ruth Towne Whiting. Through her, Dad met the entire Whiting family and would go out to their 200-acre farm in Berkshire

County on weekends. The family sensed he was courting, but because of Dad's natural diffidence, they were not sure which of the six sisters he was interested in. Once Dad made his intentions known, Ruth accepted.

Fortunately Dad's older brother Robert, president of the Guardian National Bank in Detroit, came up with an opportunity. Robert was also a stockholder in the Leopold Desk Company, a successful manufacturing company in Burlington, which had a personnel problem. Carl and Fred Leopold, the principal owners, were both reserve officers in the US Army and both had to go to war. Robert recommended Dad be hired to take over, and after taking the train out to Burlington to look it and the Leopolds over, he accepted.

On April, 18, 1918, Dad started at Leopold, and a little over a year later he returned to the Berkshires to marry my mother. They were married on June 19, 1919, on the spacious lawn of the Whiting family home, surrounded by twenty-five young girls from the boarding school operated by Ruth's sisters Margaret and Anne.

Later that afternoon, they slipped away in a borrowed car and pitched a tent on a mountaintop near North Adams and spent the night. Four or five days later, they were back at the Whiting house, to pack for the train ride to Burlington.

Ruth's mother, my grandmother, worried about her daughter's move to the "wild west" and advised her to take a shotgun. She declined.

Mother and Dad brought with them to Iowa their interest in tennis, nurtured on the dirt court on the Whiting farm. By the time I was nine, and had been playing tennis for four years, our attic was full of trophies they had won in singles and mixed-doubles tournaments in towns scattered through the cornfields of southeastern Iowa and western Illinois.

When I was twelve, I would play tennis with my father most afternoons, when he came home from work. Meanwhile, Mother, who worked on hands and knees in the gardens until mid-afternoon, would go in and prepare the dinner, take a bath, putting on one of her clean flowered summer dresses, and sit on a canvas captain's chair on our front lawn reading the day's *Hawk-Eye Gazette*. From her perch, she also could see the tennis courts up the hill and when she saw us leaving the court, she would go back into the house and warm up the dinner. By the time Dad and I had taken showers and dressed, dinner was ready.

Mother always told me to leave my sweaty clothes on the floor outside the door to my room. By the following afternoon, when I was ready to play again, they had been washed and dried and were ready for use again. I didn't realize at the time what a pleasant life I had.

This was one of many things my parents did for the benefit of their three boys. I began to feel their main thrust in life was to help and support us.

The street was mildly upscale, but the far end led into a dirt road where farmer Mark Smith lived; he regularly sold us eggs and vegetables, all hand-delivered. From him we leased our chickens. We had an acre and a half of land, apple trees, a grapevine, and a carpet of lawns front and back. The mowing of the lawns was the boys' responsibility. I came first because I was the only one then strong enough to run the lawnmower. As soon as I realized that my brother Tom was capable, I passed the honors off to him. His tenure was short-lived, as he passed the chore on to Dick.

Tennis was already my main sport, and an important part of my young life. It brought me in touch with people I would otherwise not have met. I was following my parents' lead, and tennis gave me something in common with both of them. When I was fifteen years old, I finally beat my father. But there was also familial conflict. During tournaments and intercity play, my father would stand inside the back fence (right behind the court) and offer unsolicited instructions. I wasn't old enough to deal with it directly. Years later, when he did that to Dick, who was more talented than I, Dick stormed off the court and never returned. I, on the other hand, would throw my racket over the fence or hit balls far out of the court and over the clubhouse roof in anger. These fits of anger would embarrass Dad, but it didn't stop the pressure he placed on me.

Neighborhood boys often came over for pickup basketball games at our house, where we had installed a backboard at the regulation height on the front of the garage. I played basketball in junior high, high school, and junior college, and in 1939 I eventually played in a game in the Burlington High School field house against the visiting Harlem Globetrotters, in their red, white, and blue uniforms. It was a packed house, and a great show, and an odd feeling for me to be on the same floor with those great players. This was in the earlier days, before they brought along their own opposition team known as the Washington Generals. They were always scheduled to play local teams.

But tennis remained my sport of choice. I played in tournaments all over the Middle West and was ranked nationally in the Boys Division (fifteen years and under) and the Junior Division (eighteen years and under).

I never thought of my home as austere, but there was never a drop of liquor in the house. Nor did anyone in the family drink real brewed coffee. My mother drank George Washington Coffee (the first instant coffee) or Postum, a roasted-grain coffee substitute, at breakfast. That was it. Although I was not aware of it at the time, my parents were very disciplined. As boys we never asked for any special food and always ate anything Mother put on our plates.

Along with tennis, books provided a release for me, a break from the more organized parts of life and a chance to learn about the world. Bookcases in the living room were filled with leather-bound books with gold inlay and gold on the edges that my father had bound. For a long time, that's what I thought a book was, not the simple cardboard cover surrounded by a jacket.

Mother set up a nightly reading. After we had helped clear the table and dried the dishes, we would all five assemble in the living room. Usually Mother read, sitting in a rocking chair by the fireplace. Dad stretched out on the floor and occasionally fell asleep, and my brothers and I lounged around in various easy chairs or on the couch. My mother veered from the somber to the humorous. Of all the books Mother read us, the one I still remember is *We Took to the Woods*, (which remains a much-cherished book in New England and even now, nearly eighty years later, is still in print). It's the lyrical, humorous story of Louise Dickinson Rich and her husband, who in the 1930s, when no one was contemplating a back-to-the-land movement, left city life for the wilderness of Maine. They managed to thrive without electricity, plumbing, or a grocery store any closer than forty miles away. During winter months there were only two other families in the nearby backcountry. Food sometimes ran low. Babies were born without doctors, and Louise Dickinson Rich and her husband found their roles in life.

By the time I reached my mid-teens, I was combining my interest in news with that of sports, regularly phoning in the scores of our grade-school and then junior-high athletic teams to Bill Baylis, the sports editor of the *Hawk-Eye Gazette*. In high school I was sports stringer for the *Des Moines Register*. I'd phone in the results of the evening games to one of the editors and was paid twenty-five cents for the first inch they printed and fifteen cents every inch after that. I worked on my school newspaper, covering sports and other stories, and by the end of my junior year I'd become editor in chief. In those days, Drake University gave out awards for best high-school sports stories in the state. In my senior year of the five stories selected, I came in first, second, and fourth.

Harris Coggeshall was the only man in the history of Iowa who'd had national ranking in tennis. He was a prominent lawyer in Des Moines and a gentleman, married to a very attractive woman, and I admired him. He had gone to Grinnell College, and that was enough to make me want to go there. There were fewer than 1,000 students at the school, but it had a high academic standing, an active intramural sports program, and dances in the men's halls every Friday night.

My parents didn't have enough money to pay for my college. During the year, I waited tables in the dining room. Summers I joined the work crew on campus, painting buildings and performing odd jobs. At the end of each day, the other boys and I would shower, rush to the dining room for dinner, and then head down to the Greyhound bus stop, at the only hotel, which was right across the street from the railroad station. We waited on the hotel porch for the transcontinental evening bus to see if any movie stars were arriving. I don't know

The player above was captain and No. 1 man on the Grinnell College tennis team in 1941, when the photo was taken on the varsity courts at the college. I represented Grinnell in the National Intercollegiate championships at the Merion Cricket Club (Philadelphia) in 1941 and at the same event at Tulane University (New Orleans) in 1942.

My client, Dick Schaap, took the picture above of me watching a match on an outside court at Wimbledon. He said it would be important to establish that I actually went to Wimbledon on those trips to London. (I have been to Wimbledon twelve times.)

that any actor or actress ever descended from the steps of a bus into Grinnell, Iowa, but that didn't dampen our semiserious belief that one might. (After all, Gary Cooper went to Grinnell College.)

My senior year I was president of my house—there were no fraternities or sororities—and to set an example, I was always the first to arrive for any glee-club rehearsal, and the last to leave. On the Sunday of the intramural finale, as we were all lined up in our tuxedos, ready to march off to the show ground, Chuck Sayer, our choir director, approached me: "Sterling, I think we would do better if you and Meatball"—that was Meatball Gonias, captain of the Grinnell football team, who stood next to me—"just mouthed the words." I was surprised, but not displeased, and Meatball chuckled. We obeyed Chuck Sayer and our house won.

When I graduated in 1942, our commencement speaker was the looming publishing icon Henry Luce, who had also waited tables while in college and went on to become the founder of Time Inc. Then in his prime, Luce started such publications as *Time*, *Life*, *Fortune*, and *Sports Illustrated*. I could never have imagined that nearly half a century later, one of my most prolific clients, Ralph G. Martin, would write his unauthorized, revealing, and controversial biography (*Henry and Clare: An Intimate Portrait of the Luces*, 1991).

I didn't know what I was going to do with my life, but the US Army did. I was drafted and sent to an electronics school in Des Moines at night and then to a radar school in Manhattan, Kansas. It was there that I met the then-greatest woman tennis player in the world, Helen Wills Moody, the women's singles champion at Wimbledon for eight years. She was a Californian but had moved to be with her husband, Aidan Roark, the polo player, who was stationed at nearby Fort Riley. We had a mutual friend, D. Keedy Campbell, principal owner of a nationally known sporting-goods company, Lowe & Campbell, who said he would write her to tell her I was coming. A couple of weeks after I hit Manhattan as an Army radar trainee, I was walking along a street near the Kansas State College campus when I saw her sitting in a Ford coupe at a gas station. I was young and somewhat shy, but when I saw the greatest woman player in the world, I overcame my diffidence and approached her with: "Mrs. Moody, my name is Sterling Lord, and I believe D. Keedy Campbell wrote you about me." She turned her head, batted her eyelashes, hesitated, and said, "Oh, yes, you are the junior champion of Iowa." Here was a great woman tennis player who had won eight Wimbledon singles titles, seven US singles championships, and four French singles titles. She was trying to make a young man from Iowa feel important. I was bowled over and absolutely charmed.

We played twice in the ensuing weeks on the Kansas State College clay courts, where there were about one hundred people hanging on to the fence to watch us. If I say I beat her—which I did—it was because in her time there was an enormous difference between the quality of play in men's and women's tennis.

I did my basic training in Miami Beach, billeted at the Sands Hotel on Collins Avenue, which in those days lacked any glitz. While there I met Bob Peacock, an officer in the Navy, who had been US intercollegiate doubles champion. He wanted me to be his partner in a forthcoming invitational tournament in Miami. The problem was I didn't have permission to leave the hotel to play tennis with anyone, anywhere. Although I sneaked away to play in the early rounds, when we reached the finals, he had to come and personally address the sergeant in charge for permission to take me there. His request paid off: We won the championship. Tennis would carry me only so far. I subsequently went into the Army Air Force radar training at Boca Raton, Florida, and was then shipped to Europe.

At the end of World War II, I transferred to *Stars and Stripes* (European Edition), the Army daily. I soon became an editor on *Weekend*, the weekly magazine, and by the time the Army had decided to drop *Weekend*, because it was too costly, Richard Evan Jones, who had been editor in chief, and I took it over and set it up as a private enterprise.

And this is where the fun began.

*Weekend* was a general-interest magazine of thirty-two pages, aimed at the US troops and English-speaking people in Europe. Most of the articles were on European subjects, but often we had stories that dealt with American issues, but which were of worldwide interest. Those pieces appeared under the pseudonym William Stuyvesant (to sound New York-y) but were actually concocted in our office by Richard and me or by one of the staffers we hired. Our office was in Frankfurt at the Park Hotel, across the plaza from the bombed-out Bahnhof (railroad station). Dick was the editor, and I was managing editor, supervising the production and art department, and writing and editing stories. We no longer had to worry about Army supervision, and we could produce income by selling the paper and by soliciting advertising. As an Army paper, we could not accept advertising. As we moved from Army to private auspices, we vowed not to skip even one week. We thought consistent publishing, taking advantage of a buyer's weekly habit, was our best course. But this meant we had no time to solicit investors. We had to raise money as well as tend to all the business functions the Army had previously taken care of, such as locating and dealing with printers and setting up distribution arrangements.

One of our efforts to secure investors involved the Count and Countess von Mumm (for whom the famous Champagne was named), who came over from Wiesbaden to let us take them to lunch at the Park Hotel. He was impressive and she was extremely attractive. They offered to invest, but only in exchange for a controlling interest. Well, that was that, although the comic highlight of the lunch occurred when Dick ordered a dry martini. The waiter thought he said *drei* martini, and brought him three. The seriousness of the lunch kept me from laughing out loud.

On our own, we were now competing for readers and advertising with the overseas edition of *Time* and the international edition of *Newsweek*. We were selling more copies in the European Zone of Occupation (US and British) than either one of them. Amazingly our first two issues made a profit, as we drew ads from the German occupation zone branches of US companies such as Sears Roebuck and American Airlines. The American weeklies were not going to allow this upstart magazine to usurp their readership. We soon realized that the European representative of *Newsweek* was intent on putting us out of business. He had the good fortune to be married to the daughter of a US Navy admiral, which gave him considerable clout.

*Weekend* was printed every Thursday night and distributed every Friday, and for three consecutive weeks we learned on the following Monday that our license to publish had been revoked. It wasn't until later that we understood why. Undaunted, we went right ahead preparing the next issue and waiting for our secret weapon to reach its target. Dick's brother, Russell, an Associated Press correspondent stationed in Berlin, was trying to make an appointment with his friend, General Lucius Clay, the commanding general of the occupation forces, who we knew could fix the problem. Although there were a few anxious moments, toward the end of each week the permission was granted to allow us to print the paper on schedule. We never missed a beat.

Other problems, some of national and international concern, added considerable tension. In June of 1948, West Germany enacted currency reform, changing that country, where we were publishing, from the cheapest location in Europe to print and publish a weekly magazine to the most expensive. Still determined not to miss even one week, we had to look elsewhere—and quickly—around Western Europe. Our research matched our hearts: Paris turned out to be the cheapest place to relocate and publish.

After Germany, Paris was a pleasant assault to the senses with its mad traffic full of French cowboy-like drivers and few traffic lights, its windy, narrow alleyways, the wafting smell of Gauloises, its extensive apartments hanging over the Seine, and exquisite neighborhood bakeries with buttery croissants.

In Paris we quickly made an agreement to be printed by Defosse, who also printed the overseas edition of *Time* magazine. This turned out to be a fortuitous choice; two or three months after we had set up in Paris, Defosse phoned us on the morning of the day we went to press—Thursday—announcing that we were out of paper. They suggested a resolution: We would "borrow" paper from *Time*. I never asked how that was done, or whether we ever paid *Time* back, but we agreed to their solution.

For many newspaper and magazine correspondents and photographers on assignment to do postwar stories in Europe, Paris was either a stopover or a destination. Dick and I noticed that they tended to stay at the California Hotel or the Lancaster Hotel, both near offices of the Paris *Herald Tribune*, and many of them frequented their hotel bars. We discovered that many of these journalists, even the most established and best known, were hungry for work and would do articles for us for $50, given the right subject. Even in those days—the late forties—$50 an article was an embarrassingly low fee.

Some fairly important figures passed through these hotels. When John Steinbeck and Robert Capa, the famous war photographer, came through on their way to Moscow, they stayed at the Lancaster; we tried unsuccessfully to get them to do an article for us—one of the few times we were turned down. In one *Weekend*, we published Eleanor Roosevelt, Chester Bowles, who later became a prominent figure in the Truman and Kennedy administrations, and Michael Musmanno, one of the judges on the Nuremberg War Crimes Tribunal. They weren't even paid $50. While we preferred original content, we had to fill our weekly magazine. We shelled out $30 a month for the United Press mailer, a batch of features and columns, which we often fashioned into *Weekend* articles.

We continued to look for investment money and were constantly searching for ways to attract attention and promote the magazine.

There were continuing rumors that Hitler was still alive and residing in Patagonia. At a time when Germans were not permitted to have or display pictures of Hitler, we received a newspaper series by Michael Musmanno on the general subject of postwar Germany and Hitler and ran it as our feature article entitled "Is Hitler Still Alive?" with a full-face picture of Hitler on the cover. *Weekend* was supposedly published for the GIs of the US occupation forces and other Americans working in the occupation zone, but that issue sold out overnight. The sensation this issue caused was the high point of an article *Life* magazine did about *Weekend* shortly thereafter. It was a good lesson in promotability, but it would not be enough.

Within two months of the *Life* article, *Weekend* ran out of gas. We were editorial geniuses, but we didn't know a damn thing about business. We couldn't pay the printer. Not enough advertising came in, although two weeks after we folded, our freelance French advertising salesman came in with two long-term contracts for full-page ads, which would have saved us. But it was too late.

My consolation was that while in Paris I had been able to play a good deal of tennis and to meet my wife, Dodie Yencesse, an attractive and interesting French girl who was a young sculptress following in the footsteps of her father, Hubert Yencesse, a well-known French sculptor, and a protégé of Aristide Maillol.

Through an interesting set of circumstances, I was admitted to play in the French national indoor championships (open to others besides Frenchmen) and in the first round I carried Marcel Bernard, the French national champion, 6–4 in the fifth set before losing. I had led 4–1 in the fifth but wasn't in good enough shape to finish him off. As a result, the French tennis federation gave me permission to play any time I wanted in Roland Garros, the capital of all French tennis, the same courts that Rafael Nadal and Roger Federer play on now. They also arranged for me to join a small club at Asnières, on the edge of Paris. The first day I played in a tournament at Asnières, I brought my wife Dodie with me, and while I was on the court, a French tennis official I knew took her for a cup of coffee in the club restaurant, and explained to her the appropriate social arrangement between husband and wife while the husband was playing in a tournament. No sex. Dodie was surprised but not shocked. She was French. Later I was invited to play in the first major outdoor tournament of the international tennis scene, at the Casino de Monte Carlo. The Casino would pay half my expenses, and Asnières would pay the other half. I had a free ride to Monte Carlo with Jacqueline Bouton, the city champion of Paris, and her husband.

Despite that, I didn't go. I was twenty-eight years old. I knew I wasn't good enough to play against the top American and Australian players when they started coming back to Europe the next year. And I didn't have a job in the United States to come back to. I knew I had to become serious about life. With my French wife, I came back to the United States.

Soon after I arrived, I was walking down Madison Avenue late one afternoon and was hailed by a man I knew vaguely.

"Tell me, Sterling," he said, "what was your name before you changed it?"

Where else but New York!

## CHAPTER 3

# Starting from Scratch

I had just been fired from my job as associate editor of *Cosmopolitan* magazine—this was pre–Helen Gurley Brown, the editor who transformed it into a magazine for the modern woman. At that time it was a mildly respectable, slick magazine whose readers were the wives of junior advertising executives, management said. The magazine for women was edited and managed by men, not an unusual situation in those days. I was fired by then-editor Jack O'Connell, a smart-looking Irishman who had been running *Cosmopolitan* for nine years. The magazine was not sufficiently profitable for the Hearst Corporation—and someone had to be blamed.

The fact that I had had three magazine editorial jobs in New York in two years—not by my choice—made me realize that the magazine business in the United States in the late forties and early fifties was not stable enough for a man at my level.

I'd previously had an upsetting situation at *True*, which was at that time a successful magazine for men who hunted, fished, and had workshops in their basements. In 1949, I was hired at a salary of $110 per week by Ken Purdy, the editor, a brilliant, high-strung man, who was also a colorful writer. (When he wrote about foreign cars, which he loved, you could almost hear the sound of singing violins.) Two months later, when I was about to start, Ralph Daigh, the editorial director at Fawcett Publications, and Ken Purdy's boss, called me up to his office and told me the salary would be only $95 a week. I was stunned, but I had no alternative. I had no other source of income, and I didn't have the desire or courage to make the rounds again looking for a job.

At *True* I read manuscripts, typed comments, and sometimes acted as first reader for Purdy. Ken was a talented, gutsy editor. I hadn't been with him very long when he developed an idea for a startling article and enlisted a writer named Major Donald Keyhoe, a retired Marine who had been conducting his own research on the existence of flying saucers, a phenomenon little known or publicly discussed in print up to that point in time. In a telegram to Donald Keyhoe, Purdy wrote:

NEW YORK, N.Y., MAY 9, 1949
HAVE BEEN INVESTIGATING FLYING SAUCER MYSTERY. FIRST TIP HINTED GIGANTIC HOAX TO COVER UP OFFICIAL SE-CRET. BELIEVE IT MAY HAVE BEEN PLANTED TO HIDE REAL ANSWER. LOOKS LIKE TERRIFIC STORY. CAN YOU TAKE OVER WASHINGTON END?
KEN W. PURDY, EDITOR, TRUE MAGAZINE

When *True* published Keyhoe's first article, "Flying Saucers Are Real," in our January 1950 issue, it created more publicity, more reaction than any other magazine article the publishing world could remember. According to Patrick Huyghe, author of *Swamp Gas Times: My Two Decades on the UFO Beat*, "the article caused a sensation." Later, in his book on the subject, *The Flying Saucers Are Real*, Keyhoe writes about the release of the article:

The publicity was far more than I had expected. I phoned a reporter in Washington whose beat includes the Pentagon. "The Air Force is running around in circles . . . nobody thought it would raise such a fuss. I think they're scared of hysteria. They're getting a barrage of wires and telephone calls. . . . They're going to deny the whole thing."

LORD *of* PUBLISHING

> From Washington I flew to New York, where I found *True*
> in turmoil. Long-distance calls were pouring in. Letters on
> flying saucers had swamped the mail room. Reporters were
> hounding Purdy for more information.

Keyhoe was interviewed by Mike Wallace on CBS. Among subsequent UFO stories we published was one that had been bought by *This Week*, a well-known Sunday newspaper supplement, but they had been afraid to publish it. So we did.

But my experience was not as exciting. I got in trouble once with Ralph Daigh, who often read the manuscripts we bought before okaying the payments. He didn't like the way I spelled the name of the president of Indonesia: Soekarno, which was the older spelling of the same person known as Sukarno. Daigh was dating a young lady from Indonesia, so he considered himself knowledgeable about the country. Purdy stepped in to defend me, and my spelling prevailed.

I left *True* after two years to take a position as editor in chief of a new magazine for young men—*21*—but the owners, Parents Institute, closed it less than a year later. The executive who gave me the bad news was Oscar Dystel, soon to become the innovative president of Bantam Books and someone with whom I would later do business.

My wife, Dodie Yencesse, who had been our art director at *Weekend*, selecting art and photographs, and laying out each page—she had previously sketched for Jacques Heim, the noted couturier—was a Parisian, and in her milieu, for one's husband to lose a job was a social disgrace. She was extremely upset and embarrassed by my dismissal from *Cosmopolitan*. I, too, was shocked, but I wasn't panicked. I started thinking immediately about what to do and what I could do. I needed a job from which I could not be fired.

At *Cosmo* and *21* and at *True* before that, I had dealt with many literary agents, many of whom seemed ill equipped or not interested in coping with the postwar magazines—books were almost exclusively their principal activity, and many even disdained Hollywood and film. They failed to notice that the public's reading appetite was changing. To American soldiers returning home, France, England, Germany, and even the cities of Southeast Asia were no longer strange and foreign. The war had opened their eyes to the rest of the world. Americans were becoming less parochial, more sophisticated. Before World War II, magazines were weighted with fiction. I thought the war gave writers a great sense of the possibilities of nonfiction. And I recognized that as the country was moving from an agricultural to a manufacturing-based economy, the interests of the reading public were also shifting. When families lived their whole lives in the same house, same property, fiction carried them to other worlds. But post–World War II, Americans' lives were changing. Highways were lacing the land, and mobile Americans, on the cusp of becoming middle class, were anxious to read articles that helped define and explain their changing world.

From my magazine experience, I knew some of the best magazine-article writers, and I thought that many of them could write meaningful and successful books. Even though I had never done it, I believed I was capable of representing them.

I decided to become a literary agent.

I started my agency in 1952, the year that Eisenhower was elected president, Queen Elizabeth II was crowned, and Hemingway and Steinbeck were on the bestseller lists. I began with what I knew: nonfiction writers and the magazine business. I was innocently confident I could make my knowledge of journalism, good article writers, and magazines support the agency and, in the beginning at least, that was my goal.

I had never even seen a book-publishing contract.

I realized, shortly after starting the agency and making a few sales, that my knowledge of what a New York literary agency does and how it works was very thin. Yes, it sells books to book publishers and articles and short stories (though not much anymore) to magazines, but the day a friend who was editor in chief of all the Time-Life magazines told me he didn't know what agents did or how they operated, I began to think. The agent has to know good writing and what is a good, interesting-to-the-publisher idea not only in order to judge what he can sell and what he can't, but also because often writers tried and untried will seek his advice. And he must know what to tell them.

An agent is successful if he can attract and hold effective writers; these are two different talents. You have to know and understand the lives and problems of writers and devise how to help them with their lives. If you take on a young or new writer and his first book is a rousing success, you have a different problem: Other alert agents may suddenly approach him, offering to do more for him than you do, a situation you need to be ready for if you are an accomplished agent.

The agent has to know more about every aspect of publishing—which editors and publishers are right for each writer and are experienced in the kind of book your writer is producing. He must also know the current state of the market, which changes frequently, what books or kind of books are selling, what prices are being paid, etc. If your writer turns out to know more about any one aspect of the business than you do, you have a problem—unless you recognize the situation before he or she does, and do something about it. The best agents are good judges of people—meaning, primarily, their writers. They never say anything negative to anyone about their clients. They are selective and judicious in their expressions of enthusiasm for the work they sell, so that when the time comes that they are wildly enthusiastic about a book they are trying to sell, their enthusiasm will mean something to the editor and publisher.

Knowing the important foreign publishers and the important and successful (at the moment) film producers and ebook publishers is also essential for selling in these fields.

There are many activities that are important, though not in the agent's basic training book, and are only appropriate on occasion: sending flowers, obtaining theater tickets, helping the writer's wife secure a job. The agent performs these duties only if they make the writer happy, or ease his or her personal problems and make it easier for him or her to do the writing.

Most—but not all—of the writers I knew then were young men who cherished their independence, were unconcerned about job security, and were serious about their writing. They didn't want to be anyone's employee if it interfered with their writing. They were halfway or all the way outside the mainstream and were often not interested in becoming part of the burgeoning corporate society. They had more freedom than your average American, and they drank more and laughed more and were more cynical. A few of the writers I knew who had come from corporate jobs had wives who couldn't stand the uncertainty of not knowing when the next paycheck would arrive; these writers were domestically bound to find a desk job in some office. I was attracted to the freelance writers—many of them had interesting personal stories. I didn't carouse with them, but I was totally sympathetic to them and I think they understood I was on their side all the way.

It was a fortuitous time to start an agency. I was soon selling books as well as magazine articles. Book publishing had started in Europe years before, by wealthy individuals who were interested in financing or supporting talented writers. Faint echoes of that concept were apparent in New York in the fifties, when many publishing houses were owned and managed by the fairly well-off men who had founded the companies. In those days, book publishing had been a quiet industry, although there were exceptions in the twenties and thirties, such as the more adventuresome Richard Simon and Max Schuster, two Jewish iconoclasts who'd started Simon and Schuster in 1924 by publishing the first crossword-puzzle books. Not being part of the club, they were free to innovate, and by the early 1940s, S&S had created children's books under the label "Little Golden Books," and was starting with unheard-of print runs of 50,000 copies per title, vastly reducing unit cost.

I didn't have the advantage of being a born-and-bred Easterner or a graduate of an Ivy League school or the son of a man already in publishing, as were many in the publishing world at that time, but I had the advantage of being close to the age of the writers I represented, something that I intuitively understood was important. And unlike a lot of other agents, I wanted to represent an author in as many fields as I could: books, magazine articles, and even if they wrote the messages in Chinese fortune cookies. I was dedicated to helping them do whatever they could to make a living as a writer. It was a time when most general-interest national magazines—and there were many of them then—survived editorially on the articles they were buying from freelance writers and even some major newspapers were doing the same.

The book-publishing business was growing. At least eight strong book publishers went into business in the fifties and sixties. And the literary world was becoming less confining and less puritanical. Grove Press was publishing books never before permitted in the United States, including

*Lady Chatterley's Lover* (Italy 1928, USA 1959) by D. H. Lawrence and *Tropic of Cancer* (France 1934, USA 1961) by Henry Miller. The old obscenity barriers were bent and then broken.

Almost from the start I attracted interesting, saleable clients, but I wasn't pulling the income I needed to make the agency work. Late in 1952, I had a call from Bill Wise, a friend from my days at *True* magazine. Bill had been approached by the *Police Gazette*, a popular magazine for blue-collar men interested in boxing, betting, and horse racing. The publication desperately needed help, as their top editorial employee had just left to join the Estes Kefauver Senate Commission that was investigating the Mafia. They needed Bill to come in as editor, and Bill didn't think he would like or could handle the job, but he had delayed so long in telling them, they were now desperate. Bill wanted me to take over.

I met the publisher and agreed to do it, if I didn't have to come to their offices, as my primary commitment was, of course, to the agency. They agreed and the money from that gig gave my agency a boost. That lasted seven months, and when I told H. H. Roswell, the owner, that I was quitting (it was beginning to take too much time from the agency), he took me out for a drink at the elegant Bull and Bear Room at the Waldorf-Astoria. He thought his persuasiveness and a couple of martinis would win me over; they didn't: He had no idea of the strength of my commitment to the agency or that my working for him had been a means to another end.

The *Police Gazette* took us through 1953, by which time the agency was beginning to grow on its own, but it wasn't working quite the way I wanted. And money was still short.

I also faced my first personnel problem.

My partner, Stanley Colbert, was a young acquaintance, who also had no prior agency experience but had written and sold two short pieces of fiction to *Esquire* magazine, and in those days you didn't need much more experience than that. We called ourselves Lord & Colbert. Each of us invested $95, which didn't exactly carry us far. We had to be inventive and lucky and careful with our money. For a while, Stanley lived out of our one-and-a-half room office. I agreed to it as long as he would put away his sheets, blankets, and all other traces of his living there before work began at nine each morning.

Stanley had less patience than I and a different work ethic. He didn't devote himself to the agency as diligently as I did. He talked but I worked, and after one or two rejections, he put book proposals on the shelf. I didn't. Early in 1954—by that time he had moved out of the office and into an apartment—our differences were bothering me enormously. After a weekend of thought, I confronted him. I told him how upset I was that we weren't working together effectively. I suggested that the assets of the agency were equal to its liabilities, and that if he wanted to continue without me, he could have the agency on those terms. If not, I would take over the agency on the same basis. That was on a Monday morning, and I gave him until Friday of that week to tell me what he wanted to do. If I didn't hear from him by the end of the day on Friday, the agency would be mine.

You don't make a proposal like that if you don't already know what the answer will be.

The next week I changed the name to the Sterling Lord Agency.

In the days to come, I found it embarrassing to borrow money, but I believed in what I was doing and I believed I would succeed and be able to pay people back. I could pay them back although I knew they didn't necessarily expect it. I borrowed $5,000 from my then–mother-in-law and $1,000 each from my father and a well-to-do friend of mine who had a seat on the stock exchange and was married to a French baroness.

There were only two of us at the agency, a secretary and me, and while I may not have had great reason to be, I was optimistic about my prospects, even though the business was not yet financially rewarding. But interesting projects were beginning to come in over the transom. An article in *Publishers Weekly* about my forming a literary agency with Stanley Colbert, which appeared in 1953, attracted the attention of a new British publisher, who got in touch with me immediately. It was Ernest Hecht. He had established a company called Souvenir Press in 1951, and he thought a new agency might be appropriate for a new publisher. He had already published thirty-two books and made a profit on thirty-one of them. That is an astonishing feat for a new publisher. It was then and is now. I was immediately taken with him and his lists, and was delighted to work with him. He and his family had come to the United Kingdom from Czechoslovakia in 1939, before the war. He chose the name Souvenir because he had come up with an idea to create and sell theater-related publications as souvenirs, a sort of *Playbill* that didn't exist then in the United Kingdom. (Theaters often had simple two-page hand-outs with names of cast members, number of acts, and ads for beer in them.) But he couldn't persuade the owners of the large theaters to let him sell his product, so he went into traditional hardcover books, starting with British football as a frequent subject. My instinct about him was correct. The list he built over the years includes five Nobel Prize winners and many bestsellers. Meanwhile, the British theaters now all have the type of programs Ernest originally tried to sell them. As of this writing, in 2012, he has celebrated sixty very profitable years at Souvenir Press.

Photo by Sylvan Mason

One of the great meeting places during Wimbledon is the NBC hospitality tent, shown in the picture above. Ernest Hecht, the founder and principal owner of Souvenir Press, a very successful British publishing house, is to my right, and Bud Collins, the tennis historian and former tennis correspondent for the *Boston Globe*, is to my left. I've known them both for many years. At the NBC tent, you can see and meet well-known people from various walks of life. I took Dick and Mary Francis there, as well as Lady Fiona Montague. I also brought the British hero, Terry Waite, MBE, who was a client of mine; through a friend, I got him into the Royal Box to view the men's singles finals.

In the first five months I took on five nonfiction writers whose success raised the profile of the agency enormously.

Charlie Samuels retained the gruffness of the street reporter he'd once been at the *Brooklyn Daily Eagle*. He would go on to write biographies of Jackie Gleason, Judy Garland, Lizzie Borden, Clark Gable, and Evelyn Nesbit, and he helped Ben Hecht and Billy Rose write their newspaper columns, but his best-known book was the masterpiece he ghostwrote, *His Eye Is on the Sparrow*, Ethel Waters's autobiography. The book told the haunting and painfully honest story of the popular blues and jazz singer of the nineteen-thirties, forties, fifties and sixties, whose best-known recording was her version of the spiritual "His Eye Is on the Sparrow." Even now, more than seventy years after the book's publication, many consider it the finest autobiography of a black entertainer. You can tell from the opening lines of the book that with Charlie's artistry, Waters removed all pretenses and showed herself without adornment:

> I never was a child.
> I never was coddled. Or liked or understood by my family.
> I never felt I belonged.
> I was always an outsider.
> I was born out of wedlock but that had nothing to do with all this.
> To people like mine a thing like that just didn't mean much.
> Nobody brought me up.
> I just ran wild as a little girl. I was bad.

I began representing Charlie after he'd just experienced this major triumph of his career. He came from a close family, and on Saturdays following the success of the Ethel Waters book, he'd leave his home in Nyack and go to Brooklyn to visit his father and play pinochle with him. Once, the older Samuels reached across the table, grabbed Charlie's right hand, turning it over, and finding no calluses, his father asked him how he was earning a living.

Charlie and I would meet at the Blue Ribbon Restaurant on West Forty-Fourth Street, and later at his house in Nyack, perched on a bluff with a sweeping view of the Hudson River. He took me step-by-step through his ghostwriting experiences, starting with the selection of the subject. Later, when I would introduce him to some potential autobiographical subject, he'd warn me, "Sterling, when you introduce me to a celebrity as a possible book subject, I don't mind if I immediately hate him or her; I know that by the time the book is finished, I will hate them. I will also know more about them than any person knows or has a right to know—except their psychiatrist." He opened my eyes to that part of the book business and helped me appreciably in dealing with other authors.

While we were working together, Charlie wrote many other books, including *The Girl in the Red Velvet Swing,* an account of the spectacular 1906 murder involving the seductive and photogenic Evelyn Nesbit, a red-haired artist's model who helped her nearly destitute mother by posing nude for some of the greatest artists in America. Evelyn was sixteen when she met the wealthy womanizer Stanford White, a married forty-seven-year-old architect, who derived pleasure from having nude young girls sway on a red velvet swing he'd constructed in his apartment. Evelyn would go on to date John Barrymore and marry Harry Kendall Thaw, the son of a railroad and coal tycoon, who upon encountering Nesbit's old paramour White at Madison Square Garden one night, shot him to death. When Thaw was tried for murder, his mother offered Evelyn a bribe: If she would testify that White raped her, she would receive a million dollars. Nesbit obliged, but her mother-in-law reneged, never giving her a penny.

With his reportorial skills and his novelistic approach, Charlie had a great sense of what makes a good story and how to tell it.

In addition to Charlie my other early nonfiction writers included John Keats, Rowland Barber, Ralph G. Martin, and Al Hirshberg. In the next few years, each of these four would produce books that were either on the *New York Times* bestseller list or were turned into major motion pictures. Not a bad way to begin a career.

Charlie, Rowland, and Al all wrote their most successful books as ghostwriters, writers who write or help write someone else's first-person book no matter what kind of credit he or she receives—if he or she receives any credit at all. Inspired by Charlie Samuels, I began to seek ghostwriting work for many of my writers. Those jobs helped many of them move from magazines or newspapers to books. And many have profited from knowing the subject and the people in his or her milieu.

In the fifties and early sixties, it was a question of a writer sacrificing his or her ego to that of the subject. In the eighties, nineties, and thereafter, ghostwriting was more in demand, as promotable autobiographies often involved famous subjects who had no idea how to write, and the money was often very substantial. Many writers can submerge their ego to the dollar, and I don't discredit them for that.

In this business it helps when a writer has versatile skills and interests. A writer who's a pro can take on almost any assignment, but if he or she doesn't much care about the subject, I try to dissuade the writer, as in that case the book can be just plain hard labor, as opposed to a labor of love. I saw it as my responsibility to find the right job for my writers to keep them happy and employed and solvent. In the fifties and sixties if a writer ghostwrote a successful book, publishers subsequently considered him a bestselling author and were eager to work with him on his next project.

By the end of the century, I had organized and sold seventy-five ghosted autobiographies.

John Keats, a World War II veteran, wanted to escape his life as a copyeditor and reporter at the *Washington Daily News*, and his friend Richard Starnes, the novelist, told him to come see me. John was a genuine iconoclast and a natural social critic. He was acerbic, perceptive, intelligent, witty—and a flirt. His first book, *The Crack in the Picture Window* (1957), was a diatribe against what was then new-suburban living, or what the growling Keats called "a box of your own . . . fresh air slums . . . of identical boxes . . . spreading like gangrene" through America. Money, he said, was responsible for "developments conceived in error, nurtured by greed, corroding everything they touch. They destroy established cities and trade patterns . . . and actually drive mad myriads of housewives shut up in them."

His second book, *The Insolent Chariots*, which was published a year later, was another acerbic commentary on another American obsession: the automobile, and with it the increased use of chrome, larger size, higher price of gasoline, lower gas mileage, and the greater need for broader and longer paved highways. My client was just half a century ahead of his time. He slammed Detroit as inefficient and the American consumer for stupidity. He suggested what we now take for granted: that American cars were bought not so much for what they did, but for what they said about an individual. He called the cars "over-blown, overpriced monstrosities," and he mocked General Motors for understanding the public's unspoken desire for tailfins while ignoring auto safety. He blamed Americans for not insisting upon cheap, safe, sturdy vehicles. "If one foot were chopped off the length of all its auto-mobiles, New York City would gain 80 miles of usable streets." The *New York Times* reviewed his book and, with high praise, called Keats "incorrigible." Shortly after that book was published, a major Detroit manufacturer invited John to come out, all expenses paid, to visit their plant. John and I had the same instant reaction: "Don't Do It." They would be certain to turn the event to their promotional advantage and to try to challenge John's credibility.

John was in the process of withdrawing from the society he cri-tiqued. He and his wife Margaret moved to Pine Island in the Thou-sand Islands area of the St. Lawrence River. Their home had no electricity, no phones, no radio or TV, and they cooked with propane. I know because I visited them, as I would visit many of my authors throughout my life. The Keats family spent six months each year on Pine Island. Getting in touch with John during the summer months was challenging. When I needed John, I would call the Andress Boat Works, in the tiny town of Rockport, Ontario, and tell them I wanted to talk to John Keats. Someone would board a motorboat and bounce over the two miles to Pine Island to deliver the message. Once it was received, John would hop into one of his boats and motor to the tiny Canadian general store that had the phone to call me back. It was quaint and cumbersome, but it worked. When I visited John, I insisted on seeing the communications headquarters, the dinky little store that kept us in touch.

John was not only a social critic and a scold, he was a good and interesting writer. In the early 1960s, Random House asked him to write a biography of Howard Hughes, the mysterious, eccentric, secre-tive tycoon who made millions and spent them in the aviation busi-ness and on Hollywood films. John loved the idea, but the Hughes contingent did not. They were always trying to protect Howard's name and property. Heavy legal action ensued.

In May 1966, before the publication of Keats's biography on Hughes,

Rosemont Enterprises bought the copyrights to three *Look* magazine articles collectively entitled "The Howard Hughes Story." (Hughes's attorney and two officers of the Hughes Tool Company organized Rosemont Enterprises just a few months earlier in September 1965.) The *Look* magazine articles had originally been published in 1954. In August 1966, Rosemont Enterprises argued that *Howard Hughes: The Biography of a Texas Billionaire* by John Keats, published on May 23, 1966, infringed upon their copyrights. In the end it was decided that the Keats book was for the popular market and not scholarly, so his use of/reference to the magazine articles was entirely acceptable. And, of course, Hughes's attempt to stop its publication made for great publicity! So a revised edition was published some time after the trial.

John wrote ten additional books before he went legitimate, teaching writing at Syracuse University. One book about Pine Island, entitled *Of Time and an Island*, is still referred to as a classic Thousand Islands book.

Rowland Barber had been with me at *21* magazine, which we started for Parents Institute; in fact, he'd been my entire staff at my next-to-last magazine position. He had won a Hopwood Prize at the University of Michigan and later worked as a writer at *Life* during its heyday as the predominant weekly magazine in the US. That was shortly after WWII, when *Life* was fat and rich and able to assign more stories than they needed and then pick which of them to publish. *Life* hired many fine young writers, a number of whom quit because their articles, on which they had worked diligently for weeks, often without a break, pouring their hearts into them, were never published. Rowland lived in Greenwich Village, where many writers, both struggling and successful, lived, smoked, and drank black coffee at cafés.

Over the years, I was able to arrange many book contracts for him, including *Harpo Speaks!*, the autobiography of the silent Marx brother, and my first big book, *Somebody Up There Likes Me*, written with and in the voice of Rocky Graziano.

I knew Rowland was a devotee of thoroughbred racing, and I sold his first book with me, *The 1953 Horse Racing Almanac*, to Frank Taylor, the editor in chief of Dell's paperback line. We all thought it would be a substantial success that we could repeat every year. There was not a similar book on the market. But none of us knew that a company in Buffalo, New York, already had exclusive concession rights to the major racetracks in America. We couldn't get in at all.

This sales failure made me realize that I could not rely on publishers to protect their self-interest or ours. They didn't know everything; there was no research and development, no industry-wide authority to consult. In the future, my writers and I would have to do our own research before going to a publisher, which would be better for everyone.

Neither Rowland nor I was discouraged. I thought of him immediately when Rocky Graziano, the famous prizefighter, came to me to represent him on his as-yet-unwritten life story. I liked Rocky from the beginning: He was respectful, appreciative, friendly, and straightforward with me. He was a product of the rough-and-tumble streets of Brooklyn and Manhattan's Lower East Side. His father was a failed boxer and big drinker. His mother was in and out of mental institutions, and his older brother began pummeling him when he was three. The red-haired boy stole coins from subway machines and from his grandfather. He lived on the streets, hated Jews and "fags" and anyone in authority. He was educated at Catholic reform school, Rikers Island, and Leavenworth, but no one was able to control or contain him, except himself. By the time I'd met him, Rocky had changed his name on the spur of the moment while he was AWOL from Fort Dix and the detention center at Castle Williams on Governors Island; they had given him bus and train fare to go back to Fort Dix, but instead he went to Manhattan to see fight manager Irving Cohen. Cohen had a fight lined up for him at Fort Hamilton Arena in Brooklyn. Rocky wanted the fight, but he knew that as Rocky Barbella (his original name) he would immediately be picked up by the military police. Luckily, Cohen never knew Rocky's last name—he was just Rocky Bob to Cohen— so he quickly took the name Rocky Graziano, which was the name of two of his friends—brothers—who were both in Leavenworth at the time. He won the fight, but eventually a military court would send him back to Leavenworth for going AWOL.

By July 1947 Rocky had gone legitimate and was the middleweight champion of the world. He had married a Jewish woman named Norma, and after having two daughters, he turned his life around.

After a couple of missteps—over the phone Rocky told Rowland to meet him at "the joint," but he hadn't directed Rowland to the right joint—they met and started working together. Rowland wrote a strong proposal, but it turned out to be a tough sell. Eight publishers turned it down.

I suppose the story seemed too rough and even ugly to publishers seasoned in the literary world. Rocky was not the sort of fellow they would bump into in the Algonquin Hotel lobby, the literary hangout of the day. I suspected that they didn't find Rocky an appealing character and failed to understand how his story would appeal if not to them, then to many readers.

Finally Simon and Schuster jumped for it, and Rocky and Rowland got to work. Needing office space and not wanting to shell out a lot of money, Rocky and Row persuaded Toots Shor, the noted restaurateur on West Fifty-First Street, to let them work in an upstairs room above his restaurant. *Somebody Up There Likes Me* was published by Simon and Schuster in 1955, immediately after *Look* magazine had published a two-part excerpt from Rocky's book (which I had sold them). Simon and Schuster's editors understood the popular market that the more traditional publishers failed to see. Row captured Rocky's voice, the pace of his restless life, the depths of his depravity and his instinctive ability to triumph over it.

Despite his petty crimes, Rocky had an innate decency that shone through. In prison, he started a boxing program. On the streets, he'd steal bikes to give to poor kids. *Somebody Up There Likes Me* was pumped full of adrenaline, giving readers an espresso high. It was written in such a descriptive, visual way that it would translate easily onto film. Critics and the public liked the story, which became an MGM movie starring the then-young and little-known actor Paul Newman. It wasn't a shoo-in sale. We had to get releases-to-depict signed by all the real persons who I thought were essential to the film story. The way it worked best was to have Rocky himself contact them by phone. I suggested he come into my office to make the phone calls, and he did. The toughest man to get an answer from was Rocky's former chief rival in the ring, Tony Zale, who lived in Chicago. It took days to get Zale on the phone. He seemed to duck out of the house early in the morning for unknown places. Rocky finally caught up with him and explained to Zale what he wanted. Zale didn't understand. Finally, on the second call, Rocky was getting through and told Tony, "Look, Tony, you sign for me, and when they make a movie of your life, I'll sign for you!"

At that time, as far as I knew, there was no Tony Zale movie in the works, but Tony bought Rocky's proposition.

That book and the film were important for Rocky, giving him legitimacy beyond the ring. He would go on to become a well-known comedian on a popular television show and a painter. A decade later, he played the role of a successful former boxer, Packy, in Gordon Douglas's feature film *Tony Rome* (1967) alongside Frank Sinatra as Tony, a private detective.

Shortly before *Somebody Up There Likes Me* opened, MGM gave a private screening in their New York City offices for Rocky and Rowland and their friends: About sixty of us were there. I was sitting about ten feet away from Rocky. I liked the film, and when it was over and the lights went

Lawyers, an accountant, and principals gathered at MGM's New York City office when authors Rocky Graziano and Rowland Barber signed the contract to grant the studio the film rights to their book *Somebody Up There Likes Me*. Looking over the contract, left to right, Rocky, Rowland, me, and Rocky's lawyer, Max Schultz. The resulting film was superb; it starred the young Paul Newman in one of his first leading roles.

on, we all started out. I caught Rocky's attention and said, "What did you think of it, Rocky?" His answer: "What did *you* think of it?"

"It's good," I said. "Very good." He wasn't the first person whose life was filmed who couldn't figure whether the resulting picture was good or bad.

Rocky and I kept in touch after the movie came out. In fact, the next time we saw each other was in the MGM offices on Broadway. We were there to give money, not take it. One of the men who had signed a release-to-depict for us (nobody got paid) was Rocky's one-time fight manager, Irving Cohen. He had bumped into a lawyer at a party, and the lawyer persuaded him he was a fool to let himself be depicted without being paid. The lawyer was very clever: He asked us (Rocky, Rowland, MGM, and me) to pay him a sum that turned out to be slightly less than it would have cost us to get his claim thrown out. So we all agreed to contribute proportionally—to what we had been paid for the movie rights—and that's what we were meeting about, with checks in hand.

When the meeting ended, Rocky and I went down in the elevator together, and he asked me where I was going next. I told him I had an appointment uptown. "I'll walk up Broadway with you." Broadway was Rocky's territory, not mine, but I was pleased he had suggested it.

As we started up Broadway, Rocky put his arm around me and said, "You know what I like about youse, Sterling—we talk alike." I was amused. I grinned and thanked him. I knew it was a compliment.

I saw him from time to time after that, when he came into the office to pick up money that had come in for him. His wife was the treasurer of the family and everything that came in had to be paid entirely to her—almost: Rocky persuaded me to slice off a small portion of every check before sending the balance to Norma, who apparently was very stingy about giving her husband any pocket money.

The last time I talked to Rocky was just a couple of years before he died. He phoned me at the office one afternoon; "How are you doing, Sterling?"

"Fine, Rocky, how are *you* doing?"

"Great! Where are you hanging out these days?" And before I could answer, "That's right, you don't hang out."

We talked about getting together soon, which we both wanted to do but never did. New York is a busy, seductive city, and often these friendly meetings never happen. Rocky died in 1990.

As good as it was for Rocky, the book changed Row's life even more. He was now in demand by publishers and would go on to write other books including *The Night They Raided Minsky's*, a fictional version of the story of the family whose name was synonymous with New York City burlesque. It became an MGM movie, and Row moved from New York City to Hollywood, which sounds better than it was. During those first years on the West Coast, Row would call me at night to talk about books, not yet having found anyone in Los Angeles he could talk to about them.

Ralph G. Martin and I had met when I was at *Cosmopolitan* and I assigned him an article on the Racquet Club—an exclusive athletic club, many of whose members were well-known New York City names. A few weeks later I was fired and decided to open the agency. As I was walking with Ralph down Sixth Avenue, I told him my plan. I didn't commiserate with him about the loss of my job because I knew instinctively that when you're starting a business and looking for clients, you've got to be positive. Ralph was represented by one of the giants, the William Morris Agency. I had barely finished telling him my plans when he stopped, turned to me, and said, "I want to be with you." I think the powerful agency wasn't giving him any attention, and I was young and could give him that. Plus, we had mutual friends— Andy Rooney (of *60 Minutes*), Ernest Leiser, a frequent contributor to the *Saturday Evening Post*, and others.

During World War II Ralph worked for *Stars and Stripes* and *Yank*, the Army magazine. One of Ralph's most remarkable stories for *Yank* was never published. He was stationed near the Siegfried Line in France, a German defensive line ringed with bunkers, when the Allies broke through and for the first time were fighting on German soil. He had news that Winston Churchill was to visit the line that day. As Churchill's group started walking across the field toward the Siegfried Line, Ralph joined in. He was wearing a uniform with no insignia, which was not uncommon for *Stars and Stripes* or *Yank* writers covering the war. This must have confused the generals and Churchill, but it was one of those situations where everyone assumed if Ralph was there he should be, or perhaps they were too embarrassed to ask. As they reached the line, Churchill stopped and said, "Gentlemen, it's time to take a piss," so everyone, from Churchill to Ralph, obliged, urinating on the Siegfried Line. The editors at *Yank* thought it was a little too personal to publish.

An unusually likeable and affable man, Ralph is always pleasant and upbeat, but beneath the pleasantries is a talented and determined writer. After returning to the US, he became a roving editor for the *New Republic*. His first book was *Boy from Nebraska: The Story of Ben Kuroki*, a Japanese-American who faced down prejudice to fight for this country, flying fifty-eight combat missions during World War II. The book received an excellent review in the *New York Times* and sold all over Europe.

But beginning in the fifties, it was a different ball game for Ralph: Times were tough. Ralph was freelancing and supporting himself, his wife, Marge, and their children. They were living in a small apartment on the third floor of a building just off Sheridan Square in Manhattan's Greenwich Village. The local Democratic Party headquarters was on the second floor, and while Ralph was a staunch Democrat, he wasn't pleased that their boisterous meetings sometimes spilled over onto the third floor.

Ralph began writing one book after another and, like those of many writers, they were all small books, often with small publishers or publishers who did not survive long and that had little chance of creating a major commercial success. Ralph was more prolific than most: In one twelve-month stretch he wrote three books.

I suggested that he change his approach and look for a major book idea—one I could get a larger advance for, so he could exclusively devote himself to it over a couple of years. He agreed, but we each knew that such ideas are not easy to find.

Ralph had done a photo-and-text book on Winston Churchill with Richard Harrity—a longtime friend, playwright, author, actor, and television producer who co-wrote three books with Ralph. As Ralph was researching Churchill, he came across material on Jennie Jerome, Churchill's extraordinary American mother, a major force in politics, culture, and society. He subsequently was hired by NBC as an adviser for a TV series on Winston Churchill. In the course of his research for the show, he became increasingly intrigued by Jennie. He couldn't understand why this important woman had not been the subject of a major biography. Born in New York, she lived most of her life in England, where she was married three times and had a number of lovers. She was renowned for her beauty and for her skill in shaping the lives of those around her, particularly with regard to her son Winston's career. In the December 1908 issue of *Current Literature* magazine, Jennie was referred to as "the most influential Anglo-Saxon woman in the world."

As he was walking across the Brooklyn Bridge one day in 1962 to visit the house where some people claimed Jennie was born (Ralph later found out she was born in a different Brooklyn house), he made the decision to write her biography. Immediately, he put together an outstanding book proposal. The subject was so strong and so fascinating to me that I thought any major publisher would take it. Surprisingly, many US publishers turned it down. Publishers are adept at writing insincere rejection letters (they don't want to unnecessarily hurt the author's feelings), so often an agent and author have to guess at why a book isn't bought. In the case of Jennie, while publishers may have found the concept appealing, they may also have thought it was too important a subject for the author, Ralph Martin, who was not well known in those circles. I finally had an expression of interest from my old friend Donald I. Fine, the vice president and editor in chief of Dell/Delacorte, who offered an embarrassingly small advance.

Don was fairly short, with a pockmarked face, and his approach to life was somewhat defensive. His offer reflected that: an $8,500 advance, $3,000 of which was to be paid on signing. I suggested to Ralph that we should not accept it. But by that time Jennie had become his obsession, and he insisted we sign with Don. For Ralph, Jennie was not just a book—she was a cause. This became a standard procedure for me: If I disagreed with an author, I would try to dissuade him, but if he insisted on maintaining his point of view, I would direct my total energies to support him or her in dealing with publishers. An author's strong belief and enthusiasm will affect the writing of the book and often the publisher's commitment to it. We signed with Don. Ralph used the advance to pay for a trip for himself and Marge to London, where he knew the details of Jennie's life existed—if only he could find them.

It wasn't easy for him in London. In 1964 he found some letters of Jennie's that he felt would be important in moving forward, but they had already been co-opted by Randolph Churchill, who had been writing a biography of his father, Winston. Ralph knew about the letters but couldn't access them.

Fortunately, Ralph had been corresponding with historian Robert Rhodes James, then a clerk of the House of Commons, who was writing a book on Jennie's husband and Winston's father, Lord Randolph Churchill. (The book, *Lord Randolph Churchill*, was published in 1959.) James liked Ralph and suggested that he visit the centuries-old Blenheim Palace, where the family archives were stored. Ralph knew entry to the private quarters of the Baroque palace was extraordinarily difficult, but James, who was socially well connected, arranged for Ralph to gain access. The collection was completely disorganized: No indexes, no librarians, and no one had any interest in spending money to straighten it out.

To have befriended Robert Rhodes James was part of Ralph's remarkable luck because the then–duke of Marlborough had no desire to accommodate any writer. Nor did the duke show any interest in Jennie, who was buried nearby at St. Martin's Cemetery in Bladon. Even her gravesite was in disarray. The large storage room looked to Ralph like a little-used attic jammed with boxes. He started out fortuitously with a big black box labeled "India" in the front of the room. Jennie had never been to India, but Ralph had to start somewhere. The contents of that box proved to be the most important source for him: letters, diaries, pictures, a couple of marriage contracts, and other documents.

The younger Churchill had never even rifled through the black box—which contained interesting material involving Randolph and Jennie—because one night when he and the duke of Marlborough were having dinner at Blenheim Palace, the duke ordered the television set brought in to the dining room without consulting the short-tempered Randolph Churchill. Randolph complained bitterly to his host. The duke's response: "But I always watch the telly after dinner."

"Screw you!" Randolph snipped, and that was the end of their cooperation and the opening that my client, Ralph Martin, needed. Once Ralph finished examining the treasures in the black box and started writing, he realized he couldn't squeeze it all into one volume and do it justice. He had material for a two-volume biography. Back in New York, Ralph met with Don Fine, showed him a partial manuscript, and told him Jennie would have to be two volumes. Don laughed and said, "Maybe somebody would be interested in buying and publishing two volumes on Winston Churchill, but his mother? Are you kidding?"

Ralph was not kidding, I could tell, and I respected that. I was fascinated by what Ralph had actually written, and I was well aware of the time and energy he had already given to the work. His material so far—the partial manuscript—was extremely interesting. Jennie was a colorful, independent woman who traveled in the highest social and political circles. Martin notes that at the age of seven, Jennie's personality was already taking form: Wanting to dance with the Prince of Wales at a ball her father gave, she wept when her father refused to let her attend.

Jennie's desire to be in the middle of all the action and drama carried through to her adult life. At the theater, where traditionally women wore only black, Jennie insisted on wearing a pale blue dress, even though her husband warned her to change because it was "so conspicuous."

But, as Martin posits, Jennie was more than a woman who wanted to be noticed; she was deeply involved in politics throughout her husband's career, as well as a devoted mother and adviser to Winston. She read not only the authors her husband suggested—Gibbon, Horace, and Disraeli—but also anything she could find related to British politics and the issues of the time. Subsequently she personally edited Winston's speeches, and later wrote them. But when Randolph died at age fifty-seven from syphilis, she dashed off to France, avoiding London's strict mourning rule of one year in all black clothing and another in clothes with black trimming, with no social calls for the full two years. In France it was "perfectly permissible for a beautiful young widow wearing long black bloomers to bicycle in the Bois de Boulogne," which she did.

Jennie continued to pave the "stepping stones for Winston's future." After Winston told his mother he "must go" to Cuba, she set up the contact to make the trip official. On their way to Cuba, Winston stayed with Bourke Cockran, the US congressman, who was a famous orator and Jennie's first romantic relationship after Randolph's death. Martin reminds us that Winston had already been in conversation in his young life with "Gladstone, Salisbury, Rosebery, Chamberlain, Balfour, and his own father."

Throughout the book, Martin stresses Jennie's hand in Winston's development and career. There was no limit to their combined drive, their combined determination. She had not been able to make her husband Prime Minister of England, but now she had a fresh chance with her son.

I felt it was just too good a book idea and too important historically for the book to go unpublished. I supported Ralph totally. He repaid Dell the advance money from his savings, and Delacorte canceled the contract.

Ralph and I had a heavy task on our hands: It had been hard enough to get that deal with Don Fine, but to do it all over again with another publisher, this time insisting on two volumes? At least, we now had more than a book proposal; we had a partial manuscript to show.

After many rejections, Ralph approached a friend from his early freelancing days, Eugene Rachlis. Gene had just been named editor in chief of Prentice-Hall, a house better known for business, finance, and how-to books than for general-interest trade books (although they did publish Louis Armstrong's autobiography). Gene and Ralph were good friends, and Gene asked to see the Jennie Jerome manuscript. Gene absolutely loved the material, but two volumes? They had a long dinner to discuss the book, during which Ralph kept insisting on two volumes while Gene was drinking one bourbon on the rocks after another. Gene finally said, "All right, you sonofabitch, we'll do two volumes." That was a tough decision for Gene to make. We found out later that if the two volumes had failed to sell well, Gene would probably have lost his job.

In 1969, upon the publication of the first volume, Ralph phoned me: "Sterling, they're really excited about the book at Prentice-Hall.

They're going to make it a big bestseller." Later in the conversation, I asked Ralph how many copies they were printing. It was 5,000. Ralph was so excited, I wasn't going to destroy his hopes. I didn't say anything to Ralph about the size of the printing, but in the wisdom of my youth and my brief experience in publishing I *knew* that a publisher had to start with a minimum first printing of 15,000 copies in order to make a book a national bestseller.

How wrong I was.

*Jennie* started selling immediately, even though Prentice-Hall did not take out a single advertisement until the book was in its third printing. The reading public was buying it anyway. Publishers often wait to see if a book takes off on its own, as Prentice-Hall did, before committing marketing dollars. It is a matter of judgment how long to wait and how much money to spend. I soon learned that there is almost no infallible way of successfully predicting in advance that a book will become a bestseller. If the writer's last book was a bestseller and the new one is the same genre, it probably will be a bestseller. But there are cases of bestselling authors whose next book flopped.

Particularly with nonfiction, publishers often pay advances in the millions of dollars, but not all these advances are earned out, by any means. Why do publishers pay millions of dollars for one book? They anticipate huge sales, probably feeding on the judgment of the experienced sales force, but they also do it because they need a big book to "carry the list." If they're planning a strong campaign, there are early signs, but one has to know how to interpret the signs. By early in the twenty-first century almost all publishers were announcing an exaggerated number for print size in order to impress the booksellers, the reviewers, and even the buying public with the importance of the book. You really have to know the players.

*Jennie: The Life of Lady Randolph Churchill, The Romantic Years* went to the top of the *New York Times* bestseller list and stayed on it for thirty weeks, even though the *Times* gave the first volume a mediocre review, followed eleven days later with a more favorable review that called the book "ruthlessly gossipy"—maybe the writer meant to insult but readers found that appealing—"An engrossing panorama of high life... Her beauty, warmth and brilliance light the shelf."

*Book World*, the independent review at the *Washington Post* said:

> . . . not only Jennie, but the world in which she lived, dance before the reader in magnificent display . . . He [Martin] writes with such candor, and at the same time such evident sympathy for his subject, that one is spellbound . . . There can be little doubt that the completed biography will provide the best documented and most readable account possible of this fascinating woman . . .

Three weeks after publication, Ralph came into the office so we could evaluate how the sales and publicity were progressing. Ralph asked me why *Jennie* had not been taken by the Book-of-the-Month Club. In the era before Amazon and book chains, the Book-of-the-Month Club made it possible for the reading public, such as the citizens of Burlington, Iowa, to have worthwhile books delivered to their homes. By 1946, twenty years after it started, the club had over half a million subscribers. For many years, being selected by the club was an avenue to a book's success. I didn't know why Ralph's book hadn't been selected because those rights are always controlled by the book's publisher, not the agent, but I knew one of the editors at Book-of-the-Month. While Ralph was still with me, I phoned the editor, and that's how *Jennie* became an alternate selection of the club.

Ralph had spent seven years on *Jennie*, but it was worth all that time. Counting US and foreign sales, hardcover and paperback, *Jennie* sold 3,000,000 copies.

Two years later, in 1971, volume II, *Jennie: The Dramatic Years*, was published, and this time the *New York Times* raved, declaring that Ralph G. Martin "completely succeeds in conveying the beauty and warmth of Sir Winston's mother. Indeed, to understand England's savior, one must read the story of Jennie Jerome." Volume II spent thirty weeks on the *Times* bestseller list.

As a result of Ralph Martin's books and readers' newfound appreciation of the life of Jennie Jerome, her gravesite, which had been in disarray for many years, was tidied up for the crowds that came to pay their respects.

After *Jennie*, Ralph never received an advance less than $100,000—

and often they were as high as $500,000—and his books were frequently selections of the Literary Guild or Book-of-the-Month Club. On the suggestion of Phyllis Grann—then–editor in chief of Putnam's and by coincidence a Westport, Connecticut, neighbor of Ralph's— he wrote *Charles and Diana*, which *Library Journal* declared to be superior to other books of that genre. Ralph's account was a blend of English history and *People* magazine. (On their wedding registry, the couple listed 300 items including a croquet set, two dozen champagne glasses, and a pair of Crown Staffordshire white cockatoos.)

Publishing success had improved Ralph's lifestyle. He and his family now had a waterfront house in Westport, Connecticut, with what you might call the Jennie Jerome indoor swimming pool right off the living room, and Ralph worked in a large studio joined to their home by a second-floor outdoor walkway. His success attracted attention not only to him, but also to our agency. And it certainly gave me a great deal of personal satisfaction, particularly when I think of the number of publishers who had rejected the proposal. It was a triumph to relish.

One of Ralph's subsequent books, *Henry and Clare: An Intimate Portrait of the Luces* (1991), another Phyllis Grann idea, received reviews that were not as strong or as thoughtful as those for *Jennie*, particularly from the reviewers who worked for a magazine owned by Henry Luce.

Detailing the extramarital lovers of both Henry and Clare, Ralph describes Henry's relationships with Jean Dalrymple, Mary Bancroft, and Lady Jeanne Campbell.

But two respectable and distinguished publications were very positive and appreciative of the quality of Ralph's work. *Publishers Weekly* said:

> The stormy marriage of Henry Luce (1898-1967), founder of the Time-Life publishing empire, and Clare Boothe Brokaw (1903-1987), editor of *Vanity Fair*, congresswoman, war correspondent, playwright and diplomat, was a fiercely competitive alliance marked by intense loneliness and numerous affairs on both sides. Godfearing, patriotic Henry, son of Presbyterian missionaries to China, had two great loves: theatrical producer Jeanne Dalrymple and Lady Jean Campbell,

daughter of British newspaper tycoon Lord Beaverbrook, who married Norman Mailer. Henry's affairs with these and other women drove his outspoken, brash wife to demand a divorce and attempt suicide, even though she herself had a stream of lovers. Martin (*Charles and Diana*) reveals Henry's yearnings to be a public hero and his frustrated political ambitions. He portrays Clare as a woman consumed by private demons, including knowledge of a brother's probable suicide. This riveting dual biography is both a peek inside the Luce publishing empire and a candid love story that rips away the veil of secrecy surrounding a "royal American couple."

And *Library Journal* quoted Abraham Z. Bass of Northern Illinois University–DeKalb:

In this case, an intimate portrait means every publicly available detail, along with fresh information from new interviews, about public and private activities. A Martin book means a well-integrated storyline, written from a somewhat analytical and detached perspective, told in a captivating manner for a gossip-loving general audience. The subjects are Henry Luce (1898–1967), the founder and creative force of Time Inc., and Clare Boothe Luce (1903–1987), the congresswoman and ambassador. The book is hard to put down, exactly right for a BOMC and History Book Club alternate selection. Recommended more for a library's biography section than for the media collection, since it concentrates on the personal, not the business side.

Al Hirshberg was not quite one of my first clients, but I think he felt he was. And among my clients, he was the first consistent promoter of the agency. Al traveled on book, newspaper, and magazine assignments a great deal, and once we started working together, Al was always telling friends and acquaintances about the "great agent" he had.

Some people may have been intimidated by me in part because I tend to be silent at times, observing the scene, listening and thinking before I speak, and in part because of the prominent writers I was already representing. Al Hirshberg was not intimidated. I liked his humor and informality and how he cut through all pretensions and addressed me as "Pal" and "Palsy." Al had a receding hairline and as much insecurity as any writer I represented. He talked as if we were in a bar, though neither of us were serious drinkers.

Al was not a stylist. His writing was very straightforward and highly readable. He seemed to know every major sports figure in the US, and he was successful in interviewing them because he was easy-going, not pretentious, and seemed like "one of the guys." He was also conscientious; if a subject told him something was off the record, it was kept off the record.

Al had actually started reporting as the campus sports correspondent for the *Boston Post* while he was still in high school, and he continued while at Boston University. But he was actually first paid not by the *Boston Post* but by the *Jewish Advocate*, which sent him $5 each time they accepted his weekly column. At the *Boston Post*, he had been dealing with a young assistant in the sports department, but as college graduation approached, he was hoping he could get a grown-up, full-time job with the *Boston Post*. Luck was with him: A friend who knew the city editor, Edward J. Dunn, would introduce Al to him for $35.

That was the beginning of Al's long career with the *Boston Post*.

Al started work in the sports department in 1935. He later became the best-known sports columnist in Boston, and was highly regarded in the entire American sports world. But in the summer of 1952, the *Boston Post*, which had been losing money, was sold to a man named John Fox, who tried to remedy the shaky financial condition of the paper with substantial staff cuts and changes. And just like newspapers in the first decade of the twenty-first century, many employees were fired. By November, Al was told that the sports department was being dramatically reduced. He was ordered to report to the city room for duty as a copyeditor on the foreign desk starting December 26.

Al, like many of my clients, was a stubborn man when he was crossed. In a letter to Joe Griffin, the new editor in chief, dated December 19, he wrote: "In view of the fact that I have been a member of the sports department since I was first hired on the regular staff of the *Post* in 1935, and in view of the fact that I would be completely out of my element anywhere else, it will be impossible for me to comply with your order to transfer me to the city room. Unless I hear otherwise from you, I am planning to report to the sports department on Dec. 26."

Al's final letter to Griffin, two days before the deadline, said that the orders they had given him were equivalent to a discharge, and that it was impossible for him to report to the city room. He requested his severance pay.

In retrospect, I know he was right, and I admire his tough stand.

The *Post* resisted paying Al anything, but the Newspaper Guild stood strongly behind him, and in the end Al won. He was awarded substantial severance pay—and that was the comfortable nest egg that started him on his full-time writing career.

And that's when Al came to me. He started his new career with a battered typewriter, working on the dining-room table of his apartment in Brookline, Massachusetts. He was a great storyteller, and he could recall what happened to him or where he was on almost any day of his life—although later I discovered that members of his family privately questioned his accuracy and, though they never challenged him, thought there might be an element of imagination in some of his recall. Aside from that factor, he was totally trustworthy, a quality that induced Jimmy Piersall, the Boston Red Sox outfielder, to approach Al for help with his autobiography. Al called me right away and briefly outlined the story.

Piersall had been with the Red Sox before he was put in the Westborough State Hospital in Massachusetts for emotional and psychiatric problems in August 1952. While it was typical at that time for someone leaving a mental hospital after treatment to undergo a transitional period before re-entering society, that's not what happened in Piersall's case. After his treatment, he returned to the Red Sox outfield the next season and became a valuable asset of the team. He wanted to tell his story.

It sounded highly dramatic, and I told Al, "Let's go ahead." As the two men started on the book, Al brought Jimmy and his wife Mary down to New York for a lunch at the Hyatt Hotel near Grand Central Station, hardly a publishing hangout, but convenient for the Piersalls, who came in and out by train. I liked Jimmy for his frankness and courtesy toward his wife, who was a nurse in the Boston area. Jimmy was what we then called "high-strung," but what struck me most were the steely blue eyes of his attractive wife, which made me think that she had the strength and toughness that were perhaps essential to keep him going.

I saw immediately that the two men had personalities that could work together well. Al was very low-key and could handle Jimmy's outbursts of indecision or complaint. He had his moments of anxiety, but when working with a subject he was—as he would say—cool as a cucumber. He had a rather stable home life, a wife, Margie, who was the more conversational one in a mixed social setting, and who gave him two children—a boy and a girl. The girl, Judy, was a lively one—lots of energy—but I never saw the boy who was three-and-a-half years younger. Later Al told me that Punch had been born blind—retrolental fibroplasia they called it at the time (now ROP)—and he had been in a caretaking home, the Fernald State School in Waltham, Massachusetts, since the age of nine. The Hirshbergs had a summer-house in Pocasset on the neck of Cape Cod and wintered in Florida starting in February or March, the typical sportswriter gambit to cover baseball's spring training. A pretty good life, and Al enjoyed it.

Al and Margie had a busy social life in the Boston area during the week. Their daughter, Judy, remembers all sorts of celebrities—mostly sports stars—drifting through the home, Jimmy Piersall (he was inducted into the Boston Red Sox Hall of Fame in 2010) and Bob Cousy (one of the all-time Boston Celtics greats) among them. Judy was identified primarily as Al's daughter, and her friends in high school could recognize Piersall's car immediately when it drove up.

Sundays were built around Punch's visits to the apartment. Al would drive out to Waltham to pick him up and then take him back in the afternoon. Al's relationship with Judy was quite different and showed a side of him that neither I nor his other male friends ever suspected. He would—when Judy was four, five, or six years old—put her to bed telling her a children's story of his own creation. The stories all featured Judy, Alexander, Bowser, and Tabby—those were always the four characters—and had titles like "The Day It Rained Up" and "Visiting a Cloud from Out the Window of an Airplane."

At one point when he was writing me—instead of finishing the Piersall book—I received five detailed letters from him in eight days. Throughout the letters, he referred to me as "poop," "pally," and "buddy," and signed off "Chatty Al."

The Piersall book was called *Fear Strikes Out*. The publisher had been struggling with the title until I suggested "Fear Can't Strike Me Out," which was refined by Jimmy and Little, Brown into *Fear Strikes Out*. I'd retained first-serial rights for the author. And since Al had written articles for the *Saturday Evening Post*, then one of the best-known weekly magazines in America, that's the first place I sent the manuscript. Usually the *Post* responded within a day or two, but for this book they wanted to pass it by a medical expert. Public display of one's emotional problems was still a new thing, and the *Post* wanted to be sure that it was medically accurate and sound. I thought that was reasonable, but my client was going nuts waiting for the decision. He came down to New York so I could support and comfort him while he was waiting for the answer. Little, Brown published the book in 1955, shortly after it appeared in installments in the *Saturday Evening Post* under the title "They Called Me Crazy—and I Was!" It went on to become a one-hour TV drama on *Climax!* on CBS with Tab Hunter playing Jimmy, and a Paramount film produced and directed by Alan Pakula and Robert Mulligan, two highly regarded young filmmakers, and starring Tony Perkins (who had played Norman Bates in *Psycho*) as Piersall. His story was groundbreaking. Piersall was a fairly well-known athlete and sports hero, and in the book he was openly writing about the taboo subject of his own mental illness, something that in those days was rarely, if ever, discussed—and certainly never in public. Paramount wouldn't complete the purchase of film rights until they were assured by their British office that the movie, which they considered to depict a sensitive subject, could be shown in England. That process took about two weeks, but this time, Al wasn't so nervous.

Shortly thereafter, movie studios began to realize the importance of television, and to consider it a threat to motion pictures. Unlike the Jimmy Piersall–Al Hirshberg film contract, in which we retained television rights, their contracts from that point on gave the holders of feature-film rights control of all television rights.

But what Al was most proud of was a story that appeared in *Pageant* magazine, a general-interest pocket-sized monthly, after the book came out. It described Piersall's visit to the home of a little boy in New York City who was temporarily mute. The parents couldn't get their son to talk, but they knew he was a baseball fan and they had read the Piersall book. They contacted Jimmy and persuaded him to visit the boy, and as Jimmy started telling baseball stories, the boy began to talk.

All five of these authors' successes were satisfying to me, as I realized I had helped make a substantial contribution to their lives. My commitment was always to the writer; my own financial success was secondary. I hadn't spent much time searching for clients, but with this kind of start, writers were flocking to me, editors were calling, anxious to take me to lunch, and publishers with book ideas were calling to see if I had a writer for them. They knew that if I didn't have the right author, I wouldn't try to snow them. I found that the more good writers I had, the more good writers came to me. And personally, I was discovering that giving was one of the greatest sources of pleasure in my life.

# CHAPTER 4

# Invading the Intelligence Community

As the fifties moved into the sixties, my client list continued to expand. By 1962, I had many new and important clients, including Ken Kesey, already the author of *One Flew Over the Cuckoo's Nest*; Jimmy Breslin, soon-to-become the most successful and most talked-about newspaper columnist in the United States; and Terry Southern, who was known for his satirical, witty, and poignant short stories and his hilarious novel, *The Magic Christian*, about the fictional, farcical billionaire Guy Grand, who knows that people will do just about anything for the right amount of money. Terry was also coauthor of *Candy*, a sexual romp first published in Paris and later in the US.

I acquired the rights to *Candy* from Maurice Girodias in 1964 after a drawn-out legal battle. I sold it to Putnam and *Candy* became #1 on *Time* magazine's fiction bestseller list. Terry Southern was soft-spoken with a brilliant and sometimes subtle wit. In a piece he wrote for the *Realist*—he has an imaginary interview with a male homosexual nurse—nearly fifty years ago, when people didn't say such things publicly, Terry came up with this then-provocative opening line: "Good. Well, let's see . . . now you've been a faggot male nurse for what—nine years, I believe?" It compelled people to read the rest of the pseudo-interview article.

Two journalists I started working with then—David Wise and Tom Ross—were both highly regarded newspaper reporters. Their second book with me became a #1 nonfiction bestseller on the *Time* magazine list the same week Terry Southern was #1 on the fiction list.

I was introduced to David Wise by his older brother Bill, whom I had known since the late forties, when we both worked for *True* magazine. We also had founded and published a monthly TV magazine on the side, a short-lived publication called *TV Headliner*. Over the years, Bill Wise has always been a careful, conservative, and thoughtful man. When Bill visited his father in Florida he would take a coach train from New York City, where he lived, to Virginia, to save on the fare, and then transfer to the sleeper (first class) for the rest of the trip.

In the morning, at his home in Manhattan, when he looked out the window and saw it was overcast, he both took his umbrella and wore his rubbers. He had a quiet sense of honor, and his drawl was like that of Henry Fonda. He was doing one-shots for Fawcett Publications, magazines on one subject with one issue. He had introduced me to a number of fine writers, but once I opened my literary agency, he began talking to me about his younger brother, David, then an undergraduate at Columbia University and editor of the *Columbia Daily Spectator*. He was also campus stringer for United Press and the International News Service. He left those assignments when he was offered a job as campus correspondent for the *New York Herald Tribune*, at the time a lively competitor to the *New York Times*. Shortly before graduation day, Bill appeared in my offices at 109 East Thirty-Sixth Street with his prolific younger brother, and there began a relationship that has lasted more than sixty years.

David Wise was slightly somber-looking, with glasses and a high forehead, always neatly dressed and meticulous. Looking at him, you knew he wouldn't give you any information he didn't want to divulge, which suited not only his nature, but his job. He was about to start working full-time for the *New York Herald Tribune*.

Even after I'd known and worked with David for ten or fifteen years, if I called to ask him for the phone number of, for example, another journalist in Washington, David would say, "Well, let me see!

I may have it. I'll look in my files and call you back," and while I was waiting for the return call, he would—without telling me—phone the journalist to see if he or she objected to his giving me the number. That kind of care was typical of David's professional work.

By 1961, David was the *New York Herald Tribune*'s White House correspondent, and he later became the youngest Washington bureau chief in that newspaper's history. He introduced me to his close friend Tom Ross, who eventually became Washington bureau chief of the *Chicago Sun-Times*. David and Tom came to me in June 1961 with a proposal for a book on Francis Gary Powers, the American pilot who was shot down and captured by the Russians the year before, while flying the secret Lockheed U-2 plane, the CIA's ultra-high-altitude spy craft, which the US government weakly insisted was a weather plane. The incident caused a major heating up of the Cold War, increasing distrust between the US and the Soviet Union.

The handsome young men in this picture taken in the late 1960s are David Wise, left, and Tom Ross. In preparing to write their first book, *The U-2 Affair*, they realized that they were too distracted by social demands in the Washington, DC, area (they were both single). They decided to get out of town to concentrate on the manuscript, and decamped to a coconut plantation in Puerto Rico. By the time they completed their next book, *The Invisible Government*, the book for which they are best known, they had both married and had a much calmer social life. They no longer had to leave Washington in order to report, write, and produce that book.

I'm standing with David Wise in front of his house in the Cleveland Park section of Washington, DC, in 2005. I have been representing David since the day he graduated from Columbia University—almost sixty years.

By August we had a book contract with veteran editor Bob Loomis at Random House. Loomis was one of the best editors in town. He's not a flamboyant man, but he's always had a host of top-notch writers such as Bill Styron, Maya Angelou, Shelby Foote, and Pete Dexter, because he himself is top-notch. During his flying days—he had his own private plane—he thought nothing of picking up me or another friend in Manhattan for lunch and flying us from Teterboro Airport to, say, Pennsylvania for a snack and back again. The total advance for Wise and Ross was $4,000, which at the time seemed like a fair sum for writers who had not done a book before. This would turn out to be *The U-2 Affair* (1962), one of two books they would do that were the most dramatic projects of my early years.

In researching the book, the two writers used great ingenuity. While the Air Force was still clinging to the fiction that the high-flying spy craft was a weather plane, the pair wangled their way into a U-2 plane on Edwards Air Force Base in the remote California desert. They were admitted onto the base after expressing great interest in research on cloud formations, although neither of them knew cirrus from nimbus. After examining the U-2 plane, taking turns sitting in the cockpit, and interviewing one of the pilots on how his pressure suit worked, they scrambled off again, before anybody caught on. This was typical of the two of them. They were ingenious.

Tom was a Yale man and a Navy veteran, very intelligent, suave, a seasoned reporter and a fine writer. At the end of his book-writing career and his many years in the newspaper business, he was fired from the *Sun-Times* by Jim Hoge and went to work as Assistant Secretary of Defense for Public Affairs under Secretary of Defense Harold Brown. He was so skilled at that job that the *Washington Post* did a feature about him, a very unusual thing for them to do. Later he worked for RCA and NBC.

By the end of 1961, their research done, Tom felt they should get away from the distractions of Washington, DC, to write—they were both young bachelors and easily distracted—and the Caribbean beckoned. They were dealing in an amusing way with a problem many writers have. Tom volunteered to be the advance man and flew to Puerto Rico to find a quiet place. In a couple of days, he called David, who promptly boarded a plane to San Juan. Tom was waiting at the airport with a mariachi band and a frozen daiquiri, which he handed to David.

"I've got us a coconut plantation," he said. Although alarmed at the possible cost, given their modest—even minuscule—advance from Random House, David hopped into the rented blue Chevrolet sedan, and they drove to the tiny coastal village of Mediania Alta, about twenty miles east of San Juan. Ross had found them a rustic guesthouse on the plantation grounds, right on the beach.

Their days on the coconut plantation settled into a pleasant routine. After a morning swim in the warm waves, they changed into polo shirts, Bermuda shorts, and tropical hats, and set up two card tables on the lawn in the sun, overlooking the beach, and worked all day, typing the manuscript, with only a short break for lunch. I admired their choice of workspace and later realized how well it had worked for them.

But Puerto Rico proved to have its own distractions. Juan Suarez, the owner of the plantation, showed up on the weekends with two or three attractive young women. The bedrooms of the *hacienda*, the main house, opened to a long second-floor balcony above the lawn.

Juan liked to chase the scantily clad women along the balcony and in and out of the bedrooms, amid a great slamming of doors and giggling. For David and Tom, as they recalled those days, it was like a scene out of the British play *Noises Off.* This proved somewhat unsettling to two young bachelors typing on manual typewriters below, trying as they were to concentrate not on the bikinis and the frolicking on the balcony, but on the serious business of Francis Gary Powers and his CIA spy plane. Somehow they managed.

By late each afternoon, it was time for a rum drink and a few moments of relaxation before dinner. The house came with Eusabia, a local resident who prepared the same meal for them every day— *asopao*, a chicken boiled with rice, spices, and vegetables. She would leave it on the stove and disappear without a word, reappearing the next day. After dinner, David and Tom exchanged the pages they had written and edited each other's work.

They did a miraculous job of combining their writing abilities. I couldn't tell—and I doubt anyone else could—which chapters were written by Tom and which by David.

The only other distractions were the roosters, which began crowing before first light. Annoyed, one morning David got up and went outside in the semidarkness, determined to do battle. He picked up a coconut, took what he thought was careful aim, and threw it at one of the roosters. He didn't hit the bird, but he narrowly missed one of the plantation workers carrying a three-foot machete as he slipped through the trees, on his way to chop down coconuts. The U-2 project could have ended right there, but David beat a strategic retreat into the guesthouse.

In exactly one month, which may have been something of a record considering all the distractions, they came close to finishing, and by February 1962 they were back home in Washington, DC, and had written and delivered to Bob Loomis about ninety percent of the book. They had phenomenal sources and support that went all the way to the top of the Kennedy administration. On Friday night, February 8, Tom was at a White House dinner honoring President Kennedy's brother-in-law Steve Smith, who was leaving the State Department, when the president took Tom, still with the *Sun-Times*, aside and revealed that

Powers was going to be released and returned to the US on Sunday. (That was the famous trade: Rudolf Abel, the Russian master spy the US held, for Powers, on the Glienicke Bridge in Berlin, with James Donovan, the US lawyer and ex-counsel to the Office of Strategic Services, handling the arrangements.)

Tom immediately slipped away to the nearest White House phone, as surreptitiously as he could, and called David. Secret Service agents were eyeing him suspiciously, and he feared the phone might be snatched away at any moment. I was sleeping peacefully in my apartment in New York City when my phone rang at 4 a.m. Saturday.

"Sterling, it's David Wise," a familiar voice said. He apologized for the hour of the call, with a light chuckle. "The US is about to get Powers back, and all I need to know is where I can reach you later this morning."

After David and I spoke again in broad daylight, I called Bob Loomis at home to bring him up to date. I'd sold him quite a few books, we'd developed a close working relationship, and I fortunately had his home number. As a result of that call, when Random House opened for business Monday morning, they figuratively had their track shoes on. They immediately sent the partial manuscript to the printers (rather unusual in book publication then), and publication was advanced by four months. This aided the book enormously and helped establish David and Tom as important writers in the field of espionage and intelligence.

The intelligence community had not been on David's beat, and this project opened his eyes to the fertile field of espionage.

The book was fascinating and explosive, containing many stories the public and even other newspaper reporters had never heard. The U-2 had been sent over the Soviet Union just before the Eisenhower-Khrushchev summit meeting because the CIA feared agreements would be reached that would make it impossible to overfly Russia again.

Ike worried about the program from the start. "If one of these planes is shot down," he said, as the book reveals, "this will be on my head. I'm going to catch hell. The world will be in a mess."

And, finally, the U-2 pilots were told if in trouble to push a button that would allow them time to bail out, but blow up the plane. But the pilots worried that if the CIA's goal was to destroy all the evidence, the powerful explosive would also kill them.

All this led to David and Tom breaking the secret side of the American intelligence community wide open.

A few years later, David had achieved a well-earned reputation for knowing more about the US intelligence community than any other Washington correspondent, and also for being the most security-conscious writer in the capital. Confidential information that David held was locked securely inside him. As Tom Ross once observed, "Telling something to David is like spitting down a well at midnight."

David was totally and completely secure for years, until one night in 1974, when he and his wife Joan were having dinner with their good friends Elizabeth and Seymour Hersh at the Hersh home.

David found himself sitting next to the actress and author Jane Fonda. At the time, David knew everything about the intelligence community, but little about Hollywood. He had certainly never sat next to a movie star before. Jane and David chatted about Jimmy Breslin's latest novel, and in the middle of the conversation Jane told him she'd like to meet Jimmy. She wanted to do a film based on his latest novel and she knew that both Jimmy and David had worked on the *Herald Tribune*, and therefore David would probably know Jimmy and have his phone number. David softened immediately and told Jane that if she wanted to call him at home the next day, he would give her Jimmy's phone number. She did and he did.

I learned about this later that morning when Breslin called me: "Guess what," he said. "David Wise's security has been broken—Jane Fonda did it."

If the behind-the-scenes events of *The U-2 Affair* were dramatic—Puerto Rican plantation, presidential tip-off, 4 a.m. phone call—the next book David and Tom undertook together was also high drama, most of it behind the scenes, too. They came to me about their second book, *The Invisible Government* (1964). As cautious as David was about divulging information, he knew I respected that and observed the same caution. How else could I represent him? In the years prior to the publication of *The Invisible Government*, there had been very little press coverage of the intelligence community. Although the CIA was headquartered in Langley, Virginia, near Washington, DC, neither the newspapers nor the public in general knew anything about it. *The Invisible Government* was the first serious book about the US government's intelligence agencies. It would tell the American public about clandestine and possibly illegal activities of the CIA, none of which had previously been public knowledge. Among other revelations, David and Tom had exposed the existence of the 54-12 group, also called the Special Group, a top-secret committee that approved covert operations. Its members included Allen Dulles, chairman of the Central Intelligence Agency; Gordon Gray, National Security Advisor; James Douglas, Acting Secretary of Defense; Livingston T. Merchant, Under Secretary of State for Political Affairs; and McGeorge Bundy, National Security Advisor. Because of *The Invisible Government*'s publication, the CIA gave the group a new name. The book also revealed that the CIA had tried to overthrow Sukarno (the leader of Indonesia), that a pilot flying for the CIA was shot down and captured in the operation, and that Radio Free Europe was bankrolled by the CIA. Wise and Ross also disclosed more details of the Bay of Pigs disaster of 1961 than had previously been known, including the story of four American fliers who were shot down and died there, and revealed additional details about CIA operations that overthrew the governments of Guatemala and Iran.

The CIA learned about the book's contents before publication, and agency officials were outraged. A young Random House intern—a friend, it happens, of the son of Bennett Cerf, Random House's publisher—had secretly slipped a copy of the galley proofs to his stepfather, a senior official of the CIA. Random House figured out where the leak sprang from, but for a long time they were too embarrassed to tell me.

The CIA went to extraordinary measures to keep *The Invisible Government* out of the hands of the book-buying public, but the authors and Random House fought all their attempts to censor the book or stop its publication. It became a battle between Wise, Ross, Random House, and me on one side, and the CIA and its director, John A. McCone, who made a fortune in World War II in the shipbuilding business, on the other side.

The CIA's first attempt at censorship came in the form of a phone call from Director McCone directly to Bennett Cerf. Bennett was also a high-profile personality on the TV show *What's My Line?*, a flamboyant man with a raucous sense of humor. He had founded Random House and started the business with Donald Klopfer. Bennett was a hands-on leader. He called me the morning after he had attended a cocktail party where he had met a young woman writer who was about to become my client, and he said he'd like to see her novel. On the day of the McCone call—May 5, 1964—Bennett was not in his office, so the call was referred to Bob Loomis, the book's editor, who was experienced at fending off outside attempts to interfere with forthcoming books. I knew Loomis would not cave in.

McCone was asking for the right to make editorial changes, including cuts to the manuscript. He claimed there were many inaccuracies. Loomis refused and suggested McCone check with the authors, knowing what they would say. David and Tom were invited to meet with Director McCone in his office on the seventh floor of the CIA's new headquarters in Langley, Virginia. Like Bob Loomis, I knew that even though they were up against great pressure from the highest offices, they could handle themselves. We all learned years before that it's not necessarily the smartest person who runs the show in any field. Which is not to denigrate McCone, but my authors were not about to be intimidated.

McCone attacked the accuracy of the book on one hand, and claimed simultaneously that it revealed important secrets that would damage national security. It seemed to David and Tom that his two points were in conflict. In the meeting, McCone was flanked by a CIA public-relations man and a top CIA official named Lyman Kirkpatrick. At one point, to show the writers how many CIA people they would uncover if their book came out, McCone handed my authors a two-page document marked SECRET in large black letters near the top and bottom of the first page, suggesting they take it with them to study the list of names to get an idea of the damage the book would do by revealing them now.

As it was being handed to them, Tom Ross piped up: "Do you think we are going to walk out of the building carrying a classified document?" Kirkpatrick took the document back immediately, pulled a pair of scissors out of the desk, and cut off the top and bottom of page one—where it read SECRET—and gave the document back to

Wise and Ross. Studying the list that night, Wise and Ross decided there were only four names on the list not previously uncovered, and that the rest were people widely known as being involved with the CIA. In the end, David and Tom flatly refused to make any changes. The discussion was over.

I had total confidence in David and Tom. Neither one was an irresponsible cowboy. They believed that transparency is an essential part of our democracy, and that there was no reason to censor any part of their book. Yet they were sensitive to the needs of the government. At another time, David would demonstrate that fact: When Kennedy and Salinger were in the White House, there was concern raised about the press's revealing material that would be damaging to the country. David had heard about a joint announcement to be made by Kennedy and Soviet leader Nikita Khrushchev the next day, revealing that Moscow would release two captured American fliers. David called Pierre to inquire about it. Salinger requested the *Herald Tribune* delay publication and did so again in a second phone call to David. In a third call, near midnight, Salinger said the president was asking David to delay publication. David recommended to his bureau chief that the story be held on the grounds that if the US-Soviet agreement was torpedoed by the disclosure, the fliers might never be freed and the newspaper would be blamed. The editors in New York agreed, and the newspaper was subsequently thanked publicly by JFK.

Another dramatic attempt to censor *The Invisible Government* was revealed by a well-known syndicated columnist, Marquis Childs. Childs, a fellow Iowan (whom I had never met—it's a fairly large state after all) and author of many books and a successful newspaper column distributed by United Press, wrote that high officials were considering buying up the entire first printing of *The Invisible Government* to keep it out of bookstores. He also phoned Bennett Cerf to ask whether he would sell the first printing to the CIA, which obviously intended to burn all the copies.

The clever Cerf telephoned McCone and said he would sell the first printing to the CIA, but he would immediately go back to press again, and again, and again. The CIA had, in fact, conducted research to see whether it had the legal power to buy up the first printing, but they abandoned the idea after the phone call with Bennett. The agency also appointed a task force to deal with the book. It produced a document entitled "Report of the Chairman of the Task Force," recommending, among other steps, that the CIA use "such assets as the Agency may have" to secure unfavorable reviews of the book. They had some success in Europe, David later discovered, but probably none in the US. I was surprised at the intensity of the CIA's reaction, which made me think for the first time that the CIA might very well be concealing other information the public should know as well.

Behind the scenes at Langley, other forces were at work: The authors learned that the CIA was considering the possibility of prosecuting them under the espionage laws and had approached the Justice Department with the idea. The Justice Department brushed aside the suggestion, warning that it would only help to sell more copies. In the end, the CIA thought better of their scheme.

The book was published by Random House in May 1964 without any changes and became a #1 national bestseller on the *Time* magazine list, and #2 on the *New York Times* list behind Ernest Hemingway's *A Moveable Feast*. Hemingway's preface said readers could regard his book as fiction if they wished. The *New York Times* did not regard *The Invisible Government* as fiction or it would have been #1 on that list as well. It did remain on the *New York Times* bestseller list for twenty-two weeks, and was also listed more than once as #1 in *Book Week*, the *Washington Post*, and the *New York Herald Tribune*.

It sold 500,000 copies in the US (hardcover plus paperback) and was published in eight foreign editions. And the phrase "the invisible government," which began to appear often in newspapers, magazines, and on TV and radio news-shows, became part of our language.

The last time I spoke to Tom while he was still bureau chief of the *Chicago Sun-Times* was the day of Richard Nixon's resignation. I had called him on a publishing matter, but I'll never forget his Nixon comment; "I'm so disappointed, Sterling, that we in the press were never able to tell the public the truth about Nixon."

I was very proud of my clients. I hadn't suffered through it all the way they had. It was a great vindication for the work they had done.

While all this was going on, there was a young executive in the

CIA, a former journalist named Richard Helms. He was not involved directly in the CIA-versus-Wise-and-Ross situation, but the writers were sure he knew the details. I had never met Helms, until the year 2000, shortly after he retired as head of the CIA. He wanted to write a book about his intelligence experiences and for me to represent him. I had met him at one of Kay Graham's summertime lunches at Martha's Vineyard, where she had a lovely house with a private tennis court. Kay, of course, was president of the *Washington Post*, and she seemed to know everyone, and not surprisingly many of the important and accomplished people of the time were summering in the Vineyard and invited to her lunches. She also had interesting houseguests and, through her, I met Warren Buffett and Dick Helms, among others. I had played on Kay's tennis court two or three times, and one day Kay called to invite me to play mixed doubles with her against one of the leading women tennis pros on the island and the pro's husband. Kay was not a particularly accomplished player, but she loved the game and would get a lot of balls back. To my surprise, we won the first set, and in celebration I threw my arms around her and kissed her on the cheek. Later, one of the tennis regulars told me that was the very first time that had happened to her on that court.

Buoyed by the victory, Kay invited me to Sunday lunch a few days later. There she took me aside to tell me she wouldn't be able to play with me in the coming week, as she was playing in a tournament. "But," she said, "I want to introduce you to a man here who you could play with this week. He'll beat you, but it should be fun." Kay's judgment of the ability of players was not her strong suit: Three days later, I was on the court with this young man, trying to figure out how I could give him one game in the set without his realizing it was a gift.

As Dick Helms and I were working together, we saw each other occasionally. Once he invited me to be his guest at a large banquet in Washington, and we spent the afternoon and evening together. He was a courteous host, introducing me to Sandra Day O'Connor and others. The names Wise and Ross were never mentioned by either of us. And, in a year, I sold his book to Bob Loomis.

Loomis was not only one of the most effective editors in the business but also very informed in the intelligence field, and he was made that much better informed by his experience with Wise and Ross.

Helms's book didn't get much ink, and I understood why. In the first place, by this time, readers already knew a good deal about the CIA, and he had to be protective of much information about the agency. As a result, unlike Ross and Wise's writings, Helms's revealed little about the inner workings of the CIA. Helms's book took a long time to write; Random House published *A Look Over My Shoulder* in 2003, but he had died on October 22, 2002.

# CHAPTER 5

# First Down, First Novel, First Feature Film

The transplanted cowboy above is Peter Gent, who was born and raised in a small town in the poorest county of Michigan. He became nationally known when he played basketball for Michigan State University and was selected on many All-American teams; he then played football for the Dallas Cowboys. When he'd retired from the field, he wrote an extraordinary novel, *North Dallas Forty*, which was based on his own professional football experience. He died in 2011 at age sixty-nine.

*North Dallas Forty* (1973) by Peter Gent was not my first bestselling sports novel, but at the time it was unique as the first major novel about professional football written by an insider. In recent times, few if any sports novels, before or since *North Dallas Forty*, have sold as well. In fact, it was the first bestselling book in recent years of fiction by an athlete about his own sport. Many other athletes have written nonfiction books about their lives and the sports they played, almost always with the help of a professional ghostwriter, but they didn't write novels. And fiction is generally regarded as a higher art form than nonfiction. My early experience with Peter Gent, on top of my previous ghosted nonfiction books with Rocky Graziano and Jimmy Piersall, helped me focus on what I wanted to represent in the sports field, both in fiction and nonfiction.

When I started my agency, I suspect I was the only literary agent who read the sports pages and had been reading them since I was ten years old. It was something I had in common with much of the American public. That New York literary agents thought sports were not on a plane with the literature they were representing would work to my advantage and enable me to step into the literary world sideways—as I did with Kerouac, Kesey, and Amiri Baraka (formerly known as LeRoi Jones), for example.

For me, it was only natural. As an agent, I wasn't satisfied with the story of a sports figure that had made major headlines for something he did on the field of play. There had to be more—either drama in the athlete's life, a handicap he or she had overcome, an extremely well-written story, or one with insights and drama that hadn't been explored exhaustively in the news or in previous books. *North Dallas Forty* demonstrated the latter, *and* it was exciting and gripping.

The story of Peter Gent, with all its drama, says something about book editors and feature filmmaking, and a great deal about what can be done when a writer believes strongly in his own work and takes action.

Things that most people would find impossible to attempt, let alone do—playing professional football and writing a terrific sports novel—Peter did superbly. It's quotidian life that's been tough on him.

"Only a guy crazy enough to think he could be a world-class athlete would be crazy enough to think he could write a bestselling novel," Peter once wrote, and he was right.

Peter was six feet five and wide, but not heavy by NFL standards. He was an imposing figure, both fit and strong. He was a man's man, and in a crowd he was a presence. In the early part of his days with the Dallas Cowboys, he attracted many good-looking women, one of whom he married for 120 days.

When I first met Peter, he had long hair tied in a ponytail down to a foot above his belt. I liked him immediately—his intelligence, his straightforward manner and speech—and I admired his ability as an athlete in two sports—basketball in high school and college, and professional football after that. Aside from some tennis players, I didn't know any athletes of that status who were also as articulate. (Later I met Jerry Kramer, a lineman with the Green Bay Packers and a remarkable man. Dick Schaap and I picked him out of a locker room when we were looking for a player to keep a diary throughout an entire season. Dick had seen him reading poetry in the Packers' locker room, which was enough of an indication. We took him immediately. Cowritten with Dick Schaap and edited by Bob Gutwillig, *Instant Replay* made Jerry Kramer a bestselling author.)

Peter never bragged about his sports feats; in fact he never talked about them unless asked. Despite the time he had spent in the flashy sports world, he never forgot that he came from Bangor, Michigan— a town so small it has no traffic lights. When he was growing up, local metal plants produced parts for the Big Three Detroit automakers. Small farmers grew crops for consumers in Chicago. The town had two dairies processing and delivering milk. And people didn't lock their doors at night.

Peter's grandfather owned and tended 120 acres of apple, peach, and cherry orchards. And during the Depression, Peter's father planted and cared for forty acres of pine trees. He earned his living delivering railway mail and later, rural mail, and he taught his sons lessons about life: that education was important and that they should never quit anything they started, join the Marines, or ride a motorcycle.

Peter had been an outstanding high-school athlete, playing four sports and leading his basketball team to the Michigan state title in a final game that was tied 41–41 at the end of the third quarter. Bangor High won 57–45, with Peter scoring 21 points. A middle son, he'd played high-school sports with both his brothers.

At Michigan State University, Peter was the only basketball player in the school's history to start every game, be voted Most Valuable Player, and lead the team in scoring, winning all Big Ten honors for three seasons. In his senior year he was awarded the Big Ten Medal of Honor for athletic and academic achievements and chosen for the All–Big Ten Academic Team. By the time he graduated, he was the second leading scorer in MSU history.

After graduating, Peter had offers to play basketball with the Baltimore Bullets (which later became the Washington Wizards) or football with the Dallas Cowboys. The Cowboys had a practice of inviting five or six excellent non-football-playing athletes to try out for the team, a smart practice that, as an agent (in another field, but one always interested in raw talent), I could admire. Dallas offered Peter a $500 signing bonus plus $500 more if he stayed in camp twenty-one calendar days, and $11,000 if he stayed on the roster for the fourteen-game season. The Baltimore offer was $8,500 for a hundred-game schedule—twenty exhibition games and eighty regular-season games. The $8,500 was not payable until the NBA season began. He wouldn't have to wait so long if he went with the Cowboys. Peter did the math and joined the Cowboys.

At twenty-two, Peter was not just a star athlete; he also had a fine mind, and that caused some consternation for the Cowboys' head coach. Each year the team gave the Wonderlic Personnel (intelligence) Test to all the players. Coach Tom Landry, who was tough, stoical, and single-minded, would read the test responses and then call in the players one at a time for an interview. During Landry's era, Dallas had a firm rule not to take on any quarterback who scored less than 19 out of 50 questions or any wide receiver who scored less than 12, none of which was known by the players at that time. In 1964 they gave the test to sixty-two players, but called in only sixty-one—all but Peter Gent, who was worried that he was going to be cut. It devolved that he was in the precarious position of having scored higher than Landry himself and dramatically higher than most of the other players.

Unlike Coach Landry, who wore a fedora, suit, tie, and a grimace to every game, I saw Peter's intelligence as an asset. Peter's perspective on the American sport was so inside, so dark, and so unlike the popular image, that it was uniquely honest and revealing.

The 1964 season ended with four wins, and Peter played only on the special teams. In 1965, the team lost five of their first seven games with Peter on the bench. Receivers coach Red Hickey, the creator of the shotgun offense—in which the quarterback lines up where the fullback traditionally did (about four feet behind the center), giving the quarterback a better view of the defense and the passer more time to set up—had been pressing Landry to give Peter more game time. In the previous two games, Landry had sent Peter in for a couple of series of downs only. He caught his first pass against Cleveland for a thirty-five-yard touchdown but he did not play again for two more games, until Landry put him in against Pittsburgh. During that game he caught his second pass for an eight-yard touchdown. He caught two other passes before Landry pulled him out. He spent the rest of the first half of the season on the bench, where recently demoted first-string quarterback Don Meredith joined him. Together they watched the team nosedive and struck up a friendship fueled by frustration.

Finally, facing a 2–5 season with the second half of the schedule much tougher than the first, Landry, under constant pressure from Hickey, gave Peter the starting flankerback position. At the same time, Landry offered Meredith the starting quarterback position back. Meredith refused unless he could call all the plays, and Landry agreed. Meredith was to become starting quarterback, the dominant leader of the team, and he remained Peter's friend and, some believed, his protector.

Meredith's total control of the offense made a huge difference. The second half of the 1965 season Peter became the third-down receiver, a critical spot, and with rookie Bobby Hayes, another of Peter's friends, who was an Olympic gold medal sprinter, at the other side, Dallas won five of seven games and qualified for the playoffs for the first time.

The South was still so racist that the Cowboys preseason training camps were all above the Mason-Dixon Line—Michigan, Oregon, and California—to allow the black players to live near the practice field.

Back in Texas, Bobby Hayes and the other African American players had to live in meager dwellings in Oak Cliff or South Dallas, a run-down section of town.

During his years with the Cowboys, Peter destroyed his knees, had two A/C shoulder separations, broke a leg, dislocated his ankle, fractured his vertebrae, broke his ribs, suffered partial paralysis of his lower back and left hip—caused by team doctors dragging him off the field when his back was broken—and broke his nose eight times.

He, like the other players, played through the pain, aided by free pharmaceuticals doled out by team management like candy at Halloween. Anything to keep players playing. The pressure on individual players was great but unspoken.

Peter loved playing for the NFL. He loved what he called the "talented, tormented" players. But he also recognized the futility of the game: While Americans spent Sundays roaring for their football heroes, Peter saw himself and his teammates for what they were: interchangeable parts, whose bodies belonged to the franchise that owned them.

The camaraderie, the rivalries, and the wild life of sex, adulation, alcohol, and drugs made Peter feel he "was traveling faster than I could see." And it was that experience that would provide the raw material for Peter's roman à clef.

The winter after the 1965 season, Peter did a great deal of thinking about what he wanted to do with his life. He was living with Don Talbert, a large and powerful offensive tackle for the Cowboys, who not only taught him how to be a professional football player on and off the field, but also had a great sense of humor and showed Peter a life he'd never explored. The two shared a three-bedroom duplex apartment in Dallas. Throughout the year they had a string of visitors, both other players and women. This was a new scene for Peter. It broadened his range of experiences.

He'd been interested in reading and writing since the early days, when his father would talk to him about books after school on their front porch. Peter was especially drawn to the works of F. Scott Fitzgerald and Thomas Wolfe. For a while after college he'd considered a job that involved writing and had a chance to go with Foote, Cone and Belding, a major ad agency, in their Chicago office. At the time ad agencies weren't taking men directly from college, but they wanted Peter, and he gave it a shot. Not only did he not like it, there was no writing involved and the pay was so low he could only afford a dingy room in a down-market part of town. It was so depressingly poor, Peter claimed that petty thieves broke into his room while he was still there.

He knew he had some talent for writing, and he recognized he was living and working in the world of high drama on and off the field. As an accomplished athlete in another sport—basketball—he brought an interesting perspective to the pro-football game. Football was much more demanding physically than basketball: Injuries were much more brutal. Most players who left the game or retired, left because of injuries—many of which affected them the rest of their lives. The saying in the game was "An injured player is an ex-player." And the emotional and physical rewards in basketball had been much greater for Peter.

Peter started writing while he was still playing football. His characters were exaggerated versions of his friends among the players, until he realized that as a novelist he had greater freedom. For example, there's a scene in *North Dallas Forty* in which his lead character, Phil Elliott, is having an affair with the wife of the owner. This story was not based on anything that took place in Dallas, but on something that happened in another NFL town.

During his days with the Cowboys, he and Olympic sprinter Bob Hayes, the African American Cowboys wide receiver, whose life was made more difficult by segregated Texas neighborhoods, became close friends.

Together they set up a company to sell quality engravings and printing work from a very good Dallas printer to ad agencies and major corporations. Had Peter's early forays into the world of business succeeded he might not have become the accomplished writer so soon.

Bob Hayes was not comfortable or especially effective at selling but he was so admired that all he had to do to help sales was show up; Peter would do the talking. Believing that the printer could run their finances better than they could, they made him president of their company. And it looked as though their business would be a great success. Peter was earning twice what he earned on the football field. Among the Gent-Hayes clients were two major ad agencies, plus Braniff Airlines and Neiman Marcus department stores.

Immediately after his football career, Peter continued to sell printing, but his heart wasn't in it. Nearing the end of his career, when he was traded to the Giants, he had discovered that the man he and Bob Hayes put in charge of the company had spent all the funds and run up $500,000 in debt, investing in a scheme that paid illustrators top dollar to design posters for the Texas International Pop Festival. Unfortunately, nobody had made any effort to display or sell them. The venture was a disaster. In lieu of the money the printer owed them, he gave Peter all 40,000 posters and allowed him to keep the posters in his—the printer's—storage space. But the printer's patience was short-lived. He soon grew tired of paying the rent of the storage facility and shredded the 40,000 posters without informing Peter, which is what caused Peter to realize he would have to get out of the business. He was not a businessman. Five years later, the few pop-festival posters that had survived were bringing $300 and up at art galleries and bookstores.

Peter was close to broke when he and his wife, Jody, and daughter, Holly, moved from New York City back to Dallas. They couldn't afford to ship their furniture and arranged for Delta Airlines, where Jody had been a department head, to transport their possessions from their Washington Place apartment in Manhattan back to the land of cattle and cotton.

Peter never had more than $1,000 in the bank. He knew he didn't want to be a salesman the rest of his life, and that's when he started seriously working on a novel, about a subject he knew: professional football.

Peter never sought the fame that accrued to him in high school, college, and professional sports. The longer I knew him, the more I understood that Peter was not comfortable with the fan adulation, an outgrowth of his natural physical abilities and his incredible discipline on the field.

When I spent one Thanksgiving with Peter in his hometown I couldn't help but notice that almost every car there had on its bumper a sticker that read "Annihilate Ohio State," attesting to the seriousness with which Michigan residents took the rivalry between Michigan and Ohio State. When Peter drove me past his high school, I peered through the main-entrance glass doors and could see, even from the road, Peter Gent's state championship trophy still displayed in a prominent position. But Peter is a cerebral and private person, and his move into writing was a private experience I felt suited his nature. He was a natural-born writer, writing at night and on weekends at his apartment in Dallas, sitting on a peach crate, usually in a windowless hallway between the bedroom and the bathroom. He needed privacy and didn't want anyone but the few close friends he trusted to know what he was doing. At one point during the writing he, his wife, and their eleven-year-old daughter were invited by a friend to go to Mexico for the filming of the movie *Kid Blue*. Jody was eager to go, so Peter borrowed an old Winnebago, and that is where he did his writing for the next seven months while everyone else on the set watched the filming. Peter financed the trip by borrowing $1,000 from his friend Bud Shrake, author of the movie. And somehow he got the Fox production to give him daily pay as an extra, and lodging for himself, his wife, and his daughter. Since living in Mexico was cheap in those days, that was all they needed. In fact, he only spent half Bud's $1,000 loan. During breaks in the action, actors Dennis Hopper, Peter Boyle, and Warren Oates would sit inside the production van talking about the film. Their stories, energy, and enthusiasm for their work invigorated Peter, who worked with an increasing intensity.

I had only vaguely heard of Peter before he sent me his manuscript. Two clients of mine, both Texans, had mentioned his name and told me they thought he might write a novel someday; in the spring of 1972, when I read the manuscript of *North Dallas Forty*, I was really taken with it. It was new and exciting and compelling. It ripped the cover off a heavily guarded American institution and showed how distorted the images of football players were. Peter told his story artfully by describing eight chaotic days, elevating what might have been a polemic into an existential tale full of humor and insight. The North Dallas Bulls had a druglike effect on their fans: Millionaire businessmen giggled, cops tore up their tickets, and stewardesses, cocktail waitresses, married women, and the reigning Miss Texas succumbed to them in bars and restaurants, on planes, and wherever else a player wanted to be satisfied. As long as they performed on the field, they could have whatever they wanted.

So he could play through the pain, Phillip J. Elliott, the Peter Gent–like character in the novel, gulped amphetamines, codeine, Novocain, or Demerol with his Gatorade before games. After them, he pumped his lungs full of pot. Much of what Elliott did, he did out of fear. Greater than his fear of slamming into a 235-pound line-backer was his fear of missing him. And then there was the fear of being cut from the team.

Peter's characterization of the fictional management roster was devastating. The team doctor was a shill for management, whose job it was not to heal players but to coax the wounded back onto the football field. Trainers were no more than "line workers who repaired broken club property as it was conveyed slowly, but most certainly, to the scrap heap." Anyone who advised injured players to rest, was overruled. As Gent wrote, "Numb it, bind it, but get the property back to work."

His protagonist presented a problem for management: Phil Elliott couldn't be controlled. He's chastised for cracking jokes in the locker room and for being immature. But his outlook is anything but child-ish. He sees the futility of the game, that the team is not the players but the moneymen who control them. And that players are one another's competition. That in the end, every player is alone.

Despite his five catches for two touchdowns in the last game of the season, management decides to get rid of Elliott. They hire an inves-tigator and nab him for the crime of smoking pot. Elliott's friend, the quarterback, with whom he'd been sharing the joint, betrays him and is kept on the team.

Before offering the manuscript to publishers, I recommended that Peter make a number of minor changes. When he sent the revision back to me, I was stunned. He had followed carefully every suggestion I had made. (Years later Peter told me it was the first helpful professional advice he had ever received.) I had a brief feeling of nervousness—supposing I was wrong at some point—but I marched ahead and started to submit it.

Publishers, particularly William Morrow and Random House, responded positively. But there were a few days of high drama. As I began to offer the manuscript, Peter came to New York wanting to meet editors face-to-face. He showed up in a borrowed seersucker suit, a full beard, and the ponytail down to his waist.

When he started meeting with the editors, one of them opened his pitch by telling Peter he had pulled a groin muscle playing weekend foot-ball. He kept rubbing his genitals and asking Peter for advice. Peter was surprised—none of his sports friends ever did that—but said nothing.

Peter, who was in pain every day of his life after playing for the Dallas Cowboys, and constantly on medication to reduce the pain in his lower back (I could tell the extent of his pain by watching him sit down or get up), had never met a New York book editor before, so he had no preconception of how they looked and behaved.

Another editor told Peter he would kill himself if he wasn't able to buy the book from me. Peter didn't know how to take that; in small towns in Michigan, people didn't make statements like that unless they meant it. That editor didn't get the book and continued through life anyway. *North Dallas Forty* was bought for William Morrow by its editor in chief, Hillel Black, a former writer and experienced editor, and a friend.

Black loved the book and agreed to a two-book contract. When his wife overheard him discussing the size of the deal, she warned her husband, "There goes the mortgage." But Hill knew it was a very good book and that when I sold him something, it usually was good or very good. The book was so good, in fact, that quietly Hill wondered if Peter Gent had really written it himself.

An editorial conference between Peter Gent and myself in Wimberley, a small town in the rolling hills of far west Texas, where Peter lived at one time. He was in the process of finishing one of his novels; he was very intense about it and welcomed my coming to see him. It was my first visit to Wimberley.

Hill once bought a book by a policeman and that book had done well. He rationalized, "If a cop can write a successful book, why can't a football player?" That was his logic and the logic, he believed, of book publishing, which, he said, "is no logic."

As with many writers and editors, the two—in working together— would have a few testy moments. After Peter handed in the manuscript, Hillel asked him to cut one hundred pages. Peter refused and a frustrated Hillel, who was as experienced as Peter was not, yelled at him. Hillel also wanted him to change the ending because he thought Peter's ending too dark: After being fired from the team Elliott returns to his lover, the only woman who cared about him as a man, not what he was on the football field. When he arrives at her house, Elliott finds that she and the African American man who is her friend, and apparently more, have been murdered by a rival.

Hill wanted a happier ending, one where, as he would jokingly recall years later, the characters might disappear into the sunset and live happily ever after. Peter refused, telling him the current ending was a logical progression of what happened to these characters. Peter phoned me to ask my opinion, and I told him that if he preferred the ending as he wrote it he should keep it, which he did. Hill still remembers the encounter. He told Peter, "I think you're absolutely wrong, but we're not going to change it." Years later, Hill agreed with Peter: "He was absolutely right."

When it came out in 1973, *North Dallas Forty* shocked, entertained, and educated the American public. This was not just a great sports novel, it worked as a gripping novel even for readers who might not care about sports. In the *New York Times* review, Dick Schaap wrote, "He balances shock with humor, irony with warmth, detail with insight and ends up with a book that easily transcends its subject matter." Schaap added that Peter Gent is "a far better writer than he ever was a pass catcher."

The book sold 55,000 copies in hardcover, 870,680 in paperback, and was selected by three book clubs. More than thirty years later, in 2004, *Sports Illustrated* named it as one of the 100 Best Sports Books of All Time.

We sold the film rights to Stanley Schneider, then an executive at

Columbia Pictures who at the time had a three-picture production deal with the studio. *North Dallas Forty* was to be the first of the three, but unfortunately Stanley died in December 1975, and the studio lost interest. The book spent seven years in "development hell," bouncing from studio to studio. It went through various directors from Bob Rafelson, producer of *Easy Rider* (1969) and *Five Easy Pieces* (1970), among others, to the iconoclastic Robert Altman, and in its travels was worked on by twenty-seven screenwriters. Peter grew more and more impatient at what wasn't happening to his book and more interested in writing the screenplay himself, although he had no prior screenwriting experience.

Producers and studios have different feelings about hiring the author of a book to write the screenplay. Some producers are dead set against it, on the theory that they bought what was on the pages of the book, not what is in the writer's head, which is what you might get if you hire him. I felt the authenticity that Peter would bring to the same story was extremely important. But the producers, director, and the studio didn't agree for a long time.

In 1978, Nick Nolte was seriously attracted to the book and took *North Dallas Forty* to Paramount vice president Michael Eisner (who would later become CEO of Disney). Eisner convinced Paramount that Nolte and *North Dallas Forty* were a synergistic fit. Barry Diller, president of Paramount (and subsequently CEO of the Fox Broadcasting Company), bought the rights to do the film, but insisted that he himself choose the producer and director. Frank Yablans, former head of Paramount, was chosen to produce it.

Once we learned that Nolte was pushing to do the film, Peter's interest in writing the screenplay intensified. He knew the football scene better than any established screenwriter, and Peter wanted the film to be as inside and authentic as the book. For months neither Peter's calls to Yablans's office nor mine were returned. Eventually Peter learned that Yablans and an entire production crew were in Houston, not far from the small west-Texas town of Wimberley where Peter was living, and they were about ready to start filming. Peter and his family had moved out there from Michigan a few years earlier.

Still as determined as ever, Peter drove to Houston, where the unit was planning to start work on the facilities of the Houston Oilers team. What Peter knew and, oddly, the film people did not was that the Oilers and the film people would be overruled by the National Football League, and that none of the other professional football teams would be interested in allowing the movie to be made at their facilities.

That day in Houston, Peter had a good talk with Ted Kotcheff, the movie's director, warning him about the NFL's boycott and expressing his desire to write the screenplay. Kotcheff listened and was polite, but Peter's impression was that he didn't understand the power of the NFL.

Peter was calling and keeping me informed, and I backed him completely. Our objective was obvious and plain: to get him the job. We'd worry about the terms when we got to that part. The situation was pathetic; there was no doubt in my mind that Peter would do a better job than anyone else, and he wanted the job desperately. But being good or great is never enough. You have to be wanted.

A few weeks later, on a Saturday night, Peter had a midnight call from the hard-to-reach Frank Yablans, announcing that he would start filming that coming Monday in the Beverly Hills area. They would pay Peter's expenses if he wanted to come and watch.

Once he arrived in Beverly Hills, Peter found that Nick Nolte, already signed to play the starring role, was disappointed with the screenplay, which wasn't even close to being shootable. He and Peter quickly bonded, and the two persuaded the director and producer (who had written the screenplay together) that the screenplay—all four hundred pages of it—was neither accurate nor authentic. If you are about to produce a film and have all personnel assembled, and your star hates the script, you're in trouble. That's how we got the screenwriting job for Peter Gent.

In late February 1979, they started shooting without a completed screenplay. Just before they started, Peter had a frustrating meeting with Yablans and Kotcheff about the script he was to write. The mood was tense, and tired of being yelled at, Peter, a man without pretensions or a confining sense of protocol, excused himself to go to the bathroom, from which he promptly crawled out the window. The film crew was having lunch adjacent to the building and roared with laughter when they saw Peter climbing out. Eventually, the script came in scene by scene off Peter's typewriter. Peter worked in a hotel room, first in the Beverly Hills Hotel, then in the Westwood Marquis. He would start writing in the early evening. A messenger would phone him from the lobby at 11 p.m. and Peter would deliver the next day's script to the messenger (usually a middle-aged ex-thug fighting for golden after-midnight dollars). The messenger would immediately deliver it to Kotcheff—and that is what they shot the next day. That was how the entire film was made.

You might ask why the process was not started earlier in the day. That was by design—Peter's and Nolte's. Employing the old newspaper reporter's trick, they didn't want to give Ted Kotcheff time to discuss it with Yablans, who would always insist on changes.

Peter was writing without a contract. It made me nervous. I was putting pressure on the producers to give him a contract, but by this time they knew that he was committed to doing the script.

When I was in Beverly Hills, where I usually spent time twice a year to meet with agents, producers, or studio executives with whom I was doing business or wanted to do business, I met with Michael Ovitz, president and one of the founders of Creative Artists Agency (CAA) who was interested in my writers. I said, "You know Yablans and we haven't got a contract, nor have we been paid. I'd like you to get that settled." He gave me a studied reaction and said something like "I'll have to use my personal clout," implying that this was a valuable commodity to be used sparingly.

We got the contract and the money. It was only $25,000, but Peter had the job.

Paramount released the movie in August 1979, opening in eight hundred theaters simultaneously. Critics liked the movie, though some thought it meandered. *Time* magazine wrote that it "retains enough of the novel's authenticity to deliver strong, if brutish, entertainment." *Variety*'s reviewer declared, "The production is a most realistic, hard-hitting and perceptive look at the seamy side of pro football." Much later, in 2005, *Sports Illustrated* called it one of the Fifty Best Sports Films of All Time.

Peter went on to write a number of other books, including a sequel to *North Dallas Forty*, a dark tale of greed, corruption, and murder that *Library Journal* described as "storytelling at its best" and a far more complex tapestry than the first book. In *North Dallas After Forty*, Phil Elliott suffers from debilitating football injuries and badgering by his ex-wife, a slippery lawyer. His respite comes when he's offered a writing assignment about a reunion of his old football team.

Over the years I visited Peter a number of times. I found Wimberley to be a pleasant little town overlaid with a touch of the early West. Peter and I talked a good deal, sitting in his backyard overlooking the low west-Texas hills. Sometimes I sat swinging in the hammock while Peter lay on the ground, an idyllic few moments of relaxation. After I left, Peter told his wife Jody, a tough west-Texan farm girl, how good it was "of Sterling to come down." Jody's sharp answer: "He's paid to do that."

In later years, Peter's life became more difficult. His wife and he grew apart. He wrote to me that after having "tasted money and fame," she realized that she "liked the traffic in the fast lane." Peter is not unlike some other novelists in that, while he is working on a book, and particularly as he gets toward the end, he is exclusively involved in his work. Nothing else counts. Jody wasn't flexible or interested enough to take it and shortly after he finished *The Franchise*, they divorced. It was a torturous divorce, followed by an exhausting custody battle that broke the family apart. When Texas courts temporarily allowed Peter to see his son, Carter, only four days a month, Peter engaged in what he called "the thin ice of civil disobedience," meeting his son for lunch at his elementary school and playing ball with him. As Peter would later write in his book *The Last Magic Summer: A Season with My Son*, about his days with Carter, "Neither judges nor jail were going to keep us apart forever."

At one point, Peter was arraigned in a Texas court for "enticement of a child." Had I not loaned him a few thousand dollars (all his money had gone to Jody in the divorce), they would have jailed him on the spot. The charges were later dropped and Peter would persevere, offering to babysit his son when his wife went away—she refused—and calling the boy at night to tell him bedtime stories.

"She had lived with me through fifteen years of pro football, publishing and movies," he wrote, "and she never noticed my one constant: I do not quit. That is the first rule of sport." And a rule imprinted on him by his father.

Following a three-year battle, Peter, promising to continue to pay alimony, Jody's house payments, and child support, was given custody of his son.

Peter got Carter, and Jody got almost everything else, including the forty acres of pine trees his father had planted.

The next time I saw Peter was in his hometown of Bangor, Michigan, a rural community of around 2,000 people in Van Buren County, where he raised Carter. In *The Last Magic Summer*, the ex-football player wrote about the simple pleasure of tucking his son in at night and waking him in the morning, and about eight summers of coaching Carter in baseball. With grace, Peter wrote about "baseball's redemptive and salubrious effects on my son," a description that equally applies to Peter. Father and son bonded "in the gentle joy of baseball," he wrote. "The game restored wholeness to my life."

By the time that book was written, in 1996, some publishing houses were not as concerned about the quality of their editors' work as they were in selling copies, disregarding the possible relationship between the two factors. They were overloading in-house editors with too many books to slog through and farming out manuscripts to the least-costly, but not the best, freelance editors. Peter's book, which could have been the ode to baseball and his son that it should have been, suffered.

Peter's life after the NFL and Jody was sometimes lonely, but he was back in Bangor, his hometown. We didn't speak all that many times, but when we did, Peter talked to me not just about his writing but about everything else, too, including his medical condition. I think that for Peter, I was not just his agent and friend; I had become a sort of touchstone. In his acknowledgments in the book about Carter he surprised me by writing that I had "worked long and hard" keeping him "upright as I stepped blindly into the maelstrom of the future, time after time, to try to build a life out of chaos. A quarter of a century of hard work is remembered and, who knows, I may get it right yet."

Peter had not completed anything for publication since that time but was constantly working on a long novel about the US intelligence community's use of athletes in operations against foreign countries.

But we were always in touch. Not frequently but regularly.

I called Peter on September 13, 2011, because I hadn't heard from him in some time. We had a good chat, but I knew he was in increasingly severe pain and not getting much effective medical help. A day later, I had a letter from him:

> STERLING —
> I WAS SO GLAD TO HEAR FROM YOU YESTERDAY ++
> I BELIEVE EVERYBODY CONSIDERS WHAT NEXT? THRU OUT LIFE +
> AT THIS POINT FOR SOME REASON DEATH DOESN'T SCARE ME ++ I AM SURE IT WILL EVENTUALLY ++ BUT RIGHT NOW WHAT TERRIFIES ME IS THAT I AM LIVING A LIFE WITHOUT PURPOSE ++ ALSO THE EXCRUCIATING SPINE JOINT MUSCLE AND BONE PAIN TERRIFIES ME ALSO
> MAYBE MORE THAN ANYTHING ++ I HAVE BEEN IN CONSTANT PAIN SINCE I FIRST BROKE MY BACK IN 1967 AND IT HAS NEVER EASED AND NOW GETS WORSE DAILY ++
> SO I BEGAN TO SHARPEN PENCILS AND MY WITS + ARRANGE PHYSICAL REHABILITATION TO KEEP ME MOBILE AND MAYBE ADD A FEW MONTHS WEEKS OR DAYS
> AND I BEGAN THE LAST MOMENTS OF LIFE WITH A DESPERATE HOPE THAT I AM STARTING THE NEXT LEG OF A ONE MAN RELAY RACE ++
> YOU ARE THE ONLY PERSON I HAVE CONFIDED THIS LATEST "DEATH SENTENCE" PASSED ON ME BY ANOTHER "PRACTITIONER OF WESTERN MEDICINE"
> YOU ARE THE ONE CONSTANT IN MY LIFE THAT I AM PROUD TO CALL MY FRIEND
> MORE LATER
> HOPEFULLY LOTS MORE
> PETER

I could almost feel his pain, and all I could think to do was to suggest he write a short book about his dealing with it. It might help take his mind off his condition. Four days after I suggested this, on

September 30, 2011, Peter called the ambulance from his house. By twelve noon, Peter was in the ambulance, where he died. He was only sixty-nine years old. What a man! What a loss!

A year before Peter sent me the manuscript of *North Dallas Forty*, in October 1971, Dan Jenkins, one of *Sports Illustrated*'s top writers, brought me a manuscript called *Semi-Tough*. Many writers let their words speak for them, not caring much about their appearance. Many are unshackled by convention and free to dress and behave in unconventional ways. Dan Jenkins wasn't like that. He wore a necktie and had a flashy, if studied, air about him. After I'd made a deal for him, he would deliver his manuscript as though he'd tossed it off casually. I always thought he wanted to give the impression that it was easier than it was. And, something I admired about him: Dan always had his eye on the main chance.

His book *Semi-Tough,* about two Texas jocks who play for the New York Giants, was a wonderful comic read, an insightful story of the world of professional football, seen through the eyes of Billy Clyde Puckett, a star New York Giant who has been commissioned by a publisher to keep a journal of events leading up to the epic Super Bowl game with a rival team. Even today, sports fans consider it a classic. The language can be vile, the anecdotes are politically incorrect, and Dan makes fun of just about everyone. It has been described as one of the funniest sports books ever written, and one of my first thoughts after reading and really enjoying the manuscript was that an editor who was a Texas Aggie (graduate of Texas A&M) would buy it in a hurry. But Dan asked me to send it first to Random House, as one of the editors there had done him some favors. I did, and they rejected it.

The Aggie I had in mind, Herman Gollob, was editor in chief of Atheneum Books, the small, quality publishing house—and he was a very good editor. Three days after I sent him the manuscript, he called: He'd already read it twice. Two things were obvious: that Herman desperately wanted to buy it, and that Atheneum didn't see it as a large seller; their offer was a paltry $6,000. I'm afraid I took advantage of Herman's Texas pride, persuading him to give me better-than-normal breaks in book-club and paperback reprint sales, since he was offering such a meager advance.

The book was very successful. It hit #3 on the *New York Times* bestseller list and stayed on the list for twenty-eight weeks. In 2004, it, like *North Dallas Forty*, was selected by *Sports Illustrated* as one of the 100 Best Sports Books of All Time. The splits in the contract I negotiated gave Dan $30,000 he otherwise wouldn't have had.

In December 1972 we made an interesting motion-picture sale of the book to David Merrick, the flamboyant showman who dominated Broadway for decades, producing nearly one hundred shows from *Oliver!* to *Look Back in Anger* and *Hello, Dolly!* An eccentric businessman and outrageous marketer, Merrick hated fellow producers, drama critics, and actors, whom he characterized as nothing more than misbehaving children. He was married six times and divorced five, and he wore his reputation as a misanthrope with pride.

Despite his phenomenal success on Broadway, where he vacuumed up Tony Awards, Merrick wanted to conquer Hollywood, and he wanted to start with *Semi-Tough*. The deal was negotiated by my film expert and then-wife, Cindy Degener. Merrick bought stage rights for $50,000, and later that year, before the contracts could be signed, he bought feature-film rights for an additional $50,000. In an unusual setup, Dan was to receive 2 percent of the gross receipts after the film had earned 2.7 times the negative cost. Experienced film people then and now will tell you it is extremely rare—if not impossible—for the author of the book on which the film is based to get a piece of the gross receipts. As of 2009, Dan was still receiving payment through us from the studio.

Often, there's more to a deal than simply the bottom line. Cindy and I always thought that the reason we achieved such an unbelievably good deal was partially due to the fact that David Merrick and Cindy got along so well. He was amused by her wit and recognized her intelligence and genuine interest in theater and film. There were plenty of other female agents in town, but Cindy, although she apprenticed under some of them, was different. She had handled talent, such as Marcel Marceau, as opposed to writers. David went on to become president of Columbia Artists, and she went into the literary world.

She was a graduate of Radcliffe and had an intellectual orientation, and I think he was impressed with her.

The United Artists movie was released on November 18, 1977, with three stars in the powerful roles: Burt Reynolds, Kris Kristofferson, and Jill Clayburgh, in a love triangle. A few weeks before the release, Dan's employer, Time, Inc., which owns *Sports Illustrated*, arranged a private screening. I loved the movie and thought that given the leeway that producers have making movies based on books, it was loyal to the spirit of the book and to the three characters as they had been described in the book. I can still remember Dan as he left the room where the film was shown: His face was red; he hated it. There were scenes in the movie that simply didn't exist in the book. Many reviewers liked the satirical film more than Dan did, but some regretted the fact that the book's emphasis was on the football field while the movie focused more on the absurdities of the New-Age, self-help movement. The public was more forgiving than Dan and liked the movie.

I know many authors are unhappy with film versions of their book, but as I learned early in my agency days, and have told many writers, if you take the studio's money, the movie is theirs—not yours.

## CHAPTER 6

# From Our Nation's Capital

In the course of my extensive career, I've represented many authors who began their writing careers after leaving the White House or some other high-level government position. And I could have represented one American president after he left office, but my instinct told me not to, as you'll read later.

As my client David Wise, who's spent his life writing high-profile books about the intelligence community, has written in *Democracy Under Pressure*:

> Public disclosure of intimate details of a president's life is not limited to the press relations or scandal, or the literary endeavors of White House cooks, seamstresses, and bottle-washers. His own distinguished, high-level staff assistants may be secret diarists, scribbling away at night for the sake of posterity and the best-seller lists.

Arthur Flemming, President Eisenhower's Secretary of Health, Education and Welfare, was my first politically prominent author. He was serious, bland, courteous, and detail-oriented, and was best known to the public not for any accomplishment in office, but for causing the Great Cranberry Scare of 1959. He had overreacted to reports of pesticide on the cranberry crop that year, advising Americans not to serve the red berries at Thanksgiving, the one day out of 365 that Americans relish cranberries. For his caution, Flemming earned the enmity of farmers who lost millions. Some of those who lost money were friends of my in-laws who lived near the Cape in Massachusetts, but I didn't let their anger interfere with the deal. I was still a relatively young agent when Flemming and I were on our way to *Good Housekeeping* magazine, where I negotiated a contract for him to write a monthly column. During the ride, he volunteered that he expected to pay me the normal commission. Sometimes public figures don't expect to pay the normal rate, believing that the agent would benefit simply by association, an attitude I would confront in later years. The attitude is not unlike that of a Hollywood star's expectation that a nightclub owner should comp him (or her) because his (or her) presence adds to the venue's luster. Publishing doesn't work that way.

By the time of the Kennedy administration, I had a reputation for representing some of the best, new young literary figures on the American scene. I was the hot young guy in the business, and my reputation had spread from New York to our nation's capital, where political figures at the White House—including Kennedy's phenomenally talented speechwriter, Ted Sorenson, and his loquacious press secretary, Pierre Salinger, a man with such strong features that he looked as though he left for work each day with his acting makeup on—sought me out.

Later I worked with three other cabinet members: President Carter's Secretary of Health, Education and Welfare, Joe Califano; President Clinton's Secretary of State, Warren Christopher; and Kennedy's and Johnson's Secretary of Defense, Robert McNamara. The selection of an agent by a public figure is often made on the basis of who knows whom, not on the agent's reputation or the quality of his or her work. That was not the case for these or any other clients I took on. I'm not the flashy type and I don't exaggerate; I expect my professional track record to tell the prospective client more than I can in a thirty-minute interview. I assume that if potential clients, including political ones, are really interested in doing a book or books with me, they will already know a good deal about me.

And there's one more criterion I have for public figures: They have to connect with me on a person-to-person basis. There has to be some aspect of a person's character, personality, or intellect that interests me, which leads to mutual respect, or I'm not interested. If someone's ego is bigger than his talent, he can go elsewhere.

I'm accustomed to having an amiable relationship with my authors, although Ted Sorensen was an exception. He was from Nebraska. I, being from Iowa, naïvely assumed we'd have something to talk about, but there was never any room for that. As talented as Sorensen was and as graceful as his writing was, the man lacked humor and grace in my experience. He was so direct, he saw no reason to indulge in pleasantries. Following Kennedy's assassination, Ted wrote his first book and represented himself in negotiations with the book publisher. He came to me to represent him on the film rights. During the period in which we were offering the book around, I or my then-wife, Cindy, a very experienced agent who handled our movie rights, were in daily contact with him. Two days after I'd offered the book to NBC, I received a call from a reporter at the *New York Times* asking me about our deal with the network, which was news to me: There hadn't been any offer or negotiation. I repeatedly tried to reach Ted before the story was printed, but I couldn't reach him at any of the many phone numbers he'd given me and I didn't hear back from him until the next morning, after the article had appeared. Although I apologized, Ted was not happy with the story, but not for the reason I expected. He said that if he'd known of the press interest, he would have been able to stretch the news into a two-day story. I admired him for that, and since then, I have tried to create two-day stories for other clients.

Shortly before he died on October 31, 2010, I bumped into Ted again and inquired about his well-being. He told me he was writing another book. Blunt as ever, he told me, "But I don't need an agent." I hadn't even suggested it.

Sorensen was the exception. Talented writers are usually searching for the agent who will get them the best deal or some special accommodations.

My clients come from many sources. Kerouac was sent to me by his editor. Robert McNamara came by way of Martha's Vineyard and a social connection. Maurice Herzog, a French mountaineer and the first man to climb Annapurna—which he did without supplemental oxygen and before Sir Edmund Hillary climbed Everest—was referred to me by Jackie Kennedy Onassis. And a former student of mine sent Pierre Salinger. The poet Lawrence Ferlinghetti had heard I represented Jack Kerouac, and after hearing Allen Ginsberg, whom I knew but never represented, talk about Jack and me, Ferlinghetti asked that I represent him.

My client Maurice Herzog was the first man to climb Annapurna in the Himalayas—and he did it without the use of supplemental oxygen. He then wrote a book describing his climb; *Annapurna* became an international bestseller. Herzog was later named Minister of Youth and Sport in France. Above, we are completing a discussion of his next book, while on the porch of friends of mine in St. Paul de Vence, France. From that perch, we could look down the mountain and see the Mediterranean Sea.

That was the beginning of one of the most rewarding relationships in my agency history. I sold his novel, *Love in the Days of Rage*, in a few days, but our relationship grew over the years, and I have always considered him one of the half-dozen most significant figures in help-

Photo by Stacey Lewis

Lawrence Ferlinghetti first heard of me from the Kerouac crowd, including Jack himself. Ferlinghetti founded City Lights, one of the best-known, best-run bookstores in the US–the first all-paperback store. His own book of poetry, *A Coney Island of the Mind*, has sold more than 1,000,000 copies as of 2012. He was the poet laureate of San Francisco, and his paintings have been exhibited in Italy, his family's country of origin. He is responsible for naming the street next to City Lights Kerouac Alley.

ing expand the scope of book publishing. His City Lights Bookstore was a major factor in establishing the authority of paperback books for serious readers, and of course, his personal involvement in publishing Allen Ginsberg's "Howl" was enormous. And then there are the public readings of his own poems, including those included in his collection *A Coney Island of the Mind*, which are always impressive.

Jim Webb—an extremely impressive man with a strong WWII war record, and later a US senator—came to me on the recommendation of Arthur Hadley, a client of mine. Senator Ted Kennedy came on the recommendation of his then–chief of staff Bob Shrum. I still have his signed representation agreement. Generally, everyone came to me; I didn't have to go out searching. But if I saw a book or magazine piece I really admired, I sometimes made the first move.

Toward the end of 1977, I had a phone call from the lively, high-profile Phyllis Grann, then–president and editor in chief of G.P. Putnam's Sons. Phyllis had begun as a secretary to Nelson Doubleday, moving to the publisher William Morrow, and then working for the aggressive Dick Snyder at Simon and Schuster. It was during this period that we had our first substantive discussion, which I have never forgotten. S&S had my client Ralph G. Martin under contract. Long after the contract was signed, but before Martin's manuscript was delivered, Dick Snyder, Phyllis's boss, decided he wanted to change the contract, and he asked Phyllis to get me to accept the change. It was complicated. I don't remember the details, and I think Phyllis had been given a cover story, which didn't make sense to me. I realized she was only following orders—probably Dick's—and after a good fifteen minutes back and forth, I chuckled and said, "Phyllis, I don't believe you know what you are talking about." She took it well—admitted it, in fact—and returned to get more information, and although she called me back, I never heard a rebuttal. The contract was not changed, and Phyllis and I became good professional friends.

Her desk was just outside Dick's office, and she must have learned a great deal from him. She was regarded as one of the top editors and publishers in the business, reading nearly a book a day, and she was aggressive in pursuing interesting book ideas. In that period, I usually had two or three national bestsellers with Putnam each year. Phyllis had just returned from a business trip to Washington, DC, that included an interview with US District Court Judge John J. Sirica. Her call told me she didn't want the Sirica book for Putnam's, which puzzled me until I learned more. We had done enough business together—she and I—so she had a very good feeling that I would be the right agent to handle it. And if it worked out, she would have done Judge Sirica and me each a great favor. Sometimes these things don't work, and the agent feels the publisher has sent him on a wild-goose chase. But Phyllis is extremely astute, so I knew that was unlikely. She told me Sirica wanted to meet me. We arranged to get together in his chamber in Washington, DC. It was a friendly but no-frills meeting, during which we each talked a little bit about ourselves and about the process of writing and selling the book. I was impressed.

John Sirica was the judge for the Watergate scandal proceedings, presiding over the trial of the seven burglars who, acting on behalf of the Committee to Re-elect the President (appropriately acronymed CREEP), broke into the Democratic Party headquarters in the Watergate apartment complex during the 1972 presidential campaign. Sirica insisted the president hand over the once-secret tapes he'd made in the Oval Office, tapes that revealed Nixon to be a co-conspirator.

Sirica was not a high-profile judge, until Watergate came along. A Republican, he was appointed to the federal bench—where he was known to the press as Maximum John for the long sentences he meted out—by President Dwight Eisenhower. I found him to be honest, thoughtful, and appealing, and he had an unpretentious openness. He wasn't a highbrow man; he was the direct-speaking son of an Italian immigrant barber from Waterbury, Connecticut, where the family of four had once lived in a single room at the back of his mother's grocery store. Even at the age of seventy-four, he retained the look of the lightweight prizefighter he had once been. I soon learned that he worked out daily, riding an Exercycle for half an hour every morning while watching the CBS morning news.

When he came to me five years after the trial, Sirica's name, even in an age of short attention spans, was still well known throughout the world. In 1973, he'd been named *Time* magazine's Man of the Year. He was highly regarded for his tough but fair handling of the Watergate trial, and his insistence on the primacy of the law. Despite a number of books on Watergate by Nixon's top aides, H. R. "Bob" Haldeman, John Ehrlichman, and others, he wanted very much to write his own, and had already been approached by half a dozen major publishers. But he had waited, correctly, to move ahead with it until the Watergate case had passed through the judicial appeal process, which took five years. He wanted to write about the details of the case, including his considerable efforts to protect the White House tapes (once he had them), which recorded secret and revealing conversations between Nixon and his aides. Sirica ordered a strong safe from the National Security Agency to house the tapes, and he had a US Marshal's guard protecting the safe twenty-four hours a day. A closed-circuit television system was added to monitor the door of Judge Sirica's chamber. And the combination to the safe? Sirica came up with one he would never forget: his wife's birthday 23–27–12 (December 27, 1923).

When we spoke, Sirica had one unusual condition, which he stated up front to me, and I'm sure to all publishers or agents he had met: He wanted his publisher to warrant to him for the material in the book-to-be, not the reverse. In other words, the contract would have to state that the publisher would hold the author harmless in the event there was any legal action against the book for libel, slander, defamation, or right of privacy. This was unheard of in publishing circles. Normally, in a contract, the author has to warrant to the publishers for what he writes. I had been wondering why Phyllis Grann didn't want the book for Putnam's. Now I understood; I guessed that she knew she could never get her management to okay that clause. I had never heard of a book contract with a reverse warranty in my then–twenty-five years as an agent, nor have I heard of one in the years since. Sirica had seen that kind of clause in a contract between his unlikely friend Walter Winchell, the flamboyant gossip columnist, and the American Broadcasting Company, which produced his weekly radio broadcasts. (His Sunday-night radio broadcasts during the 1930s to the 1950s were heard by 20 million people each week. I had heard them occasionally growing up in Iowa.)

I knew the reverse warranty would be a tough condition to satisfy, but I liked Sirica's frankness and admired what he had accomplished, so I plunged in. I never for a moment thought Sirica would back off from that position. He looked to me like a man who meant what he said, an unusual commodity in our nation's capital. Also, he was getting older. His wife, to whom he was extremely loyal and protective, was nineteen years younger, and he didn't want her to be confronted with any financial obligations when he died. That would have to be taken care of in any contract.

So we secured a wonderful writer, John Stacks of *Time*, in whom Sirica had great confidence, to work with him on the book, and I approached all the interested publishers, making it clear that Sirica's reverse-warranty clause was essential to any offer. On the day of reckoning, I had four substantial offers, but only one editor, George P. Brockway, chairman of W.W. Norton & Co., accepted Sirica's requirement of a warranty clause. George not only understood Sirica, he had enormous respect for him, and he considered the Watergate case the most important criminal case ever to be tried in the courts of the United States, a statement which later appeared on the jacket of Sirica's book, *To Set the Record Straight*.

When publishers did a deal with me, as one retired publisher told me recently, neither side ever felt taken. I had a reputation for hard negotiating, but also for honesty and integrity. In this case, George was responding to Sirica's needs as I had expressed them. George granted other unusual—even unheard-of—conditions in the contract. If Sirica died before the book was completed, his estate would not have to repay money Sirica had already received. Norton also took out life insurance on Sirica, but allowed him to have his own doctor give the physical exam, a highly unorthodox move. For paperback rights, which the hardcover publisher almost always controls, I had introduced George to Herb Schnall, president of the prominent paperback publisher, New American Library. I told Schnall that although he had published many, many successful books, if he joined forces with Norton, the Sirica book would be the book for which he was remembered. Herb very generously put up $500,000 for paperback rights. Norton, in turn, was generous to Judge Sirica: Although the customary split of paperback money between the hardcover publisher and author was 50-50, Norton granted Sirica 83 percent of the NAL money, probably because of their enormous admiration for Sirica, but also because I, as Sirica's agent, had secured the $500,000 as part of the publishing deal.

Even after I had accomplished all that and had sent him the contract, Sirica asked me to come down to Washington again before he signed, to meet with him, his accountant, and his lawyer, who turned out, to my surprise, to be Edward Bennett Williams, then the highest-profile lawyer in Washington, DC. A careful and loyal man, Sirica wanted the other two, who had been with him for some time, to be a part of the decision. It was an interesting meeting. I had met Ed Williams before, so the atmosphere was somewhat informal and friendly. I had every confidence that the meeting would result in no changes in the contract, but Ed, being a lawyer and knowing he should make every effort for his client, started pushing for an additional change, which I considered outrageous and relatively meaningless. He started his speech by telling me how brilliant I was, and how there was no one in the publishing scene as talented as I—it was masterful, and I was amused but didn't show it. When he finished, I said, "Ed, if I'm as good as you say I am, why am I not *your* agent?" (I knew a number of publishers would be interested in his autobiography.) That, as you might guess, technically ended the meeting.

Surprisingly, one of my editor friends asked me later if I had any reservations about meeting with the accountant and the lawyer. The answer was, not at all. We were all men doing the best we could for John Sirica. I knew I had negotiated an extraordinary contract, and further, I knew a thing more about publishing than Ed did.

Sirica's book, *To Set the Record Straight*, describes in detail the original history of the White House tape recordings, which were ostensibly meant to record all of President Nixon's White House conversations and thus confirm what the president said and when he said it. Its existence was not publicly known until July 1973, when Alexander Butterfield, a White House aide, divulged the existence of the tapes to Republican counsel on the Senate Watergate Committee and later at a bombshell of a televised hearing.

Special prosecutor Archibald Cox wanted the tapes to build his case against the president. Recognizing their importance to the case and the country, Judge Sirica subpoenaed the tapes, but Nixon refused to turn them over. In a letter to Sirica he cited executive privilege. Mindful of presidential privilege, Sirica then ordered the president to hand over specific tapes for Sirica to listen to himself. In a later skirmish over additional Nixon tapes, Judge Sirica agreed with the new prosecutor, Leon Jaworski, that the government had the right to additional tapes, but again Nixon refused. Jaworski appealed directly to the US Supreme Court, which found in his (and Sirica's) favor.

Sirica had been an obscure judge in the District of Columbia who took on the President of the United States, doing nothing less than preserving the democracy, and in so doing he became an important figure in American history. In other ways, he was a pleasant, unremarkable man who, thrust into the vortex of corruption at the highest level, could not have performed better for the American people.

Sirica never spoke conversationally of his feelings about President Nixon, whom he did not know well. Even though Nixon was at one point Sirica's neighbor in northwest Washington, they never had any one-on-one interactions there. But in the book he is very clear about his anger at Nixon's involvement with the cover-up, and ultimately disappointed with Nixon's behavior. He wrote: "Most depressing is my feeling that Nixon could have been one of the greatest presidents of this century. I say that, of course, as a long-time Republican and as one who campaigned on behalf of the Republican National Committee for the Eisenhower-Nixon ticket twice and voted for Nixon for president twice."

*To Set the Record Straight* was taken by two book clubs (one of which was Book-of-the-Month), excerpted in *Look* magazine, sold for publication in Italy, England, and other countries, and optioned for film. But more important—everyone I knew who was involved was proud to be associated with the book and with John Sirica.

Sometime in the late autumn of 1992, I heard from Robert McNamara, former US Secretary of Defense during the Vietnam War period. By then he'd become a pariah to many younger Americans, who blamed him for leading and expanding the war in Vietnam and for what they believed were 50,000 unnecessary American deaths and many times that number of Vietnamese. I had not been involved in antiwar activities, nor did I blame McNamara for the ills of the nation. I thought he was a good man forced into an impossible situation. Surrounded by generals who were supportive of the war, he made some terrible choices. Bob had been the youngest and most highly paid assistant professor at the Harvard Business School. He had served in the US Army from 1943 to 1946, as a lieutenant colonel. When he left, he went to the Ford Motor Company, one of ten former World War II officers—known as the Whiz Kids—who helped Ford modernize and become profitable again. In November 1960, he became the first non-family member to become president of the Ford Motor Company.

I had met Bob a few years before, through Patricia Bradshaw, the widow of Thornton "Brad" Bradshaw, chairman of RCA, owners of NBC, who had been Bob's roommate at Harvard Business School. Pat had been enormously helpful and supportive of Brad, so much so that the day after Brad died, Katherine Graham, president and principal owner of the *Washington Post*, came to New York to see Pat and tell her she had been "more than fifty percent of the partnership."

The Bradshaws and McNamara had summerhouses not far from one another on a quiet, wandering dirt road in Martha's Vineyard, and I had encountered Bob there a number of times.

Martha's Vineyard is a fascinating island, physically, socially, and literarily. While there I played tennis with Mike Wallace, the *60 Minutes* correspondent, and with Kay Graham. I never got around to playing with Beverly Sills, the Metropolitan Opera star and a delightful woman with a nice sense of humor. I never played tennis with Walter Cronkite, who played at a different club than I and at a different level, but I removed my shoes at his request when I joined him on his yacht. There were so many well-known people summering on the island that while buying fresh tomatoes one morning, a friend of mine bumped into Princess Diana, who was also shopping without equerry. That was the same summer that President Bill Clinton was there. Jackie Onassis summered there in a secluded nineteen-room house she built along 375 oceanfront acres. In the nineties, President Johnson's widow, Lady Bird Johnson, and her relatives vacationed there. Historian David McCullough lived there year-round, and at times TV mogul Merv Griffin's huge yacht could be seen anchored in the harbor. A book agent could wander the beach and call it work.

I came to know McNamara as a smart, charming, interesting resident of the Vineyard, with whom I played tennis several times—he was focused and eager, but not accomplished on the court. He tried to exercise one way or another, every day. People might have been critical of my association with McNamara, but I'm a literary agent and have always made a point of not letting my political feelings influence my literary decisions. If I was known as a rabid Republican, the Democrats would not seek me out. If I had a reputation as a Democrat, the Republicans would have scorned me. I've always considered it to be good business to be apolitical, which is what I am.

I never once approached Bob about writing a book, although I thought there would be many people who wanted to know what he thought and why he had acted as he did. Why didn't I bring it up? Instinct. Also, my partner, Peter Matson, had previously represented him, and I didn't want to step on any toes.

So, in late October 1992, I was pleasantly surprised to get his call. Bob explained that he had talked to Peter Matson and told him he was going to write his next book and would like me to handle it. Peter had graciously agreed. When Bob told me it was going to be a personal memoir, I was delighted. I knew I would enjoy working with him, and I thought the book would be extremely interesting if it was as frank and open as Bob had been in other areas when we had talked in the past.

Bob told me the size of the advance he wanted—$1,000,000—a substantial amount but not unreasonable. I frankly thought it would be worth that much for what he was promising to produce. I would have been stunned if he had asked for anything less. Drafted with the help of Brian VanDeMark, the young historian who was his ghost-writer, Bob's proposal for *In Retrospect: The Tragedy and Lessons of Vietnam* was his first effort to speak out about Vietnam and a dramatic admission of mistakes he and others made. Bob wrote that "the war caused terrible damage to America. No doubt exists in my mind about that. None. I want to look at Vietnam in hindsight and not in any way obscure my own and others' errors of judgment and their egregious costs, but show the full range of pressures and the lack of knowledge that existed at the time." He said that he and others in the Kennedy and Johnson administrations thought they were following "principles of this nation. We made our decisions in light of those values. I believe our judgments clearly proved wrong." Bob went on to write: "I want Americans to understand why we made the mistakes we did."

"How did it happen?" he wrote. "How can it be avoided in the future? Those are the key questions."

I thought publishers would immediately recognize the value of his story.

Bob came up from Washington to meet with various publishers, but they weren't jumping gleefully, as I thought they should. Nine of them turned it down. I had a strong suspicion that while they were all curious to meet him, they were opposed more to his politics and what he represented than to his book proposal. They turned him down for personal, not publishing reasons. The hatred that many, especially liberals in his own party, had for him, I thought improperly influenced what should have been a purely literary and financial decision.

I've seen that happen a few times with nonpolitical clients, principally with younger editors. I saw it with a very good manuscript about muckraker Michael Moore, and it became clear to me that many of the people in publishing didn't like him as a person. It's part of publishing's character. McNamara's case was just an extreme example. It also happened when Peter Matson took Mitt Romney around to publishers in 2010. Only one had seriously prepared—St. Martin's—and they got the book. The others, I think, just wanted to meet him.

Harold "Harry" Evans, then–editor in chief of Random House, may have been immune to the prejudice not only because he was a superior editor, but also because he was a British transplant and may have seen the value of a McNamara book above the political fray. He had expressed interest, but had twice broken dates to meet Bob, who was ready to come up from Washington, DC, for the meeting. Even though he had Bob's written proposal in his office, I couldn't get him to respond. I'd known Harry for years, ever since he was editor in chief of the *London Sunday Times*. In fact, he had asked me to represent his book-writing group, the *London Sunday Times* Insight team, in the US, which I did. In addition, Harry was a table-tennis fanatic, and ever since I told him I had once played Bohumil Vana of Czechoslovakia, the table-tennis world champion, Harry had been after me to play with him (I never did). But on the McNamara project, I still hadn't heard from him by the time I left for the American Booksellers Association annual meeting, which was in Miami that year.

I was flying down with my friend—and Bob McNamara's neighbor—Patricia Bradshaw, who had never been to an ABA Convention and was curious. It was on a Friday afternoon, and sometime during the flight she said, "Isn't that Harry Evans sitting back there?" I walked back and indeed it was. It turned out he was reading the first half of the manuscript of Marlon Brando's autobiography. He told me how good the Brando manuscript was, and we chatted about various publishing events. I played it cool—not even mentioning Bob McNamara. And without my asking, he said, "I know I owe you an answer on the McNamara proposal, Sterling. I'll have an offer on your desk on Tuesday," which was the first day we'd each be back in New York. He was as good as his word, and after a little back-and-forth to bring the offer closer to what Bob wanted, we had an acceptable deal: a $350,000 advance for US, Canada, and world rights.

But the best was yet to come. Harry selected his editor, Peter Osnos, to edit and publish the book. Osnos, a former *Washington Post* journalist, was running Times Books as a part of Random House then; he knew the political scene well and was skilled at his job. He prompted Bob to focus on Vietnam because he correctly understood that was what the public was interested in. Osnos published *In Retrospect* in April 1995 with an initial printing of 60,000 copies. I thought this was low and called to tell him. He was protective but optimistic.

In the book McNamara tells the story of how he reached out to President Lyndon Johnson, persuading him to extend a thirty-hour cease-fire in Vietnam that began on Christmas Eve 1965. McNamara's colleagues, including Secretary of State Dean Rusk, were on record as favoring using military power over diplomacy. On Christmas Day, Johnson himself extended the cease-fire for another day or two, but McNamara had other ideas. Two days later, Rusk called Johnson in Texas requesting permission to visit him immediately to discuss war plans. As a result of that meeting, Johnson agreed to extend the cease-fire for an indefinite period and "mount a massive diplomatic effort to move Hanoi towards negotiations."

In his final chapter, McNamara lists eleven major causes of the US defeat in Vietnam, a very rare reflective move for any secretary of defense. I've included them here, in abbreviated form:

1. We misjudged geopolitical intentions of our adversaries and exaggerated the dangers to the United States.

2. We viewed the people and leaders of South Vietnam in terms of our own experience.

3. We underestimated the power of nationalism to motivate

the North Vietnamese and Vietcong to fight and die for their beliefs and values.

4. Our misjudgments reflect our ignorance of the history, culture, and politics of the people in the area.

5. We failed to recognize the limitations of modern, high-technology military equipment, forces, and doctrine, and failed to adapt our military to win the hearts and minds of people from a different culture.

6. We failed to draw Congress and the American people into a full and frank discussion and debate on US military involvement before initiating the action.

7. After action got under way, we lost popular support because we did not fully explain what was happening and why we were doing what we did.

8. We did not recognize that neither our people nor our leaders are omniscient.

9. We did not hold to the principle that other than in response to a direct threat, US militarization should be carried out only in conjunction with multinational forces supported fully by the international community.

10. We did not recognize that there may be no immediate solution.

11. Our failure to recognize the top echelons of the executive branch to deal effectively with the extraordinary complex range of political and military issues including above all else, loss of life over a long period of time. When failure was clear, we failed to debate our actions with intensity.

Once the book was shipped to the stores, salesmen were reporting brisk sales in most major cities. Osnos sensed that it was a strong impulse buy. During the first month, while McNamara was on tour around the US, orders were pouring in. Osnos did something that many successful authors can only dream of: He committed $30,000 of Random House's money to express-mail copies to bookstores around the country so they wouldn't run out during that crucial time when Bob was touring. Osnos was in touch with McNamara by phone almost every day, so he knew precisely what the public reaction was to Bob and the book. The fervor against the war and McNamara had not subsided, and the demonstrations that sometimes accompanied his talks inadvertently helped market the book.

Although it had been thirty years since Bob had been secretary of defense and twenty years since the Vietnam War ended, when he spoke, he often encountered a great deal of hostility. At Harvard's Kennedy School of Government, Bob was questioned by John Hurley, a Vietnam vet who asked why his buddies had to die when McNamara already knew the war was a mistake but remained silent. Bob was probably too flip in his response; he told Hurley he should read the book. Hurley called McNamara and *In Retrospect* "an obscenity." Bob lost it and told him to "shut up."

I did go down to see his appearance in Austin, Texas—home of Lyndon Johnson—which went more smoothly. There was a quiet, well-organized demonstration outside the lecture hall. And inside, there were half a dozen very tough questions from the audience. But Bob did not duck any of them.

In my time with Bob McNamara—both social and professional—I found him very attentive and easy to talk to. I saw no ego protruding to take over conversations. He was thorough, too, as if he had prepared for every business meeting we had. Bob's knowledge and brilliance in many fields were apparent, but it was nothing he boasted about or described in any laudatory way. He was very straightforward.

At the end of the month, I had a date for dinner with Bob and our mutual friend Patricia Bradshaw on Martha's Vineyard. Despite the often-intense feelings against him, Bob never hid or ceased appearing in public places, even though he'd had some close calls. A few years earlier, a man attacked him on the Woods Hole–to–Martha's Vineyard ferry. The man faked a telephone call for Bob and when Bob came out onto the deck to answer it, the man unsuccessfully tried to push him overboard. Feelings about Bob would remain strong for years.

I knew Bob, who was now seventy-nine years old, had worked hard and traveled the entire month, so I thought he might cancel, or at least be too tired to go out to dinner. It hadn't been an easy time. That month alone, he'd given ninety-three interviews. His book had gone to #1 on the *New York Times* bestseller list. It would eventually sell 194,571 copies in hardcover in the US and Canada, and was published in eight other countries around the world. That Saturday we waited for him, not knowing if he would make it. He had awakened that morning in San Diego and flown to Boston, then flown on to the Vineyard.

Despite the demanding month, Bob couldn't have been in better spirits that night. I drove us to dinner in Edgartown in Patricia's station wagon. She sat next to me and Bob sat in back. He was describing in detail how he and the people at Ford had created the seat belts in Fords, which were subsequently adopted in every other car.

I am normally a seat belt–conscious driver or passenger, but that evening I hadn't snapped mine on. As Bob was telling his story, I struggled with what to do: Should I quietly buckle up or not? I felt like a kid who had forgotten to study for finals. Because Bob was sitting directly behind me, I realized that he probably couldn't see whether I had my seat belt on or not or at least was distracted by other issues. I let it go, and he never found out.

*In Retrospect's* success was due to Bob's frankness and his enormous energy in promoting it, and to the brilliant job Peter Osnos did editing and publishing it. Peter understood both the nature of the book and the lingering emotions of the sixties. He gave the book the attention it deserved. I had the feeling Bob felt a sense of relief now that he had unburdened himself. Much in publishing and in life depends not only on drive, connections, and intelligence, but also on serendipity. And I have often wondered since then whether there would have been a book at all if I hadn't bumped into Harry Evans on that plane. I would have missed one of the most effective and professional publishing jobs of my career.

A few months after Kennedy's assassination, I had a call from Charles U. Daly, a former journalism student of mine at Columbia University, who had been a special assistant to JFK in the White House and was still there serving LBJ. He told me that his friend Pierre Salinger, Kennedy's press secretary and a former journalist, was starting to write a memoir, and although he did not yet realize it, he needed help. Was I interested? I had never met Pierre, but had heard many things about him—among them, that he was a Francophile and a well-known bon vivant—from those who knew him. And, of course, he had been an intimate witness to many events in our recent history.

A few days later, Chuck called again. Pierre was coming to New York City the following day. I went out to La Guardia that Friday morning to meet his plane. When he deplaned, I recognized him immediately, of course. Salinger had a wide head, bushy hair, and bushier eyebrows, and an expression on his face that said "Harrumph." He was a bit shorter than I had guessed, carrying a briefcase and walking as if he was anxious to get someplace. He wasn't overbearing, nor did he act like a big shot from Washington. We chatted comfortably in the taxi en route to my office, starting with talk of our mutual friend. We were only halfway into my office on 75 East Fifty-Fifth Street when Pierre turned to me and said, "I want to be with your agency—with you."

That was the beginning of a rewarding relationship for each of us.

Pierre left me all that he had written: three chapters in rough draft. Mike Bessie, one of the founding editors of Atheneum, a small quality publisher, had already read the three chapters and had told Pierre he would pay an advance of $35,000 if Pierre turned in an acceptable complete manuscript.

Salinger was clearly a hot property. More than the sum of his positions, he'd become a well-known personality, a quality that would help us sell the book. About an hour after he left me for other nonpublishing appointments in the city, and before I had read one word of the manuscript, I heard from Charlie Sopkin, a client and friend of mine at the Doubleday Book Club. He was calling to see if I was representing Pierre Salinger. Someone had spotted me at La Guardia with Pierre that morning and tipped off Sopkin. Before the end of the business day, I had a firm offer of

$149,000 from Doubleday as an advance for the memoir—and they had not even seen the three chapters.

That was a very good offer in those days, and we took it. Pierre went back to Washington, DC, that night a relieved and happy man.

*With Kennedy*, published in 1966, was selected by two major book clubs and sold 140,000 hardcover copies. In the book, Pierre tells many inside stories and shares many of his one-on-one exchanges with President Kennedy. Salinger confesses he received a letter from a woman in Dallas, Texas, on November 19, 1963, that read: *Don't let the President come down here. I'm worried about him. I think something terrible will happen to him.* He wrote back, confident in the future success of the president's visit, but he never shared the letter with the president. One of the last things JFK said that day to Salinger, in an air of fatigue, as they had been traveling a lot: "I wish I weren't going to Texas."

Often documents sent to Kennedy for approval and signature came back slightly damp, or even wet, as he kept working while in the bathtub. The president took many hot baths to soothe his chronic back problems.

It was these inside-the-White-House details that made the book work. During the presidential election night, with Kennedy's narrow lead, Nixon's press secretary called to say Nixon was going to concede. As the night drew on and Nixon didn't concede, all in the room were angry except Kennedy, who said, "If I were he, I would have done the same thing." Later, the president-elect was emerging from a warm bath, when Salinger threw him a towel. Still shaken by his narrow victory, Kennedy said, "I still don't know how we did it without California." He felt he spent a day too long in New York based on incorrect advice, and thus lost the time he could have spent in Nixon's native state.

Of Kennedy's golf skills, Pierre wrote, the most effective part of his game was the "con" he gave fellow players on the first tee; "Through a complex system of betting, which only he understood fully, JFK won most of his matches before the first ball was even hit."

The reviews were barely positive, but there were a great many of them. The *Saturday Review* syndicate declared:

> This is a scrupulous, sincere, modest account of a key relationship in the mightiest power center in the world, and it is,

furthermore, sometimes gripping, sometimes funny vaude-ville. The reasons for Salinger liking the Kennedys were always obvious. Now we know why the Kennedys like Salinger.

*Harper's* magazine wrote:

It's a tough assignment—being the third close adviser to John F. Kennedy to publish a book about those days, particularly when it means following Theodore Sorensen and Arthur Schlesinger, Jr.— And his story of how he and Secretary Rusk and five other members of the cabinet learned the news of the assassination (they were in a plane over the Pacific flying to Japan) is one of the most dramatic of all the dramatic happenings of that dreadful day. . . .

*Time* magazine wrote:

"What I have attempted to write down on these pages," notes the author, "is a view of life at the center of power." Well, not quite. Pierre Salinger was at the White House during the entire Kennedy Administration, and highly visible. But as press secretary, he was not privy to history-making conversations; thus, he has little that is fresh to add to the anecdotal history of the time.

Pierre had one story of considerable interest, however. He believed that Nikita Khrushchev helped Kennedy win the 1960 presidential election.

During a visit to the Soviet Union in 1962, Salinger was drawn into a discussion with Khrushchev on the subject of Richard Nixon. Khrushchev reminded Salinger of the incident in July 1960, when a US Air Force RB-47 was shot down over the Barents Sea. Nixon, said Khrushchev, tried to use the incident to his advantage. Through an unnamed high-ranking Republican, Khrushchev said, Nixon "approached us with the request to release the crew members of the American RB-47. We of course understood that Nixon wished to make political capital out of this for himself in advance of the elections."

Writes Salinger:

> I responded that the release of the RB-47 flyers before the election might very well have won it for Nixon. "Of course," said Khrushchev. "For this reason, I said it would not be proper to do this. For you see, Nixon wanted to make it appear as if he had already arranged certain contacts with the Soviet government. And this, of course, would have played a decisive role in the election. That is why we decided to wait a while until Kennedy came to power, and only after that release the American flyers."
>
> It was clear that Khrushchev wouldn't have lifted a finger to help Nixon get elected dogcatcher. The Communist boss described Nixon as "an intellectually limited" man who "produces the impression of a slightly fraudulent, petty storekeeper, capable of selling tainted herring or representing kerosene-soaked sugar as good merchandise."

I had come to believe that Pierre was more successful at telling his own story than at crafting a new one. He was a piano prodigy and an editor at the *San Francisco Chronicle* at a young age. At the paper he wasn't known for his grace in writing but for his showmanship: pretending to be an inmate and writing a series from inside the local jail. I found him to be of much more than moderate intelligence. I suspect that during his career he learned how to be canny. He was excellent at dealing with people on all levels. Pierre became a very appreciative and supportive client, sending me a number of other would-be writers, including the curious and wealthy Baron Guy de Rothschild, whose autobiography, *Whims of Fortune*, made the point that the life of a millionaire is not necessarily deserving of envy. I sold it to Random House in 1985, making the baron slightly wealthier. In the book, he takes us from his childhood in his parents' chateau to the attempted kidnapping of his son; from the battlefield during the German invasion of France to his tireless efforts to modernize and diversify the activities of the family firm. It is frank in his views about France under the socialists, about the situation in Israel (as of 1985), and about other international affairs, which he surveyed from his then-home in New York.

During our prepublication discussions, thinking I didn't understand French, but never asking me, the baron and his wife would sometimes converse as if I weren't in the room, or couldn't understand what they were saying. Despite their great wealth, they did not always spend lavishly, especially on guests. At their apartment on Sixty-Sixth and Lexington in New York City, Pierre recalled attending one of their dinner parties where the entrée was hash.

Pierre and I did eight books together, and there were additional benefits: He was so well connected that he knew how to smuggle Cuban cigars into New York at a time when they were considered contraband. I've never been a heavy smoker—and most of my life I've been a nonsmoker—but I did enjoy an occasional Cuban cigar.

Although Pierre still considered himself a writer, by the time he came into my life, he was not only involved in politics, but also in television—he needed help.

Leonard Gross and I met in 1959 shortly after he joined *Look*. The magazine had just published an excerpt from Leonard's first book, *God and Freud*. The book describes the movement toward a courtship between the "once-hostile disciplines"—religion and psychiatry. It details the fundamentals of their differences—Freud's theory of the unconscious (sexuality and hidden drives) being directly opposed to the idea of Divine guidance. Through examples, he posits this "coming together of new science and old faith" is "one of the greatest seeming contradictions of our time." Religious leaders found psychology lent practical understanding to concepts like love, forgiveness, acceptance, and understanding, which had previously been overshadowed with strict emphasis on sin. I was impressed with the idea and the execution, and I phoned the author to congratulate him and to see if we could work together—one of the few times I approached a writer.

Pierre and Leonard had known one another since the early fifties when they were both reporting for the *San Francisco Chronicle*. They were an interesting pair. Leonard was serious, a committed writer and an excellent reporter. He was the man who would transform Pierre's antics and imaginative ideas into clear and intelligent prose. By the mid-fifties they were sharing an office at *Collier's*, a national weekly magazine, in New York City. After that magazine folded, Pierre moved to Washington, where he became the presidential press secretary under Kennedy and for a few months under LBJ, before returning to California where he was appointed a US senator to complete the term of Clair Engels, a senator who had died. Leonard, meanwhile, had established himself as a first-class journalist, freelancing for many magazines, then reporting and writing for *Look* magazine from 1959 to 1971. When *Look* folded, Leonard returned to full-time freelancing.

In 1981, Doubleday, Pierre's publisher, asked him to write a non-fiction book on the secret negotiations to free the American hostages held by Iran, a story Pierre had been the first journalist to follow. ABC had just done a news feature, *America Held Hostage*, focused on Pierre's involvement.

The centerpiece of *America Held Hostage*—the program and the book—was the story of the back-channel, secret negotiations to free the hostages. Pierre was privy to these negotiations from the outset— the only journalist who was—at one point helping to connect the Americans to an invaluable intermediary.

Pierre got a call from a French lawyer who was representing two knowledgeable Iranians, living in Paris at the time, who had information they wanted to convey to the Americans that might help start negotiations to free the hostages. Their own efforts at finding a qualified American had gotten them nowhere. The lawyer asked Pierre if he could put him in touch with someone. Before the day was over, Pierre had facilitated a long, substantive conversation between the lawyer and the political counselor of the American embassy. After the lawyer had profusely thanked Pierre, Pierre asked one favor: Would he keep Pierre apprised of developments? The lawyer promised he would, and did.

That's how Pierre got the inside track, which he followed until the hostages were released. No other journalist had the story.

I knew that the sometimes-starstruck Nelson Doubleday would be drawn in by the TV program featuring one of his authors, and I arranged to watch it with him and two of his executives. I also knew that once Nelson was committed, his assistants would concur enthusiastically. In a meeting with them after we had all seen the feature, they asked me who should write the book with Pierre. I immediately mentioned Leonard. The book carried the same title as the TV special.

Their collaboration went so well that Pierre then proposed they write a novel together for Doubleday. The novel was called *The Dossier*. Its principal characters were André Kohl, a network television journalist based largely on Pierre and his life, and Meredith Houghton, an attractive woman whose father was the director of the CIA. Pierre supplied much of the material and Leonard, of course, did all the writing. Together, they worked out the plotting. The novel was a national bestseller and a main selection of the Literary Guild.

The trouble began when Doubleday asked the two men to write a sequel. Pierre had been courting one particular woman before and during the writing of *The Dossier*, and he believed that Meredith Houghton was based on that woman. That wasn't what Leonard believed at all; as the character's creator, he considered her totally fictional.

By the time the two men sat down to discuss the second novel, Pierre and his lady friend had split. Pierre stunned Leonard with his first suggestion: "Let's kill Meredith Houghton." He was obviously trying to punish his former lady friend, but that was the last thing Leonard wanted to do. Not only was he extremely fond of the character he had created, but many women who had read the book—including several editors at Doubleday—had told him how powerfully they had related to Meredith, considering her a role model.

But Pierre's suggestion got Leonard thinking, and at their second meeting, it was *his* turn to stun Pierre: "We're not going to kill Meredith," he said. "We're going to kill André."

For some seconds Pierre looked at Leonard as though his writing partner had lost his senses. Pierre thought of André as a version of himself. "Let me explain," Leonard said. For the next ten minutes, Pierre listened in silence as Leonard told his tale: On their honeymoon in the Dominican Republic, André and Meredith are attacked by would-be assassins. André's wounds are superficial, but Meredith is gravely injured. Aboard a hospital plane commandeered by Meredith's father, the CIA director explains to André that he's a marked man and will almost surely be killed, perhaps along with his wife. The solution, he says, is to feign André's death, taking him into hiding and transforming him completely—even giving him a new voice—so that not even his wife could recognize him. Realizing that he has placed the woman he loves in danger, André agrees to the plan, even though he will be obliged not to reveal the truth to anyone—not even Meredith. A year later, in his new disguise, he is not only tracking down the people who tried to kill him, but is also courting his wife.

When Leonard had finished the narrative, Pierre uttered one word: "Fabulous."

And that's the story they told in *Mortal Games* (1988), which, like its predecessor, was a Literary Guild main selection (Literary Guild was a part of Doubleday), a national bestseller, and sold in numerous countries.

Theirs was an unusually successful collaboration. Leonard is one of the most professional, dedicated, and diligent writers with whom I have worked. He is a superb ghostwriter, working hard to be faithful to the voice of the principal (the person he is working with), yet he very much disliked being identified as a ghostwriter.

Leonard Gross wrote nonfiction books and novels under his own name, and he spent twelve years working on a play until he got it right. Leonard is from the generation most committed to and admiring of President John F. Kennedy. The play was based on the fiction that President Kennedy was not killed in Dallas in 1963 but only wounded, and that he survived to complete two terms in office. To get material, Leonard interviewed fifty people who were JFK's friends or associates. The play is essentially a lively dialogue between JFK, who has written a first draft of his memoirs that was totally unsatisfactory to his publisher, and the ghostwriter brought in to work with him. It has an astounding feeling of authenticity.

*The Memoirs of JFK* was greeted by a standing ovation when it opened in November 2003 at Diego Rivera Theater at the City College of San Francisco.

By 2001, Leonard's various books had been selected by US book clubs fourteen times, either as dual main selections or alternates. He, like other talented writers, is adept at writing about disparate subjects.

One of his most commercially successful nonfiction books, and his first book club selection, was a conditioning book. The way husbands and wives sometimes acquire one another's traits, some authors, such as Leonard, pick up the ideas and traits of the subject they're working with. Since writing the book, Leonard has been completely committed to his own fitness, which included his shooting his age in golf. Leonard wrote the book and shared the by-line with Larry Morehouse, a UCLA professor who had devoted thirty years to the field of exercise physiology. But before publication, as the publisher was trying to arrive at an appropriate title for the book, which one top editor there told me was "the quintessential Simon and Schuster book," the senior editor called and said, "Sterling, I've got the perfect title for Leonard's book: *No Sweat.*"

"Well," I said, without much hesitation, "to tell you the truth, I don't like it. I don't think it is the right title at all."

Later I learned that same editor had gone into the title meeting still pushing *No Sweat* and part of his sales pitch included using my clout: He said, "Sterling Lord likes it." Fortunately, that wasn't enough to swing it his way. *Total Fitness in 30 Minutes a Week* was published in 1975 and became a *New York Times* bestseller, selling 350,000 copies in hardcover. Mass-market paperback rights were sold for $810,000, a good price, but not unthinkable in the days of a booming paperback publishing market.

As an ex-editor of *Look*, Leonard conceived the idea in the early seventies of writing a novel about the events of 1968 (including the assassinations of Martin Luther King Jr. and Robert Kennedy) as seen through the prism of a magazine like *Look*. In the novel, he called the magazine *Mirror* and Harper and Row published it under that title in 1980.

To my surprise, when I saw the bound book, the dedication read "For Sterling Lord." I was flattered, and I told Leonard. We went about the business of selling all the subsidiary rights we could, including foreign publication. One publisher who made an acceptable offer was Alfredo Machado in Brazil, who published the book in Portuguese.

A few years later (translations can take time), the eight author's copies of the Portuguese language edition arrived at the office and my staff immediately forwarded them to Leonard in California. Two weeks later, Leonard called me at what must have been 6:30 a.m. in California. "Sterling," he said, "did you read the dedication in the Portuguese edition?" Leonard reads Portuguese and I don't.

I hadn't. "Well, they translated your name so the dedication reads 'For the Supreme God.'

Having a name like Lord has its advantages.

## CHAPTER 7

# The First Among First Ladies

In the fall of 1971 I received a call from my client Maxine Cheshire, writer of "VIP," a must-read three-times-a-week column in the *Washington Post*, and a superb reporter. (She broke many stories including South Korea's efforts to bribe US Congressmen, as well as that of President Nixon's wife, Pat, receiving millions of dollars in illegal gifts from foreign governments, the illegal donations of $1,000,000 of antiques to the Kennedy White House, and many others.) She told me about a man named J. B. West who was retiring from his post as Chief Usher at the White House. He had served six administrations and had gained the confidence of all six first ladies, and he wanted to write a book. He also had a reputation for extreme discretion, which might have been a deal breaker, but in his case, was not. That discretion was apparent in his conversations and later in his writing and television appearances. He told intimate stories, but he was never indiscreet; he never told any stories that would embarrass a former president or first lady. Discretion was built into J. B. West. As chief usher he was the head housekeeper in the White House, and had access to the personal quarters of the president and first lady.

J. B. West turned out to be articulate, pleasant, well organized, and easy to work with, and there was the added benefit that he was from

Iowa, exhibiting the solidity of the Middle West. He was amused and pleased to learn I had been born and raised there, too. In those days, a potential author with a great tale and interesting subject matter, if he or she were well known, didn't always have to produce a book proposal to make a deal. I knew J. B. West was not that well known, but his employer—the White House—was known by everyone. After introducing him to editors at three major publishing houses and getting only mild expressions of interest, I decided we needed something on paper. I asked him if during his thirty years in the White House, any articles had been written about him. He had turned away all requests from writers during that time, he told me, but once he retired he agreed to be interviewed by Mary Lynn Kotz, who had worked in the White House. (Lady Bird Johnson had chosen Kotz to research and construct a film biography of the White House and the presidents who had served up to that point.) Kotz turned her interview with J.B. into an article that she then sold to the *Des Moines Register Sunday Magazine*. J.B. showed the article to me, and once I read it, I knew we had our writer for the book. The writing was fairly straightforward, but she had accurately captured J.B.

Their first efforts at working together weren't easy, though. J.B.'s discretion was so total that he could not remember many of the events of those years, and Kotz had to begin by researching the period to stimulate J.B.'s memory.

It was a perfect match of writer and subject, and using a thorough, detailed outline Mary Lynn had prepared, plus a short proposal and a copy of the article, I sold the book immediately to Coward-McCann, a division of Putnam.

The final manuscript for *Upstairs at the White House* was delivered to my office in October 1972. I read it overnight before rushing it by messenger to Coward-McCann. It was full of wonderful behind-the-scenes stories involving Bess Truman, Mamie Eisenhower, Jackie Kennedy, Lady Bird Johnson, Eleanor Roosevelt, and Pat Nixon. J.B. painted a poignant picture of Harry and Bess Truman having dinner alone in the third floor solarium, as they did promptly at 7 p.m. most every night in the White House, occasionally joined by their daughter, Margaret. J.B. recalled that Jackie Kennedy never kept a regular daily schedule—preferring spontaneity; the only time of her day that was predetermined was the children's hour: 6:30 p.m. when she played with or read to John-John and Caroline. And while it was known that during his tenure the public didn't see Franklin Delano Roosevelt in a wheelchair, West described the extreme measures the White House staff took to conceal—even from White House guests—his inability to walk. During state dinners, FDR was seated first, then the staff would remove his wheelchair, and only then would the guests be allowed into the dining room. West also wrote that Eleanor Roosevelt treated the White House like a hotel; she would invite guests to stay overnight, but was so busy with her own demanding schedule that she often didn't know who was down the hall.

West's manuscript was a well-written and interesting read, and I learned something I didn't already know about each president and first lady it described. I liked it. I thought Coward-McCann had bought a book with major sales potential. The following day I had a call from Nancy Tuckerman, Jackie Onassis's friend. She said that Mrs. Onassis, who was then an editor at Doubleday—she had previously been an editor at Viking—wanted to do anything she could to help promote the J. B. West book. I never questioned how Jackie and Nancy were so up-to-the-minute about the status of the book, but I suspect the source was J.B. himself. I knew that often at the end of each working day he had drinks with Nancy and other women on the White House staff, who all liked him.

I thanked Nancy and asked her to thank Mrs. Onassis, but reminded her that the book wouldn't be published for at least six months. She knew that, but wanted to be sure we were aware of Mrs. Onassis's interest in advance.

Normally writers go to great lengths—as do publishers—to secure an endorsement for their book from a recognizable name or an authority in their field. Jackie had spent the years following President Kennedy's death fending off the media and trying to maintain her privacy. There probably was no one else on the planet whose name and endorsement would have been more helpful to J. B. West. And I could not remember her ever giving an endorsement to any commercial project.

J. B. West (above), with coauthor Mary Lynn Kotz, produced a marvelous book about his service as Chief Usher of the White House. The two met when Lady Bird Johnson's social secretary, Bess Abell, called Mary Lynn to research and develop a pictorial listing of the White House and the presidents who served there. The book they wrote together, *Upstairs at the White House*, was on the *New York Times* bestseller list for fifty-six weeks.

That was a remarkable phone call. And I was curious why Jackie would offer such strong unsolicited support. I called the well-connected Maxine Cheshire, correctly assuming that if anyone knew the story, she would. She told me, it is the custom that, as the president and first lady depart the White House at the end of his last term, the chief usher presents the retiring first lady with the logbook, which contains a record of everyone who entered or left the private quarters during the term of office. Just before her departure, J.B. had approached Mrs. Kennedy, full of apology, to say he was unable to locate the logbook. He knew, of course, that JFK had had a number of affairs in the White House and that those women's names were in that book. It would have been embarrassing and upsetting for Jackie to see them. Nothing was said about that, and only the apology was given. That act became an unspoken bond between J.B. and Jackie.

Ms. Cheshire suggested that her support for his book was in appreciation for his discretion.

*Upstairs at the White House* was published in 1973, with this quote from Jackie printed on the jacket:

> People used to ask me, "Who is the most powerful man in Washington, after the President?" I would answer, "Mr. West, because no President could function without him."
> Yet how many Americans have ever heard of his post: Chief Usher of the White House?
> With infinite calm, humor, a passion for anonymity and the steel of a Napoleon, he ran the White House for the six Chief Executives who served. J. B. West, often at a moment's notice, coped with their idiosyncrasies, their excesses, their crises, their longings for domestic privacy. He gave Presidential couples the one thing they missed the most in suddenly finding themselves in the maelstrom of the White House—a sense of tranquility.
> I think he is one of the most extraordinary men I have ever met.

I later learned that before Jackie Kennedy left the White House, J.B. had taken the logbook to another member of the Kennedy family, who had burned it. Although I have never been able to confirm this story, I have every confidence in my source that it's is true.

Every one of the six presidential social secretaries was at J.B.'s publication party at the Ritz-Carlton Hotel in Washington, DC, in the autumn of 1973. All the first families were represented—Kennedy by Ethel Kennedy, the wife of Attorney General Robert Kennedy, the President's brother; and Roosevelt by his daughter Anna Roosevelt—but none of the first ladies was present. The extraordinarily well-attended party reflected the affection and admiration for J.B. even after the book's publication—a remarkable tribute to a man who had served so many first families loyally.

The book went on to spend fifty-six weeks on the *New York Times* bestseller list. Eleven years after she left the White House, Jackie Kennedy Onassis went to work in book publishing, a natural position for someone steeped in literature and who knew many of the most prominent people in the world. The main function of editors had become the securing of books or subjects for political, sports, and show-business books—and Jackie could be a magnet for authors wanting to work with her. Her first job was with the excellent quality publisher Viking Press, to whom I had sent a great many authors (Kerouac, Kesey, Breslin). She turned out to be a good text editor, too, and despite her new work, she was able to maintain her haute lifestyle.

A number of people in and out of publishing sought to have lunch with her, presumably to talk about book projects—many of which never materialized. They just wanted to have a salade Niçoise or pommes frites with the most revered first lady of the generation.

Jackie might have remained there had Viking not published the Jeffrey Archer novel *Shall We Tell the President?* A former member of the House of Commons, Archer had written only one previous novel. *Shall We Tell the President?* was trashed by a *New York Times* reviewer on October 10, 1977, in a manner that was embarrassing to the Kennedy family, and its last witty line was personally embarrassing to Jackie as well as to Viking. The review read in part:

### ASSASSIN ON THE LOOSE

President Kennedy's crisis isn't Bolivia. It is gun control, to which end he is pushing a bill through the Senate. Those who make money from the manufacture and sales of guns are unhappy. They conspire to assassinate Kennedy on the day of a crucial Senate vote. The Federal Bureau of Investigation, knowing only that the target date is March 10 and that a United States Senator is involved, has six days to find the assassin and save the President.

Is Ted Kennedy necessary to this book? Clumsily plotted, indifferently written, wantonly silly as it is, did it require the last Kennedy brother to make some special point about politics and history? It did not. The noise about health insurance and gun control could just as well have been noise about arms proliferation or oil embargoes, with a fictitious President.

Does this mean that a bad thriller needed to exploit a terrible fantasy—a continuing American nightmare—in order to deflect readers from its many warts? It means exactly, tastelessly, that.

There is a word for such a book. The word is trash. Anybody associated with its publication should be ashamed of herself.

Before he bought the Archer book from Debbie Owens, the British agent, Tom Guinzberg, Viking's president, told me that he had met Jackie in her office and described the book and its contents to her, and essentially asked her permission to publish it, the same move any sensitive publisher would have made back then if a book involved the family of one of his or her editors. Jackie told him to go ahead. However, after the scathing *New York Times* review, there was a considerable uproar in the world of publishing. Everyone I talked to had seen it and was incredulous. Jackie responded by denying she knew anything about the book and immediately resigned from Viking.

A few months later, in February 1978, Jackie re-entered publishing, joining Doubleday as an editor. Doubleday assigned a bright young editor to work with her—on the theory that if a manuscript that needed to be read and responded to quickly came in on a Friday, and Jackie wanted to go foxhunting, the young editor could step in.

It was during the Doubleday phase of her life that I met her. The noted New York sports doctor Jim Nichols had asked me to represent him. Jackie knew him and had been interested in doing a book with him for some time, so she called me to see if the three of us could meet. Shortly before that, I had broken both bones in my lower right leg, when a man driving a stolen car plowed into me outside Madison Square Garden as I was leaving a New York Knicks basketball game. Every workday for the next six weeks, wearing a heavy plaster cast, I was confined to a wheelchair but I came to my office regularly. That is where we met.

Jackie was very attentive during the meeting, asking Jim Nichols a few intelligent and pointed questions. She obviously admired and respected Nichols, who did most of the talking. The meeting was inconclusive, but the next morning Jackie phoned to see if we could get together to talk about my other writers and what books I might be able to bring to her.

"Could we have lunch?" she asked.

I was beginning to understand that as charming and gracious as she was, Jackie Onassis was also politely aggressive and highly competitive.

I reminded her I was in a wheelchair and hadn't been going out to lunch, but I could offer her a homemade sandwich on homemade bread, if she'd like to join me in my office.

"Oh, I'd love to," she said. "I hate those big, noisy restaurants."

At home we had a wonderful Scandinavian housekeeper who was making hearty, delicious sandwiches with homemade bread for me every day. During those six weeks I must have had fifteen to eighteen office lunches with guests, but Jackie was the only one who didn't finish her sandwich. Now I understood how she kept that svelte figure.

The day she came to lunch she was wearing a light gray cashmere sweater, pearls, charcoal gray flannel slacks, and black pumps, all of which my then-assistant, Philippa "Flip" Brophy, remembered better than I. Jackie sat on my dark blue couch, nibbling tentatively on her sandwich, and I rolled my wheelchair up to the other side of the coffee table.

She was thoughtful and diplomatic, and before she left the office, she unobtrusively managed to meet and chat with every secretary or assistant in the agency (the agents were all out to lunch), a gesture which endeared her to our office staff.

The next time I saw her was in 1979, at the Doubleday dinner at the '21' Club for my client Pierre Salinger. There must have been fifty or sixty people at the dinner, seated in groups of eight at tables scattered around the room. There were place cards. Salinger was seated next to Jackie, and I was at a nearby table next to Nancy Tuckerman, Jackie's friend and spokeswoman. Pierre had to leave early to catch a plane for Boston to promote his new book, *Venezuelan Notebooks: Travels and Conversations with Carlos Andres Perlz.* The minute he left, Nancy turned to me and said, "Sterling, you should go over and sit next to Jackie."

So I did. I didn't know why Nancy turned to me, but I was delighted.

For an instant, I thought, "What is a boy from a small town in Iowa doing sitting at a banquet next to Jackie Kennedy Onassis, perhaps the most admired woman in the world?" Then I recalled a line that JFK had said to a client of mine, Peter Wyden, then a *Newsweek* correspondent, back when JFK was a senator and was just beginning to be mentioned as a possible presidential candidate.

Peter had been interviewing Senator Kennedy on some issue of the week, while Kennedy sat comfortably, one leg draped over the arm of his chair. But as the interview was ending and Peter was gathering his papers to put them in his briefcase, he turned to JFK and said, "Tell me, Senator, what makes you think you are qualified to be president of the United Sates?" Without hesitation, Kennedy said, "Peter, all these jobs are held by people."

Jackie and I chatted, and as the party was breaking up, I was thinking that since her escort, Pierre, had left, she would probably welcome someone taking her home. When we rose from the table to leave, I said, "Jackie, I know your escort has left; may I take you home?"

She stood beside me, with those wide-open eyes, without saying anything for a moment or two. "Sterling," she said, "I have a car and driver outside. May I take *you* home?" And she did.

My relationship with Jackie continued for a number of years.

One of my longtime clients, David Wise, an expert on the Central Intelligence Agency and one of the most trusted reporters in Washington, had had a very good relationship with JFK and Jackie when they were in the White House. I say very good, and it was, but David was one of the few journalists I knew who never dined with the notables. He never mixed business with pleasure, and any potential news source was business. David had done an unusual nonpolitical favor for the Kennedys that Jackie never forgot. David was in Palm Beach on assignment on November 25, 1960, waiting with other reporters for Kennedy to land. Just as his plane arrived, the president-elect learned that Jackie—who was pregnant—had been rushed to Georgetown Hospital. Kennedy ordered the plane to return to Washington. David stayed in Palm Beach and was in the control tower at West Palm Beach Airport when he received the news from his paper the *Herald Tribune*, that Jackie had given birth. He immediately was on the phone to the president's plane to give him the news. Pierre Salinger was with the president and took the call. After telling the president, he immediately called David back to ask if it was a boy or a girl. (It was John Jr.). Then he called again, as JFK wanted to know the color of the newborn's hair (brown).

Now, with Jackie in publishing and presumably not as covetous of her privacy, David wanted very much to write her biography or to help her write her autobiography. He mentioned this to me the moment she went to work for Doubleday.

The word around the publishing community was that Jackie would never write an autobiography. When I called her to set up the appointment for David, I said only that he wanted to talk about nonfiction book ideas; he was under option to another publisher for his fiction, I added. If I had told her David's precise purpose for the meeting, I knew she would turn me down. She was delighted to be meeting with David, and they did get together shortly thereafter at Jackie's mother's home in Georgetown.

They each subsequently reported it had been a good meeting and that they both were trying to come up with a good nonfiction book idea. Nothing was said to me in the days that followed about Jackie's autobiography. I found out later that, when they met at her mother's home, on Volta Place, Jackie began by handing David a gin and tonic, and had one for herself. David asked her if she would ever think of writing an autobiography. She promptly remarked, "Maybe when I'm ninety," to which David said, "We may neither of us be around then," and that was it for the autobiography. Jackie, David, and I did talk twice about a nonfiction idea for David, without success. Finally, Jackie called me with a new thought: "Let's have some fun, Sterling. Let's get David going on a novel!"

She had forgotten that he was under option elsewhere for his fiction, and I was not about to remind her. I plunged ahead on the assumption that if we had an acceptable offer from Jackie and Doubleday, I could find a way to make it happen.

"I want to be sure Doubleday can afford David as a novelist," I told Jackie. While I was impressed by her, I was never so awed that I would squander a chance to make a good writer more money. The truth was

David Wise interviews Jacqueline Kennedy at the Kennedy compound in Hyannisport, Massachusetts, for a *New York Herald Tribune* article published during the Kennedy-Nixon presidential campaign. It was the beginning of a long acquaintanceship. Later, when Jackie was an editor at Doubleday, David tried to persuade her to write an autobiography, with his help. They met, but she said she wouldn't want to think about an autobiography until she was ninety years old. But Jackie wanted to publish a novel of David's, and later she did: *The Samarkand Dimension*. David told me her editorial notes were excellent, and he adopted many of the revisions she suggested.

that David had written two novels that were both very well reviewed but hadn't sold well. I thought the combination of Jackie and Doubleday might give him a chance to break out. So I quoted a price that was double the advance David had received on his last novel.

A few days later, knowing nothing about the contents of the novel David would write, Jackie came back with a firm offer that wasn't what I had asked, but was still considerably higher than any advance David had previously received for a novel. "But," Jackie said, "we'll have to have a title for the novel before I can start the contractual process."

Up to this point, we'd never discussed the content of the novel-to-be, nor had I kept David informed about my latest conversations with Jackie.

I called David immediately. It was almost noon, and I wanted to get back to Jackie before she left for lunch. I knew she was not going to be available that afternoon, and I wanted to button this one up as soon as possible. I gave David ten minutes to come up with a title. David had already been thinking about a story he wanted to write, and a few minutes later, he called me back. And that was the beginning of *The Samarkand Dimension*, a novel about a mythical Russian school that taught intelligence operatives how to read the minds of foreign leaders. (The real Samarkand was part of the Soviet Union and is now—in 2012—the second largest city in Uzbekistan.)

Getting David released from the option-holding publisher was not as easy as I had expected. I knew St. Martin's wouldn't match the offer I had, as his last novel with them had not earned out his advance, but they decided they wouldn't make a decision until they had seen an outline. Two weeks later, I had a very strong fifteen-page outline from David. St. Martin's failed to make a counteroffer, freeing us to accept Doubleday's offer.

As Jackie and I were working out the details of the contract, Christmas was approaching. She announced that she would be on the job right through the holidays, but would be gone the first two weeks of January. When I asked where she was going, and whether it was for business or pleasure, she said: "Oh, I'm going to India. I have two books on Indian art I'm editing, and I have to attend to them. And then, of course, my son is in India." Attaching a personal aspect to a business trip made her sound like almost anyone else in publishing.

## CHAPTER 8

# The Bells Don't Ring All the Time

Time is the most important element in an agent's life. I once listened while a close friend and avid reader told me she thought being a literary agent was a dream job, one filled with lunches with intelligent women editors, who picked up the tab, access to all the books you would like to read, invitations to glamorous publishing parties, and the flexibility to read in the office or take a day off and read at home.

That was not the job I had. In my first fifty years in the business, I never took a day off to read, and any night I wasn't carrying reading home was rare. My weekends were usually packed with manuscripts. As for publishing parties, if I had to go, I developed the technique of quickly greeting and thanking the host, congratulating the guest of honor, and then leaving unobtrusively so I could go home for a full evening of reading.

Concern about time affects my selection of clients, too. Certain writers are more time-consuming than others. Dick Francis, the famous British former–steeplechase jockey, who turned out a novel each year, was well organized and never took up much of my time. Dick had been quite successful in his pre-writing career. He was named best jockey in the British Isles one year, and towards the end of his riding career, he was the contract rider for the Queen Mother.

As a successful mystery writer, he won the Edgar—the Mystery Writers of America top award—three times (in 1970, 1981, and 1996), and his books quickly climbed to the top of the bestseller lists of every country in the world, except the US, where he was frequently as high as #3—but never higher—on the *New York Times* bestseller list. Every year, he met his manuscript delivery deadline. Mary Francis, a former English teacher, ensured his grammar was correct, I suspect, and his US publishers couldn't and didn't change a word without Dick's permission. He was highly professional and we all—agent and publisher—took extreme pleasure in working with him.

I don't think Howard Fast and Dick Francis ever met, but they were alike in many ways. Both were gentlemen, each as knowledgeable about his field of interest—Dick's field was steeplechase and flat racing, of course, and Howard's was mostly American history.

When Howard Fast came into my life, I already knew a great deal about him and had read his books for years. By the age of sixty-one, he had already published sixty-five novels, including *Citizen Tom Paine* (1943) and *Spartacus* (1953). In 1950, when he was called before the House Un-American Activities Committee, he refused to disclose the names of contributors (the list included Eleanor Roosevelt) to a fund to support a home for orphans of American veterans of the Spanish Civil War. He was held in contempt of Congress, subsequently served three months in a federal prison, and was effectively blacklisted.

Howard became my client in 1975, after his daughter-in-law, Erica Jong, who was already a client, recommended me highly. Erica was a poet who wrote the iconoclastic and bestselling *Fear of Flying*, with its strong spirit and frank treatment of feminine sex. She was an attractive, intelligent blonde, who had married Jonathan Fast, Howard's son.

At the other end of the spectrum I had two clients who vacuumed up my time: Dick Schaap, who was an editor at *Newsweek* and the *Herald Tribune*, a sports television commentator, and author of twenty-two books, and Jimmy Breslin, the front-page columnist for the *Herald Tribune* and a select group of other papers around the country. But they were both very good, productive writers, and working with them was usually a pleasure. In choosing clients, I've found it's a balancing act between one's time and an author's talent, and I always bend in the direction of talent.

Whether a writer is just beginning or extremely well known, I have to be able to deal openly and directly with him or her. One well-known political figure came to me around 1980, accompanied by an entourage of his staff members. I recognized him from the many times I had seen his picture in newspapers, in magazines, and on television. He wanted me to represent him, and sensing a possible problem, I said I would be delighted to work with him if he could assure me I would be able to talk with him directly, not his staff. He assured me it would work that way. Within ten days, I had a call from one of his staff members about a matter he himself should have dealt with. I resigned immediately from representing Terry Sanford, who shortly thereafter became president of Duke University (1969 to 1985).

Over the years, as the money paid to writers increased dramatically, the publishing part of the agency business became less gentlemanly and more competitive, and it attracted people more interested in money than in writing. The increased power and importance of the agent became apparent in the sixties, when the paperback market burgeoned—both mass-market and trade paperback. Publishers either went public, merged, or became part of a conglomerate. And some agents introduced the practice of pilfering—luring writers already represented elsewhere. One agent who could care less about quality of the writing but blatantly pursued the dollar was the legendary Hollywood agent Irving "Swifty" Lazar. He did something I'd never previously encountered: He would negotiate a substantial publishing deal for a Hollywood star or political figure such as Henry Kissinger, without representing or even consulting them (although he did know Kissinger). If the money was sufficiently substantial—and it usually was—the famous person signed on to become Swifty's client. Or at least Swifty got the commissions. In Kissinger's case, Simon and Schuster had to pay two commissions: Swifty's and Kissinger's regular agent's. Other pursuing agents—not quite as bold as Swifty—may promise to give more attention than the writer is currently receiving or improve the writer's publishing situation, with larger advances, better sales, or more foreign sales. I have never tried to raid another agent's client list. It would go against the grain—and my own ethical standards.

The ease of seduction differs depending on the sophistication of the writer. One author who had written and published twelve books but never had a bestseller until he came to Sterling Lord Literistic, Inc., eventually left our office for a larger agency—the William Morris Agency (now William Morris Endeavor)—which promised to produce many more foreign sales for him. In fact, by 2007, the person who had dramatically improved the foreign-sales record of the larger agency had left William Morris and was employed by us to sell *our* foreign rights. William Morris was back to using much-less-experienced people. The only excuse for that is if the writer is overtly not being very well represented, but the writer should know that himself or herself rather than wait for a *competitive* agent to tell him or her. In my agency, authors can always leave by giving written notice as provided in our representation agreement. But in this business, the emotional condition and state of mind of the author—or the agent—often prevails over the written document.

I've had two cases of screaming clients, writers who took out their frustrations on my innocent staff: The late Peter Wyden, whom I mentioned in the Jackie Kennedy Onassis chapter earlier in this book, had a hot temper and would frequently scream at my staff over the phone.

As fond as I was of Peter, I didn't want my staff, who were very good, subjected to that kind of abuse and disruption. We didn't need it, and it was counterproductive. I wrote him a strong letter suggesting he look for a new agent. He did, and though I saw him occasionally after that, he never challenged the validity of that letter.

The second instance involved Peter Maas, author of *Serpico* and many other interesting books. Peter had a high-powered accountant who was an A+ screamer. After he twice screamed at my staff, I phoned Peter to tell him his accountant was harming our working relationship, and that stopped the screaming.

An agent can commit so completely to a writer that he or she may, over a period of years, devote a great deal of extra effort and time to that writer, helping him or her achieve financial success, only to find one day that the client has left the agency. There may be a psychological reason for this: A writer doesn't want to continue to be associated with the agent who has seen him at his weakest moment, once the writer becomes rich and famous. It reminds me of a situation involving my client James T. Farrell (author of *Studs Lonigan*) and Nelson Algren (author of *The Man with the Golden Arm*), who had been good friends. One drunken Saturday night, Farrell pulled Algren out of the path of a rapidly approaching streetcar, probably saving Algren's life. According to Farrell, Algren never spoke to him again.

One of the most embarrassing and discouraging experiences a literary agent can have is unexpectedly losing a longtime, highly successful client. It can feel like the death of a relative.

Jimmy Breslin first walked into my office in 1952. Bill Wise, a longtime friend from my days as a magazine editor, had spoken glowingly of Jimmy, then a writer for the *Long Island Press*—he had worked for them since he was seventeen years old, starting as a copyboy—and he had obviously described me to Jimmy in the same positive light. Bill had told me Jimmy would be contacting me. Weeks passed, and I didn't hear. Bill would phone from time to time to assure me that Jimmy really would call.

He didn't call, though; he came in person. He stomped into my office at 15 East Forty-Eighth Street one afternoon with his unkempt curly black hair, spewing apologies in his Irish–New York–Brooklyn accent and promising to return. It was a brief appearance, but he seemed to vacuum all the air in the office. He was gone before any of us had time to respond. My staff didn't know what to make of him, but I was curious. I knew he was very talented. We didn't know it then, but we were in for a long run.

It turned out to be always interesting and often exciting working with and for him, though very time-consuming. I already represented a number of fine nonfiction writers, and more were to come, but Jimmy was unique and would appeal to literary editors as well as to journalism buffs. Jimmy was both intelligent and street-smart. His

Photo by Nick Elgar

In the sixties, seventies, and eighties, any and every publisher who brought out a Jimmy Breslin book threw a publication party. Sometimes there was more than one. In 1986, when Ticknor and Fields published *Table Money*, a moving novel about Owney Morrison, a Vietnam veteran living in Queens, an aggressive freelance publicist selected a half-completed apartment building on Park Avenue for the publication party. I always thought the site revealed the Manhattan publicist's conception of what she thought Queens looked like. I'm at left, with Breslin, right, at the party.

This picture captures the moment in 1986 when Jimmy Breslin was awarded the Pulitzer Prize for his columns in the *New York Daily News*. Left to right are: Jim Hoge, publisher of the *New York Daily News*; Jimmy's long-time literary agent (me); and Jimmy about to kiss his wife, Ronnie Eldridge, while Gil Spencer, editor in chief of the paper, peeks over them.

Irish charm, his warmth, and his commitment to good work and to New York City, made me want to work with him. He was thoughtful, had a good sense of humor, and was respectful. When I learned more about his background and early years, it made these qualities all the more remarkable. Jimmy's father was a piano player—at bars, weddings, all around—who left the family when Jimmy was four. Jimmy never spoke to him again, even when, years later, he was dying in a Florida hospital and one of the nurses phoned to tell Jimmy.

He was raised by his mother who was a social worker in Harlem, and an alcoholic. He also had printer's ink in his blood; at the age of six, I found out, he founded and published a neighborhood newspaper in Ozone Park called *The Flash*. One of Jimmy's friends once pointed out that children of alcoholic parents traditionally have trouble making up their minds. However, there were many extras involved in being his agent. Shortly after we started working together, principally selling his stories to the magazines, Jimmy's wife, Rosemary, let me know that the family's finances were in a dicey state, and she asked for help. They owed money around town to half a dozen New York businesses, including Toots Shor's very popular restaurant, Gallagher's Steakhouse, and B&B Clothiers in Queens. Jimmy and family lived in Queens, less than a mile from the area where he grew up. I had never thought about Jimmy's attire until I read the B&B bills. In my office, or wherever I met him in the city he either wore a sports jacket or a dark blue suit, never a necktie. At his home, it was a sweater or shirt without a necktie—nothing fancy. But Jimmy was supporting his wife and six children on a newspaperman's salary. In the spirit of "broad support for a unique talent," I volunteered to pay off all debtors gradually with a percentage of Jimmy's earnings from my sales of his material. Both Jimmy and Rosemary agreed to the plan. After eighteen months of siphoning off the proceeds, all their debts were paid, the final payment going to B&B Clothiers in Queens.

A few days after I cleared his last debt, Jimmy barged into the office with a sheepish complaint. He loved verbal combat, and he missed the haranguing phone calls from B&B Clothiers; couldn't I reinstate that debt so he could continue his phone battles? I couldn't, of course. Jimmy would have to find another target for his assaults, and I'm sure he did.

Jimmy's ingenuity, sense of drama, and survival instinct manifested in other ways. Early in our relationship, he was much in demand at *Sport* magazine (the premier sports monthly), first with Ed Fitzgerald and then with Al Silverman, consecutive editors in chief. *Sport* would assign articles and give him a deadline. Two or three weeks before the deadline date, an editor would call Jimmy to see when to expect delivery of a story. "It's in the typewriter now," he'd assure them. In reality, this was more of a "Thanks for reminding me." The second time his editor would call about his copy, Jimmy would explain, "It just missed the messenger. You'll have it tomorrow." When it didn't arrive the following day or any time shortly thereafter, Jimmy told his caller, "The boy is on the way in with it now." Eventually, the article arrived, but knowing Jimmy's habits, the editors didn't schedule the piece until they actually had it in hand.

Ray Robinson, a well-known and highly regarded writer and, at the time, an editor of a new monthly called *Real*, didn't know the drill and was subjected to a number of sleepless nights. He assigned Jimmy to ghostwrite an article with Rogers Hornsby, a long-retired baseball great. Sensing the article could help sell the magazine, Ray made the optimistic mistake of blurbing the story on the four-color cover, which was locked up thirty days before the content of the magazine closed. To be accepted, Jimmy's manuscript needed Rogers Hornsby's signature, since it was to be published under his by-line. At the last minute, the signature arrived—and Ray, in a tremendous time bind but without proof that it really was Hornsby's signature, had to assume the signature was Hornsby's. As I remember, Ray called me for help along the way, but much as I liked and admired Ray, since he alone had made the decision to put it on the cover, there was nothing I could do.

One of those magazine sales that helped pay Jimmy's debts was an assignment I arranged for him with *Collier's*, the national weekly magazine with a circulation in the millions that competed with the *Saturday Evening Post*. He was assigned a piece on some of the famous and infamous New York characters in his life. He turned the piece in to editor Diana Hirsch the day after *Collier's* went out of business. Normally, when a publication folds, the first department to know it is accounting. All payments stop immediately and the writer is out of luck. In this case, I was able to get full payment for Jimmy, and from that moment on, in Jimmy's circle I was known affectionately as "the Robber."

In May 1963, with magazines failing around us, I drew up a contract with Jim Bellows, the astute and imaginative editor, for Jimmy to do a three-times-a-week column for the *New York Herald Tribune*, the lively #2 morning daily, behind the *New York Times*. Bellows knew what he had and flaunted it. Jimmy's column appeared regularly on the front page of the paper. Shortly after Jimmy started at the *Herald Tribune*, President John F. Kennedy was assassinated, and Jimmy was immediately on a plane to Dallas. His column "A Death in Emergency Room One" appeared on Sunday, November 24, 1963, two days after JFK's death. It began:

> The call bothered Malcolm Perry. "Dr. Tom Shires, STAT," the girl's voice said over the page in the doctors' cafeteria at Parkland Memorial Hospital. The "STAT" meant emergency. Nobody ever called Tom Shires, the hospital's chief resident in surgery, for an emergency. And Shires, Perry's superior, was out of town for the day. Malcolm Perry looked at the salmon croquettes on the plate in front of him. Then he put down his fork and went over to the telephone.
> "This is Dr. Perry taking Dr. Shires' page," he said.
> "President Kennedy has been shot. STAT," the operator said.

In one of the most moving sections of the piece, Jimmy wrote that while Dr. Perry was doing his job, he "noted the tall, dark-haired girl in the plum dress that had her husband's blood all over the front of the skirt. She was standing out of the way, over against the gray tile wall. Her face was tearless and it was set, and it was to stay that way because Jacqueline Kennedy, with a terrible discipline, was not going to take her eyes from her husband's face."

It was powerful and poignant, and I sold the article all over the world. Jimmy's understanding of human nature, his eye for detail, and his ability to sense and devise imaginative ways of dealing with human frailties and drama were all apparent in that article. Also, Jimmy was Irish, as was JFK, which added an emotional touch.

From that moment on, Jimmy was known by most every newspaperman in the US and was envied by almost every columnist who read him. He always maintained a crowd-pleasing, flippant attitude towards authority. And better than any other writer, he wrote in detail and understanding about the common man. His story about the burial of JFK at Arlington National Cemetery, "Digging JFK's Grave Was His Honor," was written from the point of view of a cemetery gravedigger. The following excerpt appeared in the *New York Herald Tribune* in November 1963:

Washington—Clifton Pollard was pretty sure he was going to be working on Sunday, so when he woke up at 9 a.m., in his three-room apartment on Corcoran Street, he put on khaki overalls before going into the kitchen for breakfast. His wife, Hettie, made bacon and eggs for him. Pollard was in the middle of eating them when he received the phone call he had been expecting. It was from Mazo Kawalchik, who is the foreman of the gravediggers at Arlington National Cemetery, which is where Pollard works for a living. "Polly, could you please be here by eleven o'clock this morning?" Kawalchik asked. "I guess you know what it's for." Pollard did. He hung up the phone, finished breakfast, and left his apartment so he could spend Sunday digging a grave for John Fitzgerald Kennedy.

When Pollard got to the row of yellow wooden garages where the cemetery equipment is stored, Kawalchik and John Metzler, the cemetery superintendent, were waiting for him. "Sorry to pull you out like this on a Sunday," Metzler said. "Oh, don't say that," Pollard said. "Why, it's an honor for me to be here." Pollard got behind the wheel of a machine called a reverse hoe. Gravedigging is not done with men and shovels at Arlington. The reverse hoe is a green machine with a yellow bucket that scoops the earth toward the operator, not away from it as a crane does. At the bottom of the hill in front of the Tomb of the Unknown Soldier, Pollard started the digging.

But Jimmy's writing in other cases was not above criticism. He would often create drama to help a column along or to make a point. He was not above self-promotion. While he was living in Richmond Hill on Long Island, he put up a sign on his lawn warning people to keep away. Reference to the sign appeared in two of his columns, but when I went to visit him, I was surprised. The sign itself and the printing on it were so small you'd have to be well up on his lawn to read it.

As his newspaper column developed, he started using me for pre-submission reactions. A few minutes before his *Herald Tribune* deadline he frequently would phone from Los Angeles, Phoenix, London, or Detroit and read me an entire column. I was flattered, but always gave it my full attention and also kept the content secret.

One afternoon when Jimmy was in England on assignment, I had an appointment with Jim Bellows to renegotiate Breslin's contract. About forty-five minutes before I was to leave for the taxi ride across town, Jimmy called from London. A call from Breslin was just part of the office furniture. Jimmy was on deadline and wanted to read me his column. A little later I was sitting in Jim Bellows's office at the *Herald Tribune* building, talking contract terms, when the door burst open and Buddy Weiss, a veteran editor who edited Jimmy's columns, blew in.

"Jim, the Breslin is in!" he exulted, handing Bellows a copy of the telex. Noticing that Weiss had a second copy in his hand, Bellows said, "Give one to Sterling."

Reading it silently and noting Breslin had made the few minor changes I'd suggested, I waited for Bellows to comment. He grinned and murmured his approval. I concurred, never acknowledging my familiarity with the piece. Jimmy had an amazing habit of turning in his copy at the very last minute or shortly after, just late enough to annoy Buddy Weiss and for a time I thought it was my pre-delivery editorial conversations with my client that were causing the trouble. Subsequent research told me he was just trying to annoy Weiss, for whom he had considerable respect. Weiss was an awfully high-ranking editor to be functioning as a copyeditor, even if it was for the front-page star, but it turned out Buddy was assigned that job when Jimmy started feuding with the man on the copy desk.

When Jimmy started with the *Herald Tribune*, we had allowed its syndicate, Publishers Newspaper Syndicate, to represent the column for the world outside New York City. But a year later we realized they hadn't sold it anywhere. I was appalled, as was Jimmy. I couldn't believe other major papers wouldn't want Jimmy. Jim Bellows, a perceptive editor (and, I subsequently came to feel, the best newspaper editor in the country), allowed me to reclaim those rights.

I regarded Jimmy as a very special talent, and I didn't see any established syndicates equipped to deal with such a talent. Having done business with quite a few newspaper editors, I set up a syndicate of our own: one sales agent, one client. In the newspaper business, our approach was revolutionary. We weren't begging papers to take Jimmy. I had a unique commodity, and in order to get into our club—to get Jimmy's three-a-week columns—a newspaper had to pay a minimum of $150 a week, although some paid more. (This was in 1964 dollars, don't forget.) We reserved the right to cancel syndication for any paper that did not publish at least nine columns in a given month. (I knew that some papers were not above buying a feature, with little intention of publishing, just to keep their crosstown rival from getting it.) One prestigious Midwestern daily didn't believe that I was serious and kept offering $25 a week, week after week. That's why Jimmy never appeared in the *St. Louis Post-Dispatch*. But we had the *Chicago Sun-Times*, the *Washington Post, Boston Herald, Detroit News,* the *Toronto Star,* the *Philadelphia Bulletin, Minneapolis Star,* and the *Trentonian.*

Reporters and columnists all over the country began imitating his writing about interesting characters and their lifestyles. The *Trentonian* ran Breslin even though they already published three regular columnists who were trying to write like him.

In the sixties through the eighties, Jimmy was the hottest newspaper columnist in the US. In 1966, Joe McGinniss, who later became well known as a successful writer of books (*The Selling of the President,* among others), was given a column of his own at the *Philadelphia Inquirer* by showing the editors a few of Jimmy's columns and saying, "That's the kind of column I want to write for you."

Jimmy, however, had many characteristics that made his talent rare, if not unique. He had a great feeling for the little details as well as a good sense of the big picture. He lived and wrote colorfully and had a high sense of drama. In 1969, Norman Mailer ran for mayor and on the same ticket, Jimmy ran for president of the city council. They didn't win, but Jimmy pulled 40,000 votes, twice as many as Mailer. And Jimmy didn't miss a single column deadline during the campaign.

I often wondered why Bellows let Jimmy continue the column during the campaign. Bellows was a stickler for ethics, I had learned very early in Jimmy's *Herald Tribune* days, when Bellows tried to tell him he couldn't do a television commercial for Piels Beer. Jimmy won the argument. Fortunately, not too long after that, Piels canceled him.

Some time after his political career with Mailer, Jimmy was warned by Rosemary that if he couldn't get home before 3 a.m., he shouldn't come home at all. The next night, as the bar he frequented was closing down, Jimmy called an ambulance company and had them come and take him home on a stretcher. It alarmed the neighbors, but Rosemary knew her husband well and knew he had the constitution of an ox; she took him in anyway.

As time went on, however, there were rumors that some of his reporting was a product of his imagination. In 1967, at the request of the *Detroit News*—one of our syndicate customers—Jimmy had traveled to Detroit to do a column or two on the continuing rioting there. A few weeks later, I was in the *News* city room waiting to meet Martin Hayden, the paper's editor in chief, when one of the *News* editors introduced himself and told me that Jimmy hadn't been on the streets of the city, as his columns implied, but had done it all from inside the city room. I doubted the editor was right. My guess was that he had been in the streets before going into the city room. Whether or not Jimmy had been on the streets, those columns were superb and reeked of authenticity. I was never aware that they were anything but honest reporting. And they demonstrated Jimmy's additional talent: Some of his facts might be debatable, but he got the essence—the truth of what was happening—better than anyone else, including those writers who *did* get all the facts.

When the *Tribune* folded, we went with the *World-Journal Tribune* for one New York minute, until that paper also folded. We then switched our New York City allegiance to Jimmy Wechsler, editor of the *New York Post*.

Ours was a creaky but effective syndicate. I did the selling, the deal making, and the contract work with the newspapers, and Jimmy, and Rosemary, took care of the delivery of the columns to the various member papers. (This was in the late sixties, years before the Internet would make such transfers of stories instantaneous.) That usually involved Rosemary making a collect call from their tree-lined home in Forest Hills, New York. For each newspaper she would clearly read the column into a tape recorder in the newspaper's city room. A typist in each newsroom would transcribe the column and deliver it to the managing editor in time for the next day's press. I don't remember a missed deadline at any newspaper.

Most writers and columnists were paying established syndicates 50 percent in that day, while I charged Jimmy only 10 percent. He was netting more through our little syndicate than all but the few top writers or columnists in the country.

As I soon realized, not everyone in the media loved Jimmy, or admired him, as I did. A local television executive, who expected Jimmy to appear regularly on his show, was on the phone immediately when Jimmy didn't appear—ever. One very high-level magazine editor had a similar—but not identical—experience. As a result, he was more or less permanently blacklisted in these markets. I realized that much of the time Jimmy followed his own star and the reason we worked so well together was that I knew enough about him to see that star. If Jimmy wanted me to get him out of a jam, he briefed me in advance. He did not brief me on either of these cases.

Jimmy's first book, *Can't Anybody Here Play This Game?*, was published by Viking Press in 1963. Inspired by material he'd written for the *Herald Tribune*, it was an account of the first year of the bumbling New York Mets baseball team. The title derived from a quotation from its first manager, the eccentric, frequently quoted veteran player, Casey Stengel. A jacket quote from Bill Veeck, a client of mine and once owner of the Chicago White Sox, St. Louis Browns, and Cleveland Indians, and three Major League clubs (not all at the same time), may have helped sell the books. Veeck called the Mets "the worst baseball team ever." Jimmy's dedication read, "To the 922,530 brave souls who paid their way into the Polo Grounds in 1962. Never has so much misery loved so much company."

In the book Jimmy makes appealing but laughable comments about the players, including "Marvelous" Marvin Throneberry, a first baseman. The opening game of the first Mets season was a one-point Mets defeat, totally caused by a Throneberry judgment error: He and the Mets third baseman were playing tag with the opponent's runner, and Marvin totally forgot there was a man on third racing home.

Speaking about the second season, Breslin wrote, "Long Island, which is considered part of New York and the new home of the Mets, is the perfect place for them. Nothing particularly good has happened to Long Island for over fifty years, so nobody is going to get unduly concerned if the Mets take more than a little while to pull themselves together."

By 1965, Tom Guinzburg, president and principal owner of Viking, and Breslin had come to know each other well. In fact, the three of us were in constant contact about new books or financial matters. Toward the end of that year, Tom had a serious problem at his warehouse in the Meadowlands of New Jersey. He had moved all the back-office operations of Viking that he could out of Manhattan and over there, and the union representing the workers, almost all of them women with children in school, was threatening to strike. There were two to three million books in the warehouse at that time, and it was essential that Viking service the orders promptly.

The shipping people were part of a union controlled by Tony ("Tony Pro") Provenzano, a well-known Teamsters boss and Mafia figure, who happened to be in prison at the time. Viking had been in negotiations with union representatives for some time and had reached a stage where both sides thought they'd arrived at a fair settlement. But then the union negotiators said they didn't have the authority to settle without Provenzano's approval. Meanwhile, the strike had started.

Knowing Jimmy had relationships with people at all levels in the metropolitan area—they varied from Mutchie, Fat Thomas, and Marvin the Torch to New York district attorney Robert Morgenthau and New York governor Mario Cuomo—and that Jimmy could be generously supportive of his friends, Tom Guinzburg called him.

Jimmy listened to Tom's story. His own books were not involved.

He asked Guinzburg if he thought the terms everyone had agreed to were fair. They were.

"I'll call you back," Breslin said.

Over the years, both Tom and I had come to realize that when Jimmy said, "I'll call you back," the chances were only around fifty-fifty that he would. But Jimmy *did* call Tom back a day or two later, instructing Tom to meet him at 11 p.m. at Gallagher's Steakhouse—a speakeasy during Prohibition—located on Fifty-Second Street just west of Broadway.

Tom and Jimmy were there only a few minutes when two swarthy men arrived to join them. There were no introductions. "Want a beer?" one of them asked. Tom and Jimmy accepted. A few minutes later, the same man asked Tom if he thought the terms of the proposed settlement were fair. "Yes. Both sides think they're fair," Tom responded.

The two men got up and left without further word.

Twenty-four hours later the strike was over. And Jimmy, who never explained, was thanked.

With Jimmy, there was something happening all the time. He often called me at home around 8 a.m. and sometimes during the evening, after my long day at the office. By 1985, I had negotiated eight book contracts for him, including *The Gang That Couldn't Shoot Straight*, a hilarious novel about the Mafia in New York City and later an MGM movie.

One of the most gracious and generous things Jimmy did for me was to fly up with me to Jack Kerouac's funeral. It was on a Friday in the fall of 1969. Thursday night at my home, the phone rang and it was Jimmy with his usual how-are-you call. As we talked, he asked me what I was doing the next day. I told him. "Sterling, nobody should go to a funeral alone." The next morning at 8 a.m., there he was at the La Guardia shuttle to Boston waiting to make the trip with me.

As we were coming in for landing at Logan, he asked me how we were going to get from Boston to Lowell.

"I plan to rent a car," I said.

Jimmy said that that wouldn't be appropriate. So when we got off the plane, he went straight to the nearest pay phone and thumbed through the phone book. He was looking for the largest limousine rental ad with an Irish proprietor. Jimmy had been appearing regularly in the *Boston Herald* and was already a legend in town. It was clear that Jimmy had roused the limo owner from his sleep. When the Irish limo owner realized that he was speaking with the real Jimmy Breslin, he was out of bed, in his car, and at the airport in twenty minutes. There was a great deal of lively two-way Irish chatter all the way to Lowell. After the service, the driver drove us out to the cemetery for the burial, then on to the Kerouac-Sampas home for the wake.

Jimmy stayed in the limo at the cemetery. When reporters discovered him, they crowded around the car, hoping to get an interview. Jimmy locked the doors. "No, no, it's his day"—he pointed to the gravesite—"not mine."

The ride back to Logan was equally lively. All that banter up and back between Jimmy and the driver did a great deal to mollify the pain of Jack's death for me. Jimmy was thoughtful and caring to have joined me, particularly since he had never met Jack Kerouac, even though they had each lived, at the same time, in Richmond Hill, on Long Island.

Jimmy's wife, Rosemary, whom I liked very much and respected, died of cancer in 1981, which was a great surprise to me as I wasn't aware she had any health problems. I never thought Jimmy could run their home on Long Island alone, and the following year he married Ronnie Eldridge—she had been friends of the Breslins—a feminist and politician who would later go on to serve on the New York City Council.

In 1985, Jimmy won the Pulitzer Prize for his journalism in the *New York Daily News*, and in 1990, his novel, *Table Money*, was reviewed in the *New York Times* by James Carroll, like Jimmy, a newspaper columnist and novelist, who called it "the great American novel." Before the year was up, we had set up a one-hour regular nighttime television show on the local ABC station with Jimmy as its host.

Over the Christmas holidays, I was planning to spend a couple of weeks with friends on an oasis in the Sahara Desert. In the process of getting ready for the trip—what do you bring to Tunisia?—and also dealing with our annual office Christmas party at a chic bistro we were taking over, I forgot the wrap party for Jimmy's television show, which had just been canceled by ABC. Jimmy called me the next day wondering why I hadn't come. I was embarrassed and apologetic. I knew it meant a great deal to him to have me there, and I had wanted to go. He had his revenge on ABC by taking out a short ad at the bottom of page one of the *New York Times*, which said, "BRESLIN CANCELS SHOW IN DISPUTE WITH ABC."

After thirty-five years, he left the agency. Shortly thereafter, he appeared on the client list of a woman agent at ICM who happened to be a longtime, close friend of Jimmy's new wife, Ronnie Eldridge.

Writers leave agents for many reasons, some rational, some inexplicable. True, I hadn't succeeded in selling Jimmy's last novel, *Forsaking All Others*, to the movies. But none of his novels since *The Gang That Couldn't Shoot Straight* had been filmed. I had a feeling that a number of his friends told him it would make a good movie, which sometimes raises an author's expectations.

Losing Jimmy was a blow. Everyone in the agency was fond of him and had been rooting for him. He left us all depressed and discouraged, not for financial reasons, but for emotional reasons. In my heart, I missed him.

Breslin was one of few writers to leave the agency. His leaving was a painful reminder that such incidents are in the nature of the business and that I should learn what I could from the experience.

To be effective as a literary agent, you have to constantly hope; you have to generate the optimism to believe that you will make every deal. One of the fundamental realities of the agency business is whether a spectacular sale or a client's departure is a triumph or a disaster, you have about ten minutes to deal with it emotionally. After that, you must move on to other business. You can't be deterred or discouraged by that occasional day when the bells don't ring.

## CHAPTER 9

# Different Hooks for Different Books

Photo by Tom Matthews

My client, Nick Pileggi, and his editor at Simon and Schuster, Michael Korda, are celebrating the publication of Nick's first major book. The book became a national bestseller and was adapted into a very successful film called *Goodfellas*. The publication of this novel was the beginning of a major change in Nick's professional life, taking him from journalism to screenplays and feature-film production.

Selling a book to a publisher or to a film or television producer is the basic move of the literary agent. In its simplest form, it means showing some material to a potential buyer who wants that particular book and then working out the deal. Often, however, the first step is a phone call or teaser letter to make sure the editor wants to see it. The proposal itself can be anything from an author's summary of the story to a completed manuscript, or in the case of a celebrity or nationally known figure, presenting that figure in person with no proposal on paper. The writer is often selected by the publisher, after he has bought the book. Despite there being no written summary of their stories, the autobiographies of Senator Ted Kennedy and Andre Agassi were auctioned off only after publishers had met the subjects. Presidential memoirs are sold the same way—no written proposal is necessary. In some cases, particularly in the fifties and sixties, I would study the author's record carefully and select the best publisher in my opinion and submit to that publisher only. If it works, it's very beneficial to all parties, and often you can raise the publisher's offer by the threat of going elsewhere. Or more common, since then, is the practice of submitting a book proposal to a number of publishers simultaneously, letting the market do the thinking for you and in most cases producing a higher price for the author. This change reflects the growing importance of money over literary values in the twenty-first century. Or there are special situations depending upon the desires or demands of the writer. There are times when special circumstances arise or are created by one party or the other, and that is what this chapter deals with.

Although the story of my sale of Judge Sirica's book is not in this chapter, it is probably the most unusual or spectacular deal I have ever done. That story you may have read in Chapter 6 of this book, "From Our Nation's Capital."

Each of the following stories involved an extra amount of perseverance, ingenuity, patience, or imagination, and as a result was particularly rewarding to the authors and to me.

*Perseverance*

March 9, 1965, was one of those memorable positive days in my agency. That was when I sold a novel by my client David Markson. Was it a million dollar deal? No. The advance was only $1,500, which was low even in 1965. And the publisher was Bobbs-Merrill, where I had never before even submitted a book. But I really loved the novel and believed in it and Bobbs-Merrill was the twenty-first publisher to whom I had submitted it. Most of the publishers had rejected it because there was a prejudice against Westerns at that time. It was the first time I had sold a book after twenty rejections. In those days, editors were not very helpful in writing rejection letters. Phrases such as "It's not for our list" or "We've just taken on a novel on a similar subject" or "Our experience is that this kind of novel isn't selling well in today's market" were common and tactful, but useless. None of these help the writer who is looking for guidance to make his novel better or saleable. And that kind of reaction made me think my time is better spent going on to another editor instead of trying to get the editor who rejected it to give me helpful specifics.

I kept going because not only did I believe in David and the novel, I also knew there was somewhere in the literary world a group of David Markson enthusiasts. I hoped to find an editor who knew that.

Later I would beat that record for number of submissions, but selling a book was rarely so sweet as this one, my first extended submission. For David, who thanked me for my patience and perseverance, and for me, the sale was a vindication of our respective judgments and beliefs. The novel was called *The Ballad of Dingus Magee*, a satire of Westerns, and Dingus was a nineteen-year-old outlaw in the fictional Western town of Yerkey's Hole, full of willful men and unattractive women who were trying to lure them into marriage. The brothel was the only business in the town, and one Native American woman, Anna Hot Water, charged only 25 cents a night.

The book was published in 1965, and it turned out that many critics liked it as much as I did:

"The most generously, unabashedly comic novel in many a season...outrageously bawdy . . . brilliantly conceived." —*Life*

"A sort of Tom Jones of the purple sage or Huck Finn of the mauve horizon." —*Newsweek*

"Incredibly intricate and beautifully laced together . . . His dialogue is perfect, his vocabulary of profanity and blasphemy awesome." —*The Washington Post*

"A bawdy, gaudy charade . . . theme is even a parallel to Don Quixote and Sancho Panza . . . splendidly convoluted." —*The New York Times*

"Wonderful . . . funny . . . Rabelaisian." —*Publishers Weekly*

"Wild, unprincipled, bawdy, and very funny." —*New York Post*

"Your ribs are tickled by Markson until you're laughing out loud . . . Never misses catching you full in the funny bone." —*Chicago Tribune*

"Genius." —*The Kansas City Star*

When he wrote the manuscript, David, his wife, Elaine (who years later became a successful literary agent), and his two children were living in New York City on his $450 monthly salary as an English instructor at Long Island University. He wrote the book in three and a half months, and it was so well written that his editor never changed a word.

The $1,500 helped a bit but not enough; essentially, David and his family were living at poverty level. Front-page newspaper columnist Jimmy Breslin, who visited David for a story about him, described his apartment in the February 23, 1966, issue of the *New York Herald Tribune* as follows:

Johanna, the three-year-old, got her hands on the shade and pulled it. The shade was old and it ripped across the top. One edge stayed on the roller and the shade flopped across the window. Now the ripped shade is the first thing anybody sees when he comes into David Markson's six-flights-up apartment on 11th St., in Greenwich Village. Everything else in the apartment is in a condition approaching the shade. What isn't ripped is faded or falling apart.

Just a few days before the Breslin column appeared, we completed the sale of film rights to Metro-Goldwyn-Mayer for the then-unusual price of $100,000. When I called David to tell him the news, he was stunned. He not only didn't know we were in the market with it, but he had never had a check for his writing anywhere near $100,000. He immediately called his department head at Long Island University and canceled the dinner scheduled for that night; he couldn't leave his wife on a night like that. Instead of going out, he called a friend to bring some booze over, stayed home, and got drunk celebrating with his wife. As soon as they had the money, the family took off for two years in England, Italy, and Spain. The film sale removed them from the shadows of the tattered shade, substantially changing their lives. Meanwhile, MGM was shedding writers in its search for a workable screenplay, including David's friend Joe Heller, whose recent novel *Catch-22* had been very successful, but whose screenplay was only partially acceptable (although Joe received shared credit). MGM finally settled on one that appealed to Frank Sinatra. Although he was older than the nineteen-year-old Dingus, Sinatra took the starring role, and the title was changed to the slightly sexier *Dirty Dingus Magee*.

The movie, which was released in 1970, however, stimulated a different reaction. Roger Ebert, of the *Chicago Sun-Times*, one of the best-known, highly regarded movie critics in the US, said:

> *Dirty Dingus Magee* is as shabby a piece of goods as has masqueraded as a Western since, oh, "A Stranger Returns." It's supposed to be a comedy, and it was directed by Burt Kennedy, who is supposed to be a director of Western comedies ("Support Your Local Sheriff" wasn't bad), but its failure is just about complete.
>
> I lean toward blaming Frank Sinatra, who in recent years has become notorious for not really caring about his movies.

Gail Rock of *Women's Wear Daily* commented:

> A sleazy, dreadful film, based on David Markson's hilarious

book . . . All of Markson's fine writing style and feeling for humor are missing, and the ribaldry has been reduced to fourth-grade smut . . . Frank Sinatra is dreadful . . .

Once the film was released, David jokingly referred to it as "Joe Heller's film" whenever they met, and Joe called it "David's film." Neither wanted to be associated with it.

The Markson sale and two other subsequent sales (after twenty-three rejections for one and twenty-nine rejections for the other) made me realize, perhaps erroneously, that my judgment of material was better than that of many editors. Also, if my strong commitment to a book was apparent to an editor, that would help. Years later, I sold a debut nonfiction book to a top editor at a top publishing house for $75,000 (which I thought was very good for that kind of book at that time and for a writer's first book). I had started by calling the editor, describing the book. Years later, she told me that the subject matter had not interested her at all, but she was totally impressed by my enthusiasm.

Selling a book to a publisher is, of course, totally different from selling film rights for that book to a producer or studio. In a sense, the writer is in business with the publisher and editor on a continuing basis, often helping sell it to the public. In the film sale, once you sign the contract it is the buyer's, not yours anymore.

## The Strawberry Statement

In 1956 in a private elementary school—called the Fay School—in Southborough, Massachusetts, an eight-year-old day student from the neighboring town of Marlboro won a prize for a speech he had written and read to the faculty and the rest of the students, most of them boarding students from well-to-do families in New York City. The speech was entitled "The Problem Generation: Adults." It was the beginning of an antiestablishment writing career.

I didn't meet the young iconoclast until 1968. It was a normally hectic morning in my office, when I had a phone call from Clay Felker, the founder and editor of *New York* magazine. I was never too busy to take a call from Clay: He was the hottest magazine editor in New York City, and *New York* was the most-read magazine in town. He and I did many things together with my clients Nick Pileggi, Jimmy Breslin, Dick Schaap, Fred Graham, and others, and we each respected and appreciated the other.

"Sterling," he said, "we have started publishing a very interesting young writer and he has at least one good book in him, but he needs a top agent. His name is Jim Kunen and you should call him. He will be expecting your call."

A few days later, Jim—a sophomore at Columbia University, who was demonstrating with hundreds of other students on campus against the university—came into my office. He was wearing jeans (they were called dungarees then), bright red socks, and dirty tennis shoes, which my then-secretary, Carol Brissie, has not forgotten to this day. Jim was asking me what he had to do to write a book and get it published. I told him about outlines and proposals, and shortly he left without comment.

Two weeks later, I had a letter from him—the original of which has been lost—probably due to self-immolation—but it started with a vehement statement, "I'm not going to write an outline," and continued for two pages of anti-establishment rage. It was beautiful and I knew the editor who would respond to it. That was the document that moved Random House, and its editor in chief Jim Silberman, to give Jim a contract for a book.

I was curious as to how an undergraduate, unpublished in national magazines, could get to Clay Felker, the man almost every writer in town, or any place in the English-speaking world who wasn't already published in *New York* magazine, wanted to know. It was as if Jim had started at the top of the writing world, and I don't think he realized his good fortune. It turned out he had been writing for many years, having contributed editorials and columns regularly to Andover's weekly paper, *The Phillipian*. *The Phillipian* was the launchpad, too, for Seth Mydans and Jonathan Alter, among others, who went on to careers in journalism.

But when Jim got to Columbia, he avoided writing for *The Daily Spectator*, because he was exhausted after four years of writing for the weekly paper in prep school. Instead, he rowed crew.

Jim's Andover roommate, John Short, had become an editor at the *Harvard Crimson* in 1968. He asked Jim to send him an account of the student rebellion at Columbia while it was still in progress. Jim wrote it, and John published it in the *Crimson*, and sent Jim a bunch of copies, suggesting that he submit the story to magazines, because it had been a big hit in Cambridge. Jim shoved the copies in a drawer and forgot about them. A week or so later, a Columbia friend ran up to him on the street and said, "Kunen, you're famous! John Short called. He says the *Crimson* sold your story to something called *New York* magazine and it's coming out tomorrow!"

Jim called Short, who gave him the name and number of Clay Felker. Jim called Clay, who confirmed that *New York* magazine was running his story.

"The Diary of a Revolutionist" by Simon James was published in the May 27, 1968, issue of *New York* magazine. (Jim used a pseudonym to avoid getting in trouble with Columbia or with the law.)

Jim went down and met with Felker, who asked him to continue writing about what was going on at Columbia. So he did. He got paid $700 for the second story and a similar amount retroactively for the story that had been in the *Crimson*.

After *New York* magazine came out with Jim's first story, he got a call from someone at Pegasus Press, offering him $1,000 to expand the magazine article into a book. Jim went to Clay Felker and with great excitement told him this news. Felker asked Jim how much they were offering. "One thousand dollars," he said.

"Not enough," Clay Felker said. "You need an agent."

Jim wrote the book quickly, and when Random House came out with it—*The Strawberry Statement*—there were strong reactions among young and old readers and Jim was a folk hero in the New York writing world. John Leonard, the eminent *New York Times* critic, wrote on May 8, 1969:

> James Simon Kunen, whose Columbia diaries appeared in *New York* magazine last spring, is immediately sympathetic. He likes baseball and Eugene McCarthy. He is upset by violence. He drifted almost inadvertently into the April ugliness, and usually managed to escape through a commune window

every afternoon for crew practice. His radicalism began with an unexceptional intuition: "Isn't it singular that no one ever goes to jail for waging wars, let alone advocating them? But the jails are filled with those who want peace."

He is, moreover, an elegant literary stylist, always seeing himself as though through an ironic eye on the ceiling above the scene of action, in command of an affecting wistfulness that makes him seem a sort of politicized Dustin Hoffman. His "Strawberry Statement" refers to a declaration by a Columbia dean that "whether students vote 'yes' or 'no' on an issue is like telling me they like strawberries." When Kunen concludes that, because this country is 192 years old and he is only 19, "I will give it one more chance," the reader actually feels grateful.

I already knew Jim was a baseball fan, so I gave a party at my apartment in his honor and invited my friend Hank Greenberg, the celebrated former first baseman for the Detroit Tigers from 1933 to 1947 (the first Jewish superstar in American sports and a lovely, thoughtful man in my opinion), along with Jimmy Breslin and Tom Wolfe, both of whom were pretty hot items in the writing world, and who paid little attention to Jim. But Hank Greenberg was different. He recognized a baseball fan when he met one, and he also admired *The Strawberry Statement*, which he had read. Jim later told me, "I was awed by his presence. When I shook his hand, I was impressed by how big and strong his was."

*The Strawberry Statement*, sold in hardcover (Random House) and paperback (Avon), was snapped up for film by the very successful producers Robert Chartoff and Irwin Winkler for MGM. It was directed by Stuart Hagmann and starred Bruce Davison as Jim Kunen. It won the Jury Prize at the Cannes Film Festival in 1970.

Jim went on to tackle many interesting and varied projects, including volunteering as an auxiliary policeman, and wrote four more books: *Standard Operating Procedure* (1971), *How Can You Defend Those People?* (1983), *Reckless Disregard* (1994), and his latest, *Diary of a Company Man: Losing a Job, Finding a Life*, an autobiographical story published in 2012.

He has been my client for forty-four years.

## Ingenuity

Fred Graham had sent me a book proposal I thought was excellent. Fred was a great, self-effacing, and articulate man, a former Marine, and son of a Presbyterian minister who retained the soft speech of the South, where he was raised. At the time he delivered the book proposal, he was the law correspondent for CBS News and the former law correspondent for the *New York Times*. His credentials were superb for the book he proposed: a close look at the US Department of Justice's Witness Protection Program. Fred had graduated from Yale (where he'd had an academic scholarship) and Vanderbilt Law School in 1959, and while on a Fulbright Scholarship, he received his Diploma of Law from Oxford University in 1960. Prior to writing his book about the Witness Protection Program, he had written *The Self-Inflicted Wound* (Macmillan, 1970), about the Warren Court, and *Press Freedom Under Pressure* (Twentieth Century Fund, 1972), on the news media and the First Amendment.

The story he brought me in 1976 focused on Gerald Martin Zelmanowitz, a three-time loser picked up for carrying stolen securities from New Jersey to Florida. He had agreed to testify against notorious Mafia capo Angelo ("Gyp") DeCarlo, a member of the Genovese crime family who ran loan-sharking operations in New Jersey. In exchange for his cooperation, the feds guaranteed Zelmanowitz protection in the Witness Protection Program. The Justice Department gave him a new name—Paul Maris—and transplanted him, his wife and daughter, and other family members to San Francisco.

Back then the public knew almost nothing about the protection program, despite the fact that the Justice Department was transplanting hundreds of witnesses and their families, and manufacturing identities, Social Security cards, driver's licenses, and fictional résumés in exchange for testimony against mobsters and other criminals.

In San Francisco, Maris worked for a women's clothing manufacturer and eventually became its president. Although he'd been warned to keep a low profile, Maris couldn't help himself. His business prospered, and he lived high and by his own rules. He loaded the payroll with ranks of his relatives. While Maris benefited from his financial acumen, his investors were not so lucky.

Unfortunately for Maris, a disgruntled major investor, New York Milton Stewart—head of Creative Capital—was tired of not getting answers to his financial questions. He hired a San Francisco private detective, Harold "Hal" Lipset, who was best known for his bugged-olive-in-the-martini and other electronic-surveillance devices and for his appointment as chief investigator of the Senate Watergate Committee, from which he resigned after it was disclosed he'd been convicted of electronic eavesdropping. Lipset discovered that all members of the Maris family had sequential Social Security numbers. Obviously, they could not all have been born on the same day in quick succession and at the same location. The Witness Protection Program had made a crucial mistake, and Maris and his staff were forcefully and physically ousted on a day known in some San Francisco circles as Black Friday.

I submitted the book proposal to seven publishers, with no success. I was stumped, as I thought it was an excellent proposal. At that point I reread it to try to determine why it wasn't selling. I realized that with little change, the proposal itself was a valid and exciting magazine article. So I sent it to Clay Felker at *New York* magazine, and Clay bought it. That was in 1976, when almost everyone in book publishing read the magazine early and carefully, looking for book ideas and previously undiscovered writers. Editors even schemed to get a look at its articles before they were published, to beat out their competitors.

At that time Little, Brown and Company—the Boston publisher—had just hired Bob Ginna, an art historian, film writer, and producer who had written and edited for *Life, Horizon,* and *Scientific American* and was involved in the founding of *People* magazine. He was to be Little, Brown's editor in chief, but he had not yet taken office. Almost immediately after he was hired, he called his friend Clay Felker. Did Clay have any articles in the works that might be good book material? With my permission, Clay showed him the as-yet-unpublished Fred Graham article. Bob promptly called me and made an offer of $30,000. And that is how Little, Brown acquired the book and published it in 1977 as *The Alias Program.* The book contained many photographs, but only one blurry snapshot of Maris/Zelmanowitz, who had since disappeared.

Fred's book detailed how they got Maris/Zelmanowitz. Most fascinating was the careful account of the drama on the day Maris/Zelmanowitz was caught, "the like[s] of which San Francisco had never seen before."

[Lipset's] mission was no less than to stage a corporate coup d'état, to recruit a platoon of men to surprise and physically oust the top-level management of a corporation from its premises. [He had] never before been hired to use paramilitary tactics to enforce a corporate shake-up. He had about thirty men—private investigators borrowed from other agencies, free-lance detectives, off-duty watchmen, and former cops— and each was given a specific assignment to carry out when the time came to invade the building. Meanwhile, an attorney was at the courthouse, meeting with a judge in his chambers. The lawyer had a thick stack of temporary restraining orders already prepared, alleging that Maris and his supporters in the management could cause irreparable damage to the corporation unless they were ordered out of the building to stay. The papers included a recitation of the walkout and alleged removal of records following Maris's previous dismissal, and the judge was persuaded. He signed the orders. Shortly before noon the lawyer arrived at Lipset's house, with the court orders in his hand.

Milton Stewart was still not satisfied. He was afraid that there might be violence. As he put it to reporters when it was all over later that day: "When there is a significant change involving a substantial number of people, who knows who will get uptight about what?" But to Lipset, Stewart was more specific. He was worried about Maris, who he said was tricky and excitable.

It was a few minutes after noon when the men in blue burst into the factory and swept through the building. They calmed the ladies who were shopping in the factory store and then led them outside, explaining that "an emergency" was in progress. Guards were posted at all exits, and the employees were told to stay quietly at their places. Then Lipset and twenty of his men each stepped up to a selected member of the Maris staff, handed each one an envelope containing a restraining order addressed to him, and chanted something like this: "You are hereby served with an order of the superior court, commanding you to immediately leave the premises of the Paul Maris Company, and restraining you from taking anything with you as you leave."

Then each victim was escorted down the stairs and out the door, where they found themselves empty-handed, on the sidewalk, without even the personal effects of their desks. The last to go were Kat Walker and Paul Maris. Lipset personally did the honors for Maris, and he described it later to the press: "He was a lamb. He didn't get rough, fortunately."

As of 2011, the Witness Protection Program (also known as the Witness Security Program) was still functioning under the US Department of Justice. It is supervised by the US Marshals Service and receives relatively little publicity, which, I would think, improves its effectiveness.

I felt that Fred did a superb job in telling the story, and I was pleased I had found an imaginative way of getting it published.

Immediately after Black Friday, Maris disappeared from public view. As one reporter said, he organized his own witness protection program.

*The Importance of Title*

Charlie Sopkin always followed his own star. I had been representing him for several years before I learned that his father, Henry Sopkin, was conductor of the Atlanta Symphony Orchestra, and Charlie's wife, Victoria, was the daughter of Herbert Mayes, the illustrious editor of *Good Housekeeping* magazine. None of that was apparent. He was full of ideas, enthusiasm, and media gossip. He had graduated from Emory University, spent two years in the US Coast Guard, worked for two Southern newspapers—the *Atlanta Constitution* and the *Louisville Times*—and then earned a degree in journalism at Columbia

University where I taught him in 1968. He wrote his first book, *Money Talks*, profiles of millionaires, when a million dollars was a million, published by Random House in 1964, followed by a book springing from a typical zany Sopkin idea. In 1967, he set up seven television sets in one room of his Eighty-Third Street Manhattan apartment and for one week, watched TV day and night. Although it was a gimmick, Charlie focused his journalistic binoculars on our nascent pop-media culture. At the end of the fourth day, I dropped in to see my client, who was filling up on soaps and game shows. I found him bleary-eyed but laughing. *Seven Glorious Days, Seven Fun-Filled Nights* was published by Simon and Schuster in 1968, and Charlie's advice at the end of it was, "I recommend the experience for all Americans, living or dead."

Despite his continuing jobs in publishing—he was managing editor of Doubleday's Literary Guild, one of the two major book clubs in US publishing, and later formed his own publishing company, Seaview Books (named for the location of his summer place on Fire Island), then sold out to Playboy where he became managing editor of Playboy Press, Inc.—Charlie still had time for writing. He occasionally wrote for magazines, and one morning late in 1968 he called me. "Sterling, I'm working up a piece on the advertising business, and the *New York Times Sunday Magazine* wants to do it. Will you call them and make the deal?" He wouldn't tell me anything about the nature of the article except to suggest that I wouldn't be interested in the subject.

On Sunday morning, January 26, 1969, I opened the *Times* Sunday magazine at home and read Charlie's article, "What a Tough Young Kid with Fegataccio Can Do on Madison Avenue." "Fegataccio" is Italian for chutzpah. Charlie told the story of a thirty-year-old adman, who along with other outliers—Jewish admen—did not fit nicely into the WASPy world of advertising. Charlie portrayed Jerry Della Femina as a man unencumbered by tradition, with great humor, and the ability to prick the establishment's hot-air balloons and attract the attention of the apathetic consumer. Charlie wrote: "When flocks of young men of uncertain etiquette and astronomical salary begin shaping the industry, critics begin emerging from the woodwork."

The signature story about Jerry Della Femina, as Charlie reported, occurred when Jerry was working for Ted Bates & Company, as the company's new creative supervisor hired to bring some sparkle to an established firm. It was Jerry's first day on the job. The department heads were meeting to devise a slogan for Panasonic. It was a struggle, as Panasonic was one of the first Japanese companies to invade the US economy since World War II, when Japan was our enemy. Jerry broke the silence: "I've got it. I've got it. How about: from those wonderful folks who gave you Pearl Harbor?"

Shortly thereafter, at his own agency, Della Femina and Partners, he did things that would become commonplace in the dot-com era, but he was decades ahead. He played rock and roll at his desk, and when that upset colleagues, he was given an office, which was reason enough to throw a party. Once he had his own company, Charlie noted, employees wandered in and out of Della Femina's office, shockingly, without knocking.

Della Femina was the percussionist at the picnic, initiating such iconoclastic ad slogans as "If you're going to look like a clown in a hairpiece, we'd rather you stayed bald." For a foot lotion: "What's the ugliest part of your body?" And for a feminine-hygiene product: "Five years ago most women would have been too embarrassed to read this page." It's hard to imagine now, but back then the story was extraordinary.

I called Charlie at home right away that Sunday morning, even though it was only 9 a.m. (He was not a late sleeper.) "Charlie," I said, "that's a beautiful piece—and that's your next book. Get a hold of Jerry Della Femina and let's do his first-person book!" An hour later he called me back—Jerry was on board and we were ready to go.

In the years since then, I've often thought that in telling me originally that I wouldn't be interested in his article, he was putting me on. He knew all along it would be a good book.

The actual sale of the book idea to Simon and Schuster was not difficult. I thought it was a perfect S&S book, and just like Charlie, it was colorful, a little zany, and had a moderately promotable author—Jerry Della Femina, who was flashy, quick-witted, and drenched with outrageous Madison Avenue anecdotes. Long before AMC—the network responsible for *Mad Men*—mythologized the breed, Della Femina was the authentic Mad Man. Charlie was already under option to S&S and already had an editor, Richard Kluger, so it was just a matter of having Kluger read the article, and then arranging for Charlie and Jerry to meet Kluger. Simon and Schuster offered an $18,000 advance. This was not a try-for-$1,000,000 project; this was a lot-of-fun project. And Della Femina (and Charlie) wanted to take it. The two men finished the manuscript in five months, but there appeared to be a major problem: the title. The discussion involved Kluger, Dick Snyder, the president of S&S, who considered himself an excellent marketer—and he was—and Jerry and Charlie. I was also involved from the beginning, because many of my authors—Charlie among them—ask my opinion as they know I have come up with a number of interesting, saleable titles in the past.

The title of the book and the design of the jacket are vital elements to the saleability of a book and became even more important as book publishing evolved into more of a business—rather than a cultural event—through the twentieth century. A title should be descriptive of the book, but also memorable. That is particularly helpful in creating word-of-mouth interest. You shouldn't have to tell your neighbor about the wonderful book on advertising—that won't have the same results as if you told him or her to read *From Those Wonderful Folks Who Gave You Pearl Harbor.* As for the jacket of a book, in general it should be simple—not cluttered—and strong. And the color of the jacket is important. Some colors attract, others repel or are off-putting. If you are trying to say this is an important book, certain colors— including a substantial use of red or blue—can convey that message. And the art director in charge of the jacket has to envision how—or if—it will stand out against the designs of other books that will be displayed in bookstores or on websites beside yours.

I have talked to many people who, years after the Della Femina book was published, could remember its title even if they were vague about its content.

The title conversation went on for months. All parties were wavering except me. I held out for what became the title of the published book. It was such a great and memorable line, I thought, one that would easily be remembered. Apart from everything else, it was created by Jerry. From the beginning of the title discussion, I couldn't see how you could do better than that. After weeks of discussion, all parties were tiring of the title debate. I remember Charlie telling me as he and Jerry went over to S&S for probably the last title discussion that he and Jerry were so worn out, they didn't care what the title was. My choice won out. Finally it was *From Those Wonderful Folks Who Gave You Pearl Harbor: Front-Line Dispatches from the Advertising War.* It was funny, outrageous, and unforgettable. And I thought people who laughed at the title would find the book not only entertaining, but informative. It was written by an insider.

In John Leonard's *New York Times* review of the book, Jerry was quoted as saying, "I honestly believe that advertising is the most fun you can have with your clothes on."

But this is what Leonard had to say:

> "Mr. Della Femina is the last of the laissez-faire philosophers: business will produce the best of all possible cars, pies, sausages, and thalidomides because the best is easier to market; corrupt and tasteless advertising will be rejected by the public without the interference of some bureaucrat who wants real windows put into window-cleaning commercials, who wants marbles taken out of soup commercials. We've been lied to so often that we're used to it."

The book became a *New York Times* bestseller.

As I was writing this story in 2011, I phoned the people who had participated in the title debate years ago, and none of us could remember any of the discarded titles.

*Finding the Big Book*

Nick Pileggi did it the old-fashioned way. When I met him, he was a serious, career-oriented writer who started at the bottom, as a "gofer" for the Associated Press in New York City, and in 1956 was raised to reporter. He began his freelance writing career with a nest egg of good experience. Assigned to the New York City Police Department, he got to know the men who would become his important sources for almost everything he wrote. By September 1973, he had also begun to write for the magazines. Insiders knew that Nick kept astounding files; for years before the Internet did it for him, he clipped daily every newspaper available to him on the subjects of Mafia, cops, and crime. It was a rich treasure trove for the kind of articles and books Nick would be writing. I liked Nick from the very beginning of our relationship. He is well organized, clear about what he wants—short range and long range—and respectful in a manner that evokes respect in the person with whom he is dealing.

He came to me because he wanted to move forward in his career, to increase and upgrade his magazine work, but also to write books. Publishers and editors were a bit skeptical; they would say, "Of course, Sterling, his magazine articles are excellent, but how do we know he can write a book?" It seemed like a silly publishing position, but we accepted it.

Meanwhile, Nick had come across an interesting private detective named Irwin Blye, and we worked out the contractual relationship between them. I took the proposal first to Charlie Sopkin, editor of Playboy Press and a client of mine, who bought the book overnight. I had had him in mind as our possible publisher, as I knew he wanted Nick as an author, and he was a sucker for clever book titles. *Blye, Private Eye* was published in 1976. It was not a big-selling book, but it was a well-written one, and no one had to ask me again if Nick could write a book.

Now we had reached the next step, looking for a big book idea. Nick was doing articles on crime and the Mafia, primarily for *New York* magazine, the publication every alert book editor in the city was reading diligently. You often have to be patient, waiting or looking for the big idea and to recognize it when you see it. So when a New York lawyer named Robert Simels called to tell Nick and me about his client Henry Hill, who went to work for the mob when he was only eleven and was involved in a cornucopia of crime, Nick and I swung into action. Hill, we would learn, had a reporter's eye, and he possessed a fine memory. As a boy, he was impressed by the big men with their flashy gold belt buckles and twinkling pinkie rings who alighted from long, black Cadillacs and Lincolns that lifted up when the important men climbed out. He not only participated in major crimes, he was also an observer, noting not only the spilled blood of those who crossed the mob but also the mobsters' sense of their own civility when they stretched handkerchiefs against their cars before pressing up against them in their expensive silk suits.

I set up a meeting with Nick and Michael Korda, editor in chief of Simon and Schuster. Korda liked Nick's take on the material and the fact that Nick knew all the players from his days as a newspaper reporter. This might sound surprising to people outside the industry, but the deal was struck without any written proposal. The material was rich and in an area Korda knew something about, and he had read enough things Nick had written to have every confidence in him. I never met Henry Hill, and during the writing of the book, Hill, who turned state's evidence and had joined the federal Witness Protection Program, was a wanted man. Nick would go out to meet him from time to time, but I never asked when or where that was taking place. I reasoned that if I didn't know, nobody could get it out of me.

Nick had done many favors for many people over the years, all of whom were now looking forward to reading his book, *Wiseguy*, and to helping Nick in any way they could. The book would also sell itself. It would be hard for anyone to read the opening paragraph and not want to commit to the rest of the story. It began:

On Tuesday, May 22, 1980, a man named Henry Hill did what seemed to him the only sensible thing to do: he decided to cease to exist. He was in the Nassau County jail, facing a life sentence in a massive narcotics conspiracy. The federal prosecutors were asking him about his role in the $6 million Lufthansa German Airlines robbery, the largest successful cash robbery in American history. The New York City police were in line behind the feds to ask him about the ten murders that followed the Lufthansa heist. The Justice Department wanted to talk to him about his connection with a murder that also involved Michele Sindona, the convicted Italian financier. The Organized Crime Strike Force wanted to know about the Boston College basketball players he had bribed in a point-shaving scheme. Treasury agents were looking for the crates of automatic weapons and Claymore mines he had stolen from a Connecticut armory. The Brooklyn district attorney's office wanted information about a body they had found in a refrigeration truck which was frozen so stiff it needed two days to thaw before the medical examiner could perform an autopsy.

Pileggi continued: "He was only a mechanic, but he knew everything. He knew how it worked. He knew who oiled the machinery. He knew, literally, where the bodies were buried . . ."

The prepublication word around both New York publishers and Hollywood studios was strong. Nick had already married Nora Ephron, who was well known in both New York and Hollywood creative circles, and that may have helped, but Nick was known and respected on both coasts, and Michael Korda knew everyone in L.A. and New York. Before I started to formally offer movie rights, I had calls from a dozen producers looking to buy them. I had sold first serial rights to *New York* magazine, which published excerpts in two consecutive issues, each as the cover story. Even before this exposure, the movie producers had started calling.

*Wiseguy* was published in 1986 and became a bestseller. Unlike other such tales, Pileggi's did not romanticize the mob.

The time was right to strike a deal with Hollywood, but the right people were not yet in place. I didn't think any of the producers who called were strong enough or important enough on the Hollywood scene to buy film rights themselves and produce a first-class film from this book I valued so highly. In those days, movie sales were usually option deals as opposed to outright purchases. The producers or studios would offer a modest amount of money to control the movie rights for a limited time, usually for one year or eighteen months, giving them time to put the pieces together—screenwriter, director, stars—before they finally completed the purchase.

How to clear the air and establish the fact that we wanted a first-class producer? I called my client and told him, "Nick, I'd like to put a firm price of $500,000 on the book, no options." He agreed. I asked if he would be interested in writing the screenplay, and he said no, which was the right answer. (It could be extremely time-consuming unless you were working with an experienced cowriter or a first-rate director.) The $500,000 price worked—it scared away all the producers we didn't want.

A couple of weeks later, two things happened. First, Martin Scorsese, one of the very top directors in the business, called Nick at home. He wanted to direct the movie and write the screenplay—with Nick. Nick said yes, which was also the right answer.

Shortly thereafter I had a call from Irwin Winkler, producer of *Rocky, The Right Stuff, Raging Bull*, and *True Confessions*. I had known Irwin for some time and had previously sold him and his then-partner, Bob Chartoff, film rights to three other properties (two were magazine articles, one a book—all called "properties" in the film world) as he and Chartoff were starting their producing careers. At the time of his call, Irwin was shooting a film in Paris entitled *'Round Midnight* and had heard I wanted $500,000 outright, no option, so he did a clever thing: He offered me a $150,000 option and a $550,000 purchase price. That was hard to turn down, and we didn't.

During the latter part of this deal, I had been working with Michael Ovitz, the head of Creative Artists Agency (CAA), the hot new Hollywood film and television agency. When Scorsese came aboard, Mike had told me there was a problem, but he would take care of it. The problem was that Scorsese was then represented by an agent who always insisted on producing every film Scorsese directed. And Ovitz assured me the agent was not strong enough to carry the heavyweight film we were putting together. (What Ovitz knew that I didn't yet was that Scorsese was becoming his client.) That was the last I heard of the problem. Mike called a few days later to ask me if it would be okay if he represented Winkler as a producer. It was okay with me if it was okay with Winkler. A few days later, Ovitz, with Winkler's consent, made a deal with Warner for financing and distribution of the projected film. The deal not only covered Winkler's personal $150,000 outlay, it also gave him a higher producer's fee than he had ever had up to that point. So we now had the property (*Wiseguy*), the screenwriters (Scorsese and Pileggi), the director (Scorsese), the producer (Winkler), and the studio (Warner). With all the major pieces in place, it was strong enough to attract top-notch actors Robert De Niro, Joe Pesci, and others.

Pileggi and Scorsese started work a month later. Things usually don't happen that efficiently in the film industry, but this was a very high-profile project, and we were lucky.

The film, called *Goodfellas* (the title *Wiseguy* had been used for a TV series in 1987), was released September 21, 1990, and was #1 at the box office with a first-weekend gross of $6,368,901 ($10,906,882 in 2010 dollars). The #2 movie was *Postcards from the Edge*, and the #3 movie was *Ghost*. *Goodfellas* ran for nine months in US theaters and earned $46,836,394 at the domestic box office ($80,208,346 in 2010 dollars). Nick and Martin Scorsese were nominated for the Academy Award for Best Adapted Screenplay. I subsequently sold Nick's book *Casino* to the movies, and Nick and Marty did that one together as well.

Nick Pileggi does not write magazine articles or even books anymore. The film work keeps him extremely busy. The film-agency commissions on Nick's work now, usually 10 percent of the gross, are almost as large as the entire publisher's advances were when he was writing books.

Everything that happened to *Goodfellas* supported my original belief in the book *Wiseguy* and in Nick. Stories about crime and the Mafia were very much in demand at that time. They were often fascinating book subjects. But Nick, who had not written a book on the subject previously, was absolutely the best man to do such a book—it was almost all familiar material to him. And when I started reading his manuscript, I realized how right I was. It sang.

*Timing*

I met Dr. John L. Marshall in 1978, when I went to the Hospital for Special Surgery in Manhattan for advice on treating a knee that was bothering me on the tennis court. Years before, he had founded the hospital's sports medicine clinic, where he treated high-school athletes as well as world-famous sports stars. He was also a professor in the department of anatomy and surgery at Cornell University Medical College. I learned his major interest was in helping women achieve a status equal, or closer to, that of men in physical achievement and sport, and he wanted to write a book on that subject. I was impressed with his knowledge and experience. I felt he probably had some very interesting material for a good book. As I got to know him better and he became my client, I began to feel I was getting a little better medical treatment than I may have otherwise, but his advice had helped me from the beginning.

As I didn't feel I had an appropriate writer among my regular clients, I introduced him to Heather Barbash, whom I had met through my then-secretary, Barbara Holden. Apart from cowriting a novel, Heather had not done that much with books, but after a long interview with her, I thought she would be a good choice to work with Dr. Marshall. She was intelligent, articulate, a good listener, and had some experience in the medical field—as I remembered, her husband was a doctor. The two produced what I thought was a strong proposal, and I felt the subject was just right for the times.

Unfortunately, seven editors at seven publishing houses did not agree. It was a time when there were many books on women's health on the market—they burst onto the scene as though everyone had suddenly learned that physical fitness appealed to women, too—and although I had sent the proposal to publishers who did not already have a book on that subject on their lists, I realized what had been happening. Each house had an editor—in this case it was a woman— who was designated to handle any submissions in the women's-health area, though you couldn't call them experts. Once they had the Dr. Marshall proposal in hand, they would go down to the nearest chain store or to their neighborhood bookstore and see what existed on the same subject. Seeing many titles already on display, they were discouraged. I thought that Dr. Marshall's book was different and distinctive, but once I realized what was happening, I put his proposal on the shelf and waited for the heat to subside. I didn't tell him I was doing this, as I calculated he was so heavily committed that he would never ask me about it. I was right.

Meanwhile, I carefully kept my eyes and ears on the marketplace. Four months later, as I could tell the women's-health-book fad was fading— no new titles had appeared in that time—I arranged a lunch with Betty Kelly, senior executive editor at Delacorte Press. I had looked over various publishing staffs and thought she would be the best choice. Although I knew her, I had never done a book with her and had not sent her the proposal the first time out. Betty was a University of Michigan graduate, and—more relevantly—a product of the Radcliffe Publishing Training Program, which over the years had brought many talented people into publishing. She had worked for the *New Yorker*, and for the feisty, imaginative book publisher and editor Don Fine. Most importantly, she was alert, smart, and lively. The lunch at the French restaurant Chante-clair on East Forty-Ninth Street went well, and after I described the John Marshall proposal, she asked to see it. My instincts were right: She bought the book immediately. Originally, I thought the proposal strong enough that I didn't have to make a personal appearance with each submission. I had just proved my change of approach worked. Four months earlier, I had been hoping to get an advance from a publisher of $75,000. Betty paid $87,500—it had been a very good lunch at a first-rate French restaurant. Once the deal was signed, she and Heather sat down together at Betty's Park Avenue apartment to organize and complete the manuscript.

Working with a writer who had not done a nonfiction book before and a subject who was rarely available because of his busy professional schedule, the writing rested on Betty's shoulders, and it came out very well. *The Sports Doctor's Book for Women* was published in 1981 with a strong foreword by Billie Jean King, the tennis great, who had been one of Dr. Marshall's patients. Unfortunately, Dr. Marshall was not able to read the completed manuscript, nor to experience the pleasure of publication. A consultant to the US Olympic ski team, he died in a plane crash on February 19, 1980, on the way to the Lake Placid Winter Olympics. He was forty-three years old. I quote from *Who's Who in Orthopedics* by Seyed Behrooz Mostofim:

> Dr. Marshall was Director of Sports Medicine at the Hospital for Special Surgery in New York City, having founded [that clinic] in 1971. At the time of his death he had become a world-renowned figure in orthopedics and sports medicine.

The irony of his death was that Dr. Marshall was an accomplished pilot, though only a passenger in the small plane in which he lost his life.

The book was very readable and did moderately well, though not nearly what it would have sold had he been alive to promote it.

But the book's unsung hero was its editor, Betty Kelly, whose role increased with the death of the book's author. She was not only totally committed to the book, but also an extremely sensitive and successful working editor.

*Imagination*

In 1956, when America appeared to be uniformly churchgoing, buttoned up, and puritanical, Rinehart & Company published *Chocolates for Breakfast*, the shocking sexual adventures of educated girls with pageboy hairdos and long white gloves. Pamela Moore was eighteen years old when this, her first novel, became a publishing sensation. Her way with words and her graphic descriptions of liaisons with inappropriate men reflected a maturity beyond her years. Critics likened her pull-up-the-blinds writing to that of J. D. Salinger, and a *New York Times* writer compared her to Françoise Sagan, international bestselling author of *Bonjour Tristesse*, and added that while Moore "owes nothing to the French authoress . . . some sections of her novel make Mlle. Sagan look a trifle prudish." Pamela's tale of youthful misery and sexuality among the spoiled children of Hollywood and Manhattan focused on a pair of jaded girls: Courtney Farrell, who compensated for her unhappy childhood through sex and an attempted suicide, and her more promiscuous friend Janet Parker, who buries her angst in sexual exploits and—after being attacked by her father—by killing herself. The book, which had early musings of feminism, became a national bestseller for Bantam Books to which Rinehart had licensed the paperback rights, which raced through eleven printings. It was published in France and England and in a total of eleven languages, and sold over 1,000,000 copies.

Pamela was the daughter of a Hollywood and New York writer, editor, and TV producer (he was the producer on CBS's Thursday show *Climax!*, to whom I sold dramatic rights to Jimmy Piersall's *Fear Strikes Out* in 1953) and his author wife. Pamela was educated at Rosemary Hall (which became Choate Rosemary Hall when the Choate School and Rosemary Hall merged in 1971 to become coeducational), where her teachers gave her top marks for her academic abilities, but poor marks for "respect for school regulations." Intelligent beyond years, she entered Barnard at sixteen, where she was an A student majoring in ancient and medieval history.

I met the dark-haired Pamela after her initial success and found her to be serious, smart, quietly aggressive, and ambitious. She had large, handsome features with oversized, brooding eyes and dramatic eyebrows. She didn't smile often. Her writing obviously served as an outlet for her personal pain, but in person, she hid her sorrows well— at least from me.

Despite her success at Rinehart & Company and Bantam, Pamela came to me because she wanted a new publisher. She wanted to be regarded as a "literary" writer, and Holt, Rinehart, and Winston (recently formed), she felt, was a "commercial" publisher, or at least did not carry sufficient prestige. Pamela wanted to be published by Knopf—at that time a distinguished publisher of many of the best American and European writers, including John Hersey, Elizabeth Bowen, Albert Camus, and Jean-Paul Sartre.

By this time, Pamela had become discouraged by the American literary journalists who seemed more interested in her sex life than in the novel, or in her as the writer of her novel. She sailed to France, where she hoped the reaction would be more serious.

By 1957, she had already started on her second novel, which was based on what had happened to her as a result of the publication of *Chocolates for Breakfast*. I jokingly suggested she call it *Chocolates After Breakfast*, but a sense of humor was not her strong point; she called it *Prophets Without Honor*.

I had a portion of the manuscript to submit, but the problem was how to get Knopf, a distinguished publisher, interested in a young woman who had just written an obviously commercial—not literary— novel. Her new novel had slightly more serious content, as she had been influenced by the French reaction to *Chocolates*. One imaginative thought came to me: Blanche Knopf, Alfred's wife and, of course, an important editor at the company, went to Europe—principally Paris—most years, scouting for new European talent. Pamela's slightly rewritten book was also a bestseller in France.

I arranged for Blanche Knopf to "discover" Pamela Moore in Paris through the French publisher René Julliard, whom I knew was one of Blanche's first stops. It worked and Pamela signed the contract with Knopf for *Prophets Without Honor* in 1957, but, unfortunately, when the Knopf editors read the completed manuscript, they rejected it. Pamela put it aside.

Pamela wrote four more novels for other publishers, but none achieved the high level of sales and recognition that *Chocolates for Breakfast* did.

We stopped working together in 1961. Three years later, she was in the midst of writing her final novel, *Kathy on the Rocks*, about a failed writer who penned a suicide note in which she described shoving a .22 caliber rifle into her own mouth and pulling the trigger. Then Pamela put the barrel of a .22 caliber rifle into her own mouth and pulled the trigger. In her suicide note, she requested that the note itself be added to her final, unfinished novel. She was twenty-six and believed she was washed up.

*Caring*

Frank Deford, a gifted writer, and his daughter, Alex, who was six years old in this picture taken in their front yard in Connecticut. Alex died at age eight of cystic fibrosis. Frank was so strongly moved by the experience that he eventually became chairman of the Cystic Fibrosis Foundation. As a supportive gesture, my agency donated our commission to the CFF on any article Frank wrote about the illness.

Frank Deford, whom I have represented since he graduated Princeton in 1961, is probably best known for the essays he delivers every Wednesday morning over National Public Radio, or for his many prominent and excellent articles in *Sports Illustrated*, or because he was the editor in chief of the *National*, a daily (Sunday through Friday) national newspaper devoted solely to sports, or as senior contributor to the weekly HBO show *Real Sports* with Bryant Gumbel.

My most poignant memory of Frank involves his book *Alex: The Life of a Child*. Despite the title of this chapter, this story about Frank Deford does not describe my efforts at selling his book in the way other sections of this chapter do, but it does describe what an author who deeply cares about the subject of his book goes through. Frank is the principal character here, not his agent.

Frank is an intelligent, thoughtful man, tall—usually wearing something purple—sensitive, and relatively soft-spoken. He has been called by competitors the best sportswriter in the US, although he won't write a piece about a well-known athlete if that athlete doesn't interest him as a person. He is also generous. One of his earliest books was a biography of tennis great William "Big Bill" Tilden, in which Frank dealt openly with Tilden's sexual aberration. (He was attracted to young boys.) A number of years later, when my friend, A. R. "Pete" Gurney, the well-known playwright started writing a play about Tilden, Frank generously contributed his knowledge and information and allowed Pete to quote from his book. And when Pete asked Frank to come in with me to critique a pre-opening run-through of the play, Frank didn't hesitate.

In 1982 Frank sent me his nonfiction manuscript about Alex, his daughter who had died of cystic fibrosis at the age of eight. This was his first nonsports manuscript that I had seen, but I knew it would be very good, knowing Frank as a person and a writer as well as I did. I knew in advance it was the story of her life and death two years before, but I was totally unprepared for the power and level of intimacy of the writing. From his opening line, Frank wrote poignantly: "Even now, so long after she died, even now it's still difficult to go through all the little objects of her life that she left behind. There is not that much that a child leaves . . ."

I started reading it the first free moment I had and was immediately caught up. I began experiencing a strong, emotional reaction—so strong that I eventually had to put the manuscript aside to catch my breath. In my first sixty years as an agent, this was the only manuscript that hit me so hard I had to stop and pull myself together in the middle of it. I was overwhelmed at Frank's ability to write so intimately and sensitively about a personal tragedy that must have torn at him and his wife Carol more than anything else in their world could.

After sending it to Viking, Frank's publisher, I started offering the prepublication magazine rights to get things started to expose it to the public and, in effect, pre-advertise the book. At this time, *People* magazine had an extremely talented managing editor—the top job on the magazine—Patricia Ryan, who I knew was an admirer of Frank's work. Pat was high enough up at *People* so that she wasn't actually editing articles or books herself. But after reading Frank's story, she refused to let anyone else edit the manuscript.

We also offered the film and television rights and found an excellent buyer—the experienced, successful, and sensitive Leonard Goldberg, best known for *Charlie's Angels*, a popular TV show that featured three beautiful young women with lustrous hair and calendar bodies who worked for a private investigator. How and when I offer film rights is a matter of experience and instinct. It varies from book to book. In this case, I thought the story was so unique, so distinctive that I wanted to find the right producer before the wrong producers started calling me.

When Joan Brandt, my senior agent, who was handling film and television sales for me, told Frank that Leonard Goldberg was interested, Frank wondered why the producer of the fizzy *Charlie's Angels* would be appropriate for Alex, who was a very sensitive young lady struggling against cystic fibrosis. Joan told him Goldberg had made enough money from that show to afford to buy Alex.

When Joan presented Frank with Goldberg's terms, Frank told her, "The terms are acceptable, but I won't sign until I have met Leonard Goldberg." That was a highly unusual request in the business, but, I thought, totally justified in this case. Frank and his wife Carol were naturally concerned about whether the man producing *Charlie's Angels* was the right producer for such a sensitive story. He didn't want to cede control over Alex's story until and unless he had a sense of the man himself. He was putting his daughter's legacy in the producer's hands. It turned out Leonard, too, thought the meeting a good idea. Frank and Leonard met for breakfast at the Century Plaza in Beverly Hills, and he impressed Frank most positively. Leonard was very much up-front in saying that once the Defords signed the contract, they would lose control. That is normal in any film sale, but as the production moved along, the role was slightly modified. Sensitivity and intelligence were exercised.

The spirit of cooperation and understanding of the sensitivity prevailed throughout the production. The two screenwriters, Carol and Nigel McKeand, came east and spent a day with Frank and Carol at their home in Westport, Connecticut, and later on they showed Frank the script for his reaction and comments, a rather unusual move. Frank made some minor comments, and they were accepted.

Carol and Frank and their son Chris, then fifteen, and daughter Scarlet, then five, spent a day on the set in Toronto. Not wanting to interfere with the production, they stayed only that one day. As a favor, Frank and Carol asked that Chris be hired. He was, as an extra, and it gave him a big thrill.

The movie, which had the same name as the book, was shown on ABC on April 23, 1986.

As Frank wrote me later: "The movie was well done, we liked it, and it gave cystic fibrosis [Frank was the chairman of the Cystic Fibrosis Foundation from 1983 to 1989] extraordinary publicity, which it had never had before. Alex really became the face of the disease. Until very recently [written in 2011] I received letters from people who say the book (more than the movie) literally changed their life. Several young women chose medicine or physical therapy as a career because they read the book, and many daughters were named Alexandra (which was then a fairly uncommon name). Altogether, the experience was nerve-racking, but it worked out beautifully."

Decrying maudlin TV dramas, the *New York Times* reviewer found *Alex: The Life of a Child* to be an exception: "This is an instance where a television movie decidedly transcends its formula," the reviewer wrote.

When dealing with a writer as fine as Frank, on a subject as sensitive and meaningful as this one, you naturally go that extra mile, devoting extra attention, thought, and care to make it work. I didn't have to think that out—it came naturally. And I think it came naturally to Patricia Ryan, to the editors at Viking Press, and to all the creative people involved in the television film. We all liked and admired Frank and knew how much Alexandra, the book, and the film meant to him and to Carol.

# CHAPTER 10

# Unimpressed by Power and Prestige

Early in 1956, I had a phone call from Professor Richard Baker, the assistant to the legendary dean of Columbia University School of Journalism, Carl W. Ackerman. Ackerman, a nationally known correspondent during World War I, had covered the execution of the czar and his family in the Bolshevik Revolution. In 1931 he was brought in to head the journalism school, and at the time Baker called me, the school was still operating under the format he had developed. Would I be interested, Dick Baker asked, in teaching a seminar in magazine article writing? Before opening the agency, I had been assigning, buying, and editing articles for three national magazines. Later, as a literary agent, selling articles to magazines was an important part of my early days in business. So the idea intrigued me, particularly when Dick agreed that it would not involve any of my time except 9 a.m. to noon Mondays during the school year. I thought I could find out something about talented people of that younger generation. It didn't occur to me that this might be an opportunity to acquire a few clients, although that is what happened. Actually, I was more interested in seeing what talent of that age group looked like professionally.

The start of college classes that fall was the beginning of what turned out to be a five-year run, which ended when I realized my business was growing so rapidly that I could no longer take that time away from my agency. Also, I had discovered that author anxieties increase over the weekend, waiting for the chance to talk to their agent Monday morning.

Columbia University School of Journalism was—and still is—regarded as the premier journalism school in the United States. It is also home to the Pulitzer Prizes, the most respected journalism awards in the country. The journalism school's one-year program was then limited to under eighty students. (As of 2010 the enrollment had reached 275.) The school's effectiveness was enhanced by the large number of Columbia graduates working in various branches of journalism in New York City—a hop, skip, and a paycheck from the Columbia campus—who were available to guest-lecture, and also to steer new graduates toward job opportunities. By the time they graduated, most of my students had two or more job offers.

A number of very talented young men and women took my seminar on magazine writing, including Dick Schaap, who emerged as a versatile journalist, author, and broadcaster; Tom Congdon, who established his own book publishing company, Congdon & Lattes (later known as Congdon & Weed); Everett Rattray, who shortly thereafter became editor in chief and publisher of the *East Hampton Star*; and Christopher Wren, a staff writer at *Look* until it folded in September 1971 (as was my student Jack Shepherd) and then a prominent foreign correspondent for the *New York Times*.

One day in April 1967, six years after I taught him, I heard from Chris Wren, whom I remembered well. He and Jack Shepherd, his *Look* colleague and friend, had just left the office of Peter Schwed, then–editor in chief of Simon and Schuster, where they had pitched him an idea for a nonfiction book. When Peter, who was interested, asked who their literary agent was, Chris and Jack looked at one another. They didn't have one. So they rushed out and phoned to ask if I would represent them.

When Chris told me the idea, I chuckled. It was a wonderful idea. Like many others around the world, Chris and Jack were aware of the tiny-format book that recently had been published in China, *Quotations from Chairman Mao*, which consisted solely of brief words of wisdom from the Chinese leader. Here are some examples:

> Revolutions and revolutionary wars are inevitable in class society, and without them it is impossible to accomplish any leap in social development and to overthrow the reactionary ruling classes and therefore impossible for the people to win political power.
>
> —August 1937

> People of the world, unite and defeat the U.S. aggressors and all their running dogs! People of the world, be courageous, dare to fight, defy difficulties and advance wave upon wave. Then the whole world will belong to the people. Monsters of all kinds shall be destroyed.
>
> —November 28, 1964

> Our educational policy must enable everyone who receives an eduction to develop morally, intellectually and physically and become a worker with both socialist consciousness and culture.
>
> —February 27, 1957

> People who are liberals look upon the principles of Marxism as abstract dogma. They approve of Marxism, but are not prepared to practise it or to practise it in full; they are not prepared to replace their liberalism with Marxism. These people have their Marxism, but they have their liberalism as well—they talk Marxism but practise liberalism; they apply Marxism to others but liberalism to themselves. They keep both kinds of goods in stock and find a use for each. This is how the minds of certain people work.
>
> —September 7, 1937

It had become the required bible of the People's Republic of China and very popular among left-wing students around the US. In fact, leaders of the Black Panther Party, needing money to buy guns, bought

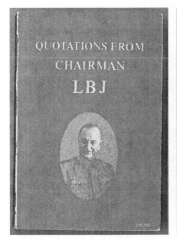 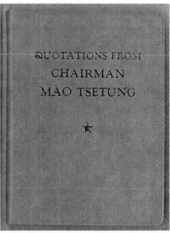

Notice how precisely the LBJ book (left) follows the format of Chairman Mao's original. Christopher Wren and Jack Shepherd created *LBJ* in their after-hours at *Look* magazine. Simon and Schuster bought it instantly, and the book-reading public consumed it ravenously until March 31, 1968, when President Johnson announced on national television that he was not going to run for reelection. At that point, book sales abruptly stopped. Many political observers felt that *Quotations from Chairman LBJ* contributed to his decision to step down.

cheap copies of what was called the *Little Red Book* in San Francisco's Chinatown and hawked them for a profit on the Berkeley campus.

In 1967, public sentiment about President Lyndon B. Johnson, his secretary of defense Robert McNamara, and the Vietnam War was turning negative. When Johnson became president in 1963, there were 16,000 Americans "advisers" in Vietnam. By 1968, at the height of the war protests, there were 500,000 US soldiers fighting in the jungles of Vietnam. The demonstrations started on college campuses and spread to the major cities—the rallying cry was "Hey, hey, LBJ. How many kids did you kill today?"

Chris and Jack's idea was a book entitled *Quotations from Chairman LBJ*, composed of quotes from President Johnson's writings and speeches. Chris told me that when he first handed Peter the red-jacketed dummy, which he and Jack had assembled on the sly at *Look*,

Chris could "see dollar signs" in Peter's eyes. I negotiated a contract for them, and they delivered the final manuscript in July 1967. Simon and Schuster published it in a 3 ⅝" x 5 ¼" paperback format with a red cover, about the same size as and the identical color of Mao's ubiquitous *Little Red Book*, and priced it at two dollars. Among the Johnsonisms:

Hello down there. This is your candidate, Lyndon Johnson.

—Texas, 1948

I'm not smart enough to make a President. I come from the wrong part of the country. I like the Senate job; it's the best job I've ever had. I want to stay here.

—June 22, 1953

Yes, we are a mighty nation. We know it and they know it. We covet no one's territory. We seek to dominate no people. We know it and they know it. That is why you gain nothing from bravado; that is why you gain nothing from rattling your rockets and bluffing with your bombs. That is why you get nowhere by saying you'll lob one into the men's room in the Kremlin.

—October 30, 1964

So peace—peace, that simple little five-letter word—is the most important word in the English language to us at this time and it occupies more of our attention than any other word or any other subject.

—August 25, 1965

Public confidence in the elective process is the foundation of public confidence in government. There is no higher duty of a democratic government than to insure that confidence.

—May 27, 1966

We cannot tolerate conflicts of interest or favoritism—or even conduct which gives the appearance that such actions are occurring—and it is our intention to see that this does not take place in the Federal Government.

—May 9, 1965

The book was scheduled for release in late February or early March 1968. The press got wind of it in advance; coverage was widespread. One story concerned an early copy that someone in the White House press corps had acquired. He waved it in front of a White House aide who tried to grab it, and and a scuffle ensued. The wire services reported the scuffle and also the fact that when LBJ saw what he called "That Damn Little Red Book," he threw it across the room in anger. The writers couldn't have asked for better publicity.

All this happened a few weeks before publication—which was quickly pushed forward by Simon and Schuster. When the book came out, *Time* published a short article about it, and the book took off. Over a period of six weeks, Simon and Schuster shipped 300,000 copies. One Simon and Schuster executive wrote in a February 16, 1968, letter to the authors: "At the moment, you might as well know the booksellers of America not only expect to sell one million copies, but they seem to think they are going to sell that million copies within the next two weeks. In other words, it's a smash." By Friday, March 29, after checking with some of their major accounts, S&S was ready to go back to press with another printing of more than 100,000 copies to be completed on Monday. Chris and Jack were in San Francisco, where they had been promoting the book—and they incredulously watched it fly off the display tables in local bookstores. Chris later received a phone call from one of the Simon and Schuster promotion people predicting, "You're going to be rich!"

But just as news events fueled massive sales, so, too, did a historically important news event put an end to them. That Sunday night—March 31, 1968—in a broadcast that stunned the nation, President Johnson announced, "I shall not seek, and I will not accept, the nomination of my party for another term as your president." Some analysts suggested that the bestselling *Quotations from Chairman LBJ* influenced his decision not to run. Chris Wren and his wife, Jacqueline, arrived back in San Francisco from a ski trip to Sun Valley just in time to watch the broadcast. She immediately turned to him and said sagely, but with regret, "Well, we're too young to have our lifetime financial problems solved!"

Neither Simon and Schuster nor its major accounts reacted as Jacqueline Wren did. However, the publisher checked with the same major accounts again on Monday, and all confirmed their interest in more copies. So Simon and Schuster went ahead and printed and shipped the 100,000 copies. In publishing, books are sent to bookstores with a full-return privilege, and it happened that every one of those copies came back. The fun was over. The target had disappeared.

Chris and Jack went on to write a similar satire of Richard Nixon and a comic novel about hippies. When *Look* folded, they joined *Newsweek* as writers, until Jack quit to earn a PhD and teach environmental sciences at Dartmouth. He wrote six more books. Chris went to the *New York Times*, where he had a distinguished career overseas as its bureau chief in Moscow, Cairo, Beijing, Ottawa, and Johannesburg, and wrote five more superb books. My agency has represented them for four decades, and the two friends are once again collaborating on yet another book.

As I've said elsewhere in the book, I'm not a political person. As an agent, I've always been apolitical in my selection of clients. An author has to be a good writer or an interesting subject, no matter the politics—although, as the owner of my own agency, I could choose not to represent an author or subject for any reason at all. And if I didn't like or respect someone, that was a good reason not to represent her or him, no matter how vaunted her or his position or how many books we could have sold.

There were many books to be written about the Johnson administration, and while LBJ was still in office, some literary agents were salivating at the prospect of selling his account of his years in the White House.

It's considered an honor to be chosen by the president to represent him, no matter what the public's feeling about him. Starting late in the twentieth century, books by presidents usually garnered a substantial advance, the figure depending upon the publisher's estimation of presidential popularity, what he will discuss in the book, and how frank he's likely to be. Simon and Schuster paid a $7,000,000 advance to Ronald Reagan, Knopf paid Bill Clinton an $8,000,000 advance and ex-president

George H. W. Bush, already a wealthy man, interviewed at least one agent, but, in the end, decided not to write the traditional memoir of his years in office. The number of presidents who have written books (with professional help), and the large advances they have received, usually stimulates more recent presidents to succumb to writing.

Interestingly, publishers recognize that the books written by former first ladies tend to be better and franker, as they don't have the kind of political baggage their husbands carry. Such books are often more open and revelatory than those written by their mates. Hillary Clinton's book is not a relevant example, as she was leading a political career in addition to being a president's wife. Still, there's no substitute for being an ex-president, and a president's book will sell more copies: He's simply better known and involved in more views and decisions that affect the public.

I have never sought to represent a president or taken the initiative in trying to contact a president, but I have been called twice and interviewed by their representatives. I thought a third president (Jimmy Carter) had asked me to represent him, but it turned out to be a misunderstanding—between him and his intermediary, Patrick Anderson, one of his speechwriters and a client of mine. Apparently President Carter did not carefully read the memo from Patrick. By the time he did read it carefully, I had sold a collection of his speeches to Simon and Schuster for an advance of $50,000, which was an extremely strong advance for a collection of presidential speeches.

Not too long after President Johnson announced he was not running for re-election, I had a call from Sam Gelfman, a former literary agent whom I liked and respected and who was working for Arthur Krim, president of United Artists, the motion picture–production company, in its New York City headquarters. Among the films UA produced during his term there: Ken Kesey's *One Flew over the Cuckoo's Nest*. He was also close to and an important supporter of President Lyndon Johnson. I had never met Mr. Krim, but I knew he was a former law partner of Louis Nizer, the famous New York lawyer, and was finance chairman for the US Democratic Party. Would I meet Mr. Krim, Sam asked, to discuss the literary future of President Johnson? I didn't think either Gelfman or Krim knew I had anything to do with the book that may have nudged LBJ to step down. I didn't want to ask.

Our meeting took place in the UA offices on Broadway, a few blocks north of Times Square. I was informed that President Johnson wanted $1,000,000 for his memoirs, which in those days was a substantial and unusual sum. I knew that would be impossible because LBJ was not very popular. I based that opinion somewhat on my knowledge of the newsstand sales of *Look* magazine, then a very successful biweekly with a strong promotion department, and I knew that when the magazine put John F. Kennedy on the cover, sales climbed. But when it published a photo of LBJ, Richard Nixon, or Charles de Gaulle on the cover, newsstand sales dropped. So I told Mr. Krim the $1,000,000 would be difficult.

Midway through our meeting, I was breathing easier as I realized neither of them knew of my connection with the *Little Red Book*. Krim suggested that for the honor of representing President Johnson, I should charge less than my then-normal commission of 10 percent. I didn't hesitate to answer: "I couldn't do that, Mr. Krim. It wouldn't be fair to the writers who have been with me so many years and are all paying me 10 percent." Despite my noncooperative answer, the meeting continued, and he eventually asked me to send him a brief biography he could take to President Johnson, which I did, even though as each day passed I found myself with diminishing enthusiasm.

A troubling aspect of the meeting was the fact that no one ever mentioned anything about a writer or what Johnson wanted to say in his book. It was all about the money. Sam Gelfman, the knowledgeable former literary agent, was sitting beside me during the meeting, and he didn't say a word.

I had never met President Johnson either, although by chance I was in the White House as a guest of my client Tom Ross, the *Chicago Sun-Times* bureau chief, just outside the oval office, the morning he called a press conference to announce the Tonkin Gulf Crisis. At the time I was there, Johnson's popularity was diminishing steadily. And I was one of those members of the public that didn't approve of his policies or his boorish ways.

A day or so later, I had made up my mind. I didn't think LBJ would give much of himself to the book, and I didn't see how it could be successful without that. Also, he had such a strong personality, I felt he could easily try to take over my life, and I didn't need that. I knew I was representing a number of writers who had been strongly against LBJ for years. So I wrote a letter to Arthur Krim withdrawing my name from consideration as LBJ's agent. I understand from eyewitnesses that when he read the letter, he was very upset. I never received an acknowledgment or an answer, but I didn't really expect one.

LBJ reportedly received his $1,000,000 through the assistance of Dr. Frank Stanton, the number-two man at CBS. But for that amount, Johnson had to give CBS three exclusive television interviews and, it was rumored, Lady Bird's own book to Henry Holt. His book was published by Holt, which at that time was owned by CBS. He hired Doris Kearns (who later became Doris Kearns Goodwin), then a young aide, to help write his book and an experienced Texas editor—Maggie Cousins, for years the managing editor of *Good Housekeeping* magazine before retiring—to edit it.

*Vantage Point: Perspectives of the Presidency* by Lyndon B. Johnson was published in 1971. Many of the reviews were not supportive, and many commented on his presidency as much as on the book itself.

In the *New York Review of Books*, William A. Williams wrote:

> The issue here is how we read a document. For how we read determines what we learn.
>
> So far, at any rate, we have not been learning much from this slyly honest witness. Mostly we have heard a frustrated (and therefore angry) complaint that Ol' Lyndon did not go naked down to the river and confess his sins in chants of unconditional surrender.

In *Harper's*, Garry Wills wrote:

> It was not the best in us, it was very nearly the worst, that despised him. No wonder he despised us back. But it makes for unpleasant reading, nonetheless. The quintessential American became, by accident, an interloper; considered not only an intruder, but the Usurper.

And Arthur Schlesinger had this to say in *Life*:

> More than most Presidents, Lyndon Johnson was many men. He could be the brilliant and masterful executive, passionate in his commitment, astute in his strategy, unrelenting in his presence. He could be the egotistical, mendacious and brutal bully, determined to humiliate everyone around him. He could be the Texas charmer, confiding and beguiling, telling wonderful southwestern tales with wit and gusto. And he could be the pious statement—this was his usual television role—the archbishop of consensus, bland, sanctimonious, self-serving . . . It is mostly in this last mood, alas, in which he has written this account of his presidency.
>
> Those who followed public affairs in the 60s will find limited documentation and few surprises.
>
> For the rest, the material is generally familiar. President Johnson takes legitimate pride in the sweep and imagination of his domestic program; but he does not add much to our knowledge about it. He has little space for politics or for characterizations of his colleagues and opponents.

Interestingly, the *Arkansas Historical Quarterly* hit the nail on the head more precisely than any other periodical:

> Most reviews of this book have said more about the writer than the contents. And, not surprisingly, most of the reviewers were grinding axes of one sort or another. The temptation to pass sentence on Johnson the president and not Johnson the author has been irresistible. Memoirs of public men, admittedly, invite such judgment as they are written with posterity foremost in mind. One cannot, moreover, reasonably expect literature of high order from heads of state, certainly not from former presidents of the United States.

David Halberstam, the noted journalist and author, in his review of LBJ's book in the *New York Times* wrote: "The real story of the Johnsonian Presidency is not to be found in this book. It is his story as he would have it, his view of how he would like things to be."

I have never had a moment of regret that I turned down LBJ.

# CHAPTER 11

# The Most Prolific Bears

For many years, the men who ran hardcover publishing houses in the United States—and almost all were run by men in the first half of the twentieth century—did not aggressively pursue children's books, nor did they take them seriously as assets. It was not until the period between World War I and II that major publishers set up children's-book departments.

Random House was one of the last to be serious about them. They had a very conventional children's-book publishing program, started in 1936, when Louise Bonino took over and brought in authors like Walter Farley, who wrote the Black Stallion books; Laurent de Brunhoff, who continued work on his father's Babar series; and Noel Streatfield, author of *Ballet Shoes*. In the 1940s, Bennett Cerf, a founder and president of Random House, was still referring to some of his children's books as "baby books." He obviously was not referring to all his authors, as he already had Ted Geisel (Dr. Seuss), whose first children's book with Random House, *The King's Stilts*, was published in 1939. The Geisel books tapped into Cerf's own passion for punning and word play. But following the enormous success of Simon and Schuster's Golden Books (founded in 1942), Cerf, jealous of his rival—he played bridge on weekends with Richard L. Simon, Max Schuster, and one of their creative executives, Albert Leventhal—took a new stance. The Golden Books' publication of four-color books with large print runs and very modest cover prices was partly possible because they were the first to use the distribution techniques of magazines and newspapers, selling principally on newsstands.

Building on the conventional list of Walter Farley and Laurent de Brunhoff, Cerf ultimately broadened his children's list to include the highly successful Beginner Books and First Time books, whose motto was "I can read it all by myself." As the titles imply, both series were aimed at younger readers. It was the beginning of publisher-created concept books, which often became predictable sellers. By the 1960s, Cerf had one of the most successful children's-book departments in the US, aided in part by the zany and wildly popular Dr. Seuss, who was also an extraordinary editor. He joined Phyllis Cerf, Bennett's wife, to create Beginner Books, of which they were principal owners. (Phyllis and Ted had worked together in 1939—sharing the same desk—at McCann-Erickson, a major ad agency.) But Bennett Cerf and Random House kept a small part of it, because, after all, Random House was the distributor of the books.

By 1960, Stan and Jan Berenstain, two artists who for many years had been drawing magazine cartoons and illustrating occasional advertisements, were ready and eager to start writing children's books. They had already published a number of family-oriented books for adults: *The Berenstains' Baby Book* (1951), *Sister* (1952), *Tax-Wise* (1952), *Marital Blitz* (1954), *Baby Makes Four* (1956), *It's All in the Family* (1958), and *Lover Boy* (1958). All were Dell paperback titles.

Several publishing people they knew and who knew their work assured them that if they were going to write books, they needed an agent. I have been asked many times how a writer should go about attracting and acquiring an agent, but the Berenstains instinctively knew how. They asked the same friends in publishing to suggest names. Each of their friends gave them a list of three or four agents to interview. Fortunately, I was on all the lists, and when Stan asked one of the editors why Sterling Lord had been recommended, she said, "He's flexible. He's open to trying things." Later I found the publishing friends were impressed by the fact that I had booked Jack Kerouac into a Village bar/coffeehouse to read his work.

It's human nature that I, along with other agents, am more likely to give greater consideration to a query letter from a prospective client if it mentions the name of the writer or editors who recommended they come to me or, better still, if the introducing writer is well known, calls me directly, and has read material by the writer he is calling about. Writers lacking those contacts have to either work to contact known writers or call or write the agent in an effort to draw his or her attention or interest. The letters, of course, must be well written or contain info that would attract the agent's attention—or both. And an agent's time is precious, so the presentation must be organized and succinct. I was already familiar with the Berenstains' work. I had seen their feature, "It's All in the Family," in *McCall's* magazine, where it had been appearing since 1956. It was imaginatively conceived and reflected common child-parent conflicts. Always interesting to me— not because I was a parent yet. And years before, I had seen their busy multicolored *Collier's* magazine covers jammed with people—unique for a major national magazine—and I was looking forward to working with them.

When Stan appeared in my office, we had a good, constructive conversation. He'd later describe himself as a hick in Manhattan, and I realized that as intelligent and talented as he was, he was slightly uncomfortable but knew this was the step he should be taking. Stan had a different look. He was around five nine, dark-haired, with an intelligent face and the suggestion of a sense of humor hidden there. He was wearing a sport jacket, which I could see he wasn't accustomed to wearing, but he was serious about what he and Jan did for a living and serious about his meeting with me. I liked him.

In that meeting, I learned a good deal about Stan, and I suspect he had a good sense of what I was all about. Stan seemed to be determined, ambitious, sharply focused, and he listened. I felt immediately that we would work well together. He was obviously serious about his work. That's how he supported his family. I had never in my life tried to sell a children's book, but I could see Stan was a man who knew what he wanted. All I had to do was learn specifically what he wanted and then I could get it for him. That proved to be the pattern of our work together.

I would soon learn what a team Stan and Jan were. No important decision was made without Jan's approval. When Stan called me a few days later to tell me it was okay with his wife and full partner (so we were in business together), I asked if there was anything he'd like me to do for starters. The Berenstains were already impressed with Ted Geisel, who wasn't a doctor but a brilliant writer, illustrator, and editor of children's books. I arranged to have lunch with Phyllis Cerf, who was Geisel's partner. She was the administrative head of Beginner Books.

The first manuscript the Berenstains offered to Ted Geisel, *Freddy Bear's Spanking*, was a simple, well-illustrated story about a boy bear who misbehaved and didn't want to be spanked. It's not the sort of book that would work in the twenty-first century—in those days spanking children was as much a part of child rearing as punishing a child by taking away his cell phone is today.

While the meeting with Phyllis went well, the first meeting with Ted Geisel was demanding, highly unconventional, and dramatic. And the Berenstains, who'd felt quite good about their talents and their story, left intimidated and discouraged.

Ted had plenty of humor: The signs leading up to his office read "This way to Dr. Schmerecase" and "etaoin shrudlu," the most common letters in the English language in the order in which they appeared on linotype keyboards. The humorous letters ended at the entryway to Geisel's office.

On three walls Ted had thumbtacked every page of the Berenstains' book, the better for him to dissect almost everything they'd done. He called the process "storyboarding" and said it was something he'd learned from his Army friend Frank Capra, who had directed such movies as *Mr. Smith Goes to Washington* and *It's a Wonderful Life*. Ted couched his words in a praise sandwich: He loved the drawings, he loved the bears, but just about everything else was wrong. If the Berenstains just followed his advice, they'd have a fine children's book. First, though, he needed to know much more about the bears, pushing the Berenstains to see the lumbering creatures as real people, asking such pointed questions as "Who are these bears? What are they about? What does Papa do for a living? What kind of pipe tobacco does he smoke?" He saw things the Berenstains didn't see: "It seems to me," said Ted, "that you've got something pretty interesting going with Papa and Small Bear."

Next he delved into what he called "the guts of your story." "There's a helluva lot wrong with it," he said. Ted thought the story was too long and too complicated, the sentences were too long, there were too many contractions, the Berenstains used too many "female rhymes" (meaning a rhyme that ends in a soft sound, like you/through, while a "male" rhyme ends with a hard consonant, like mat/hat). And the middle of the book didn't work. He wanted a story line and drama. The account had to build. The story had to be a page-turner to keep children's "eyeballs glued to the page." It wasn't only the story that Ted focused on; he also cared about the title page, the type, the paper, every phrase, every word, every rhyme, and every drawing. When the meeting was winding down, Ted became warm and charming, and he said he couldn't tell them how happy he was to be working with them.

But those words had little impact.

Had there been only one Berenstain, I don't know that he or she would have recovered from the savaging of their first book. It was several days before they even looked at it again. But when they did, they began to address Ted's concerns, and they realized his advice was extremely intelligent. In the years that followed, I came to understand this was characteristic of them. They would always seriously consider any advice they thought was intelligent.

They rewrote and redrew following Ted's guidelines, and what had been a book with a saggy middle and sloppy verse became a tight story that worked. In the process, Ted Geisel taught the Berenstains how to be children's-book authors. They would teach him that not every book should become a Dr. Seuss story.

After their fourth draft, Ted wanted the bears to behave less like people/bears and more like the zany characters in a Dr. Seuss tale. Jan, the quiet member of the couple, called him on it: There were already enough Dr. Seuss books, she said. Geisel considered her statement; he sat back for a moment, and then he agreed.

210

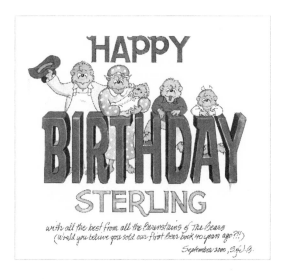

These two Berenstain drawings show how the Berenstains would communicate with me on certain personal events in my life, such as my eightieth birthday and my hospital stay after being hit by a car. I was touched!

211

The very early days of the Berenstain Empire, in 1959. From left to right, Stan, sons Leo and Mike, and Jan in the studio at Elkin's Park, Pennsylvania, where their stories began. I have marveled at the family's inadvertent corporate planning: Leo grew up to be a writer, Mike to be an artist. In later years, when the parents had passed, Leo became the family business controller, and Mike took on the entire creative end of the growing empire.

In 1979, the happy, busy, talented couple is already beginning to enjoy the success of the Berenstain Bears books. Here they hold some of their early artwork. By the time this photo was taken, the Berenstains had moved to a two-story home in Bucks County, Pennsylvania, and had immediately built a substantial wing on the ground floor, which became their studio. Having the studio attached to their home made it possible for Stan—who often worked in the middle of the night—to tramp downstairs from the bedroom, write a complete children's book, and go back to bed.

The story about the bear's spanking morphed into *The Big Honey Hunt*, a lively and endearing tale about the bungling Papa Bear and Small Bear setting out to find honey by following a bee, only to have the bees chasing Papa Bear into a pond. He and Small Bear buy some honey for their breakfast table, which is what Mama Bear wanted them to do all along.

When they met Ted in his office at Random House after *Big Honey Hunt* was completed, Ted told them it would be published the following year—1962—and he encouraged them to think about the next book.

"But don't make it a bear book," he said firmly. There were already too many bear books for kids, he said. And besides, "If you do, you'll be typecast."

They were dismayed and unhappy as they reviewed the meeting on the train back to North Philadelphia (the stop for Elkins Park, where they lived). The bears weren't just a story to them; the Berenstains identified with their characters and were committed to the concept. But Ted Geisel was the expert. They thought about their choices. Stan saw a Kools cigarette ad that featured a cute penguin. If bears were on the no-play list, they thought they could substitute with a lovable penguin. They set to work drawing penguins and telling penguin stories.

By the time they next met Ted to go over their new penguin manuscript, the *Big Honey Hunt* had been published. Ted examined their work, expressed approval, but then said that something had been happening with their first book: The Random House salesmen in the field were reporting very strong positive reactions from buyers; the book was already going into its second printing. Ted was usually right, but the market was *always* right. He asked them how they felt about doing another bear book and turning it into a series. What a relief! That was the beginning of perhaps the most successful children's-book franchise in US publishing history.

From the start, the Berenstains had a couple of elements in their favor. They maintained their running feature in *McCall's*, giving them a public presence, and the paperback books they had been doing conveyed an important message to parents: that their stories were safe and that parents need have no concern about the appropriateness of the content for their children.

Their work was very much like them. Jan Berenstain is a rather laid-back, attractive, and slight woman with a delicate smile. She's always had a positive thrust to her life, as far as I know, and I've never seen her down or discouraged. Stan was more outgoing. He had a large, handsome face with prominent eyebrows. They met each other before World War II at the Philadelphia Museum School of Industrial Art. During the war, Stan served as an artist in the Army doing finely illustrated drawings of facial plastic-surgery techniques while Jan worked in Philadelphia as a riveter. When the war ended, they married. He was Jewish and she was an Episcopalian, but while he read a good deal about Jewish history, neither of them was religious. In public Stan was the front man, whom I eventually talked to three or four times a week. Jan preferred to work behind the scenes. Over the years, I was in a number of meetings held at their house with prospective buyers, merchandise creators, or middlemen, when there would be extended debate and discussion between Stan and the other party. The dialogue would often begin in the Berenstains' living room, partially decorated with some of Jan's non-ursine art, and continue in the dining room, where Jan would have prepared a simple but tasty lunch. When the tempo receded, Jan would quietly come up with the solution to the problem, and Stan would immediately recognize she was right. She was the quiet power in the partnership.

Their writing was straightforward. Their stories were deceptively simple. Their art was neither intricate, nor did it attempt to be beautiful, but it had something more important: consistency, friendliness, and child appeal. The characters were readily identifiable. Papa Bear always dressed in blue overalls and a yellow shirt, Mama Bear always wore her lumpy, long turquoise dress splattered with white polka dots. And their stories subtly and sometimes not so subtly taught a child to be good.

Their second book, a simple story based on Stan's attempt to teach one of their sons to ride a bike, was called *The Bike Lesson*. Ted Geisel put on the cover page "Another Adventure of the Berenstain Bears." Until then, the bears had not had names other than Mama, Papa, and Small Bear, and it hadn't occurred to any of us to give them names. Ted also took the Berenstains' own names, Stanley and Janice, and turned them into part of the rhythm: *Stan and Jan.*

A literary dynasty that would last more than a half a century was born. One book would follow another: *The Bears Picnic, The Bear Scouts,* and *The Bears' Vacation.*

After a dozen years of Berenstain Bears, the author/artists bought themselves a vacation house on the Jersey shore, and four years later a large wooden house in the middle of a quiet valley surrounded by dark green fir trees and a broad green lawn in bucolic Bucks County, Pennsylvania.

The first five or six times I visited them, I spotted a wild deer bouncing casually across the lawn and disappearing into the trees. I accused Stan of scheduling those appearances for my benefit. The house was an attractive rambling building, and the Berenstains added to that effect by building a studio wing as their literary, artistic, and business headquarters for the Berenstain Bears. It all worked well under the same roof.

They were gracious hosts, always offering to take me to the best restaurant in the county. They lived just a short two-hour drive over a variety of highways from New York, but Stan prepared a detailed and infallible sheet of directions. They were only five minutes beyond the Delaware River and New Jersey. One bright autumn day, I was driving along the extended stretch of New Jersey highway leading up to the Delaware River Bridge, when a cop car sirened me to the roadside. The officer got out of his car, came over, and we chatted amiably. I had been more than slightly ignoring the speed limit and was expecting what I deserved: a speeding ticket. When he asked me where I was going, I said, "The Berenstains." He must have had children and have felt he owed them, because that was enough to let me off.

Stan and Jan worked with Ted Geisel for many years. When he began a children's-book line for very young children called Bright and Early Books, he asked them to come up with new characters and stories that were shorter and simpler. They wanted to stick with bears, but they knew they couldn't combat Ted's excitement and determination. It took a while for them to give up on their bears and find another kidlike animal to anthropomorphize. They fell for a wacky gorilla and a big beaked crow with a beret. But by the time they presented it to Ted, he'd decided they should stick with . . . their bears.

Their first book for the new division, *Inside Outside Upside Down*, told the story of Small Bear climbing into a box and being transported to town, where the box falls off a truck. Small Bear returns home, telling his mother, "I went to town inside, outside, upside down!" The Berenstains told the whole story in fifteen drawings and sixty-six words, and it was a great success.

*The Berenstain Bears Go to School* (which had sold 3,520,554 copies in North America by March 2009) and *New Baby* (4,149,130 copies) did so well, they proposed a series that Jan dubbed "First Time Books," about experiences that young children have growing up—from visiting the dentist to coping with a sibling. They proposed and Random House agreed. Their stories included *The Berenstain Bears and Too Much Junk Food* (3,766,635 copies) and my personal favorite, *The Berenstain Bears and the Messy Room* (3,952,770 copies.) Another interesting and ultimately successful book was one that Stan and Jan opposed initially because of the subject matter. Eventually Random House persuaded them they were wrong, and *The Berenstain Bears Learn About Strangers* sold 3,533,348 copies to the public by March 31, 2009. And there were books on videocassettes, board books, and chapter books. Random House would publish more than fifty books in the First Time series.

As the Berenstains had one bestseller after another, their initial naïveté gave way to wisdom. Stan was not only a fine illustrator, he was a good businessman, and representing them was never an arduous task. Stan not only read every royalty statement carefully, he insisted the publisher send him all statements whether or not there had been earnings on that book due to the Berenstains that period. Often, in the twenty-first century, you don't get these non-earning statements without pressing the publisher for them.

Ted Geisel stayed involved for the first sixteen books. Much of the time he was back in La Jolla, and a young editor named Mark Frith stood in for him at Random House. But Ted was in charge. Only once did the Berenstains have to go to La Jolla to work things out. The Berenstains adopted many of the standards that Ted Geisel had imposed on them as they continued without his hands-on work and became just as demanding of themselves and their publisher as he had been with them.

Random House appreciated what the Berenstains did for their bottom line, and they were allowed to pursue their stories with almost no editorial changes. Jan, Stan, and I worked like a well-oiled machine. I never sought out other children's-book authors—if you are clearly representing the king and queen, it is not as tempting to represent the jacks.

Although their book career was growing rapidly, early on the Berenstains were having trouble on the magazine front. In 1970, *McCall's* hired a new editor in chief, the temperamental and sometimes imperious Shana Alexander, who lived in California and agreed to take the job if *McCall's* installed a sauna on the premises. One of Alexander's first acts, along with firing former first lady Eleanor Roosevelt as a columnist, was to cancel *McCall's* longest-running feature, "It's All in the Family" by the Berenstains. I immediately sold it to *Good Housekeeping.* Shortly thereafter, Alexander, beleaguered by unhappy reader mail, wrote an essay of apology to readers for letting the Berenstains get away. Before the essay appeared, she had an editor call me to see if they could lure the Berenstains back—apparently she didn't read the competitive magazines. The *Good Housekeeping* relationship, unfortunately, was short-lived. The Berenstains realized they no longer had the time to do the monthly feature. Books, books, books.

In June 1976, we started licensing merchandising rights to the Berenstain Bears. Our first transaction, stuffed bears with Knickerbocker Toys, taught me an important lesson. All the bears produced by Knickerbocker came out cross-eyed. I couldn't believe it; neither could Stan or Jan, and I felt a sense of responsibility for the disaster. From that moment on, with the Berenstains' support, I demanded approval rights for the Berenstains for *every* product we licensed, which included dolls, toys, games, puzzles, figurines for McDonald's, theme-park attractions, and the forty-eight half-hour animated television shows licensed to the Public Broadcasting Service (PBS).

As overwhelmingly successful as the Bears became in the US and Canada, the rest of the world was not responding as enthusiastically. Stan and I were both concerned. True, I told myself, the Bears were very,

very American, but children are children all over the world. By 1968, I had persuaded the Berenstains that we should go to the preeminent worldwide children's-book fair in Bologna, Italy. I had never been, but I knew how important it was and how well attended by publishers, editors, and writers from many, many countries. So on April 6, 1968, Stan, Jan, and I boarded an Air France plane for Paris, then Paris to Bologna.

It was an interesting three or four days. So many foreign publishers had never heard of the Berenstains, but when I mentioned the substantial sales figures we had achieved in the US, I suddenly got their attention. Sales to Germany, South America, and France resulted, and we realized we should return the following year.

In 1969, we took Lufthansa to Munich, then on to Bologna, and spent April 6, 7, and 8 at the fair with equally good results, and then decided to treat ourselves with a trip to Venice, where I had American friends living in a fourteenth-century home. We then drove to Pisa and flew to Paris for what was, for me, the surprise highlight of the trip. Except for our layover at the Paris airport the year before, Stan and Jan had never been to the City of Lights and of course, had never been to the Louvre. But going through the Louvre with Stan was stunning, like touring with the most experienced guide. He knew where every painting was located and the history and importance of each. Astounding. And what a pleasure. What a great way to tour the Louvre.

Flying back to New York the next day, we found ourselves in the same plane as and sharing an overhead compartment with Jerry Lewis, the entertainer, and his family. He had just completed a successful tour in Paris (where he was widely loved in the fifties and sixties). The family turned out to be major Berenstain Bears fans and were thrilled and delighted to meet the authors, whom they invited to come back and sit with them.

The trips to Bologna were helpful in many ways: They helped promote interest in the Berenstains throughout the rest of the world, and gave Stan and Jan a clearer idea of what children's books were being published outside the US.

Working with the Berenstains has always been stimulating for me. They were full of energy and ideas, and Stan was so clear about what he wanted that he was easy to work for and with. Stan and Jan would collaborate in books and in life well past their fiftieth wedding anniversary. There was a great deal of mutual respect between then, as expressed in the way they treated each other at home, in their studio, or in my New York office. I never saw them argue.

Often Stan woke up in the middle of the night and would head downstairs to the studio to write an entire story before climbing back to bed. Jan did most of the art—in broad daylight—although each did both at times. Their two sons, Leo and Michael, were what you might call their corporate staff. Growing up, they were marvelous models for the child behavior in the Berenstain magazine panels and then for the Berenstain Bear books. Leo, the older by three years, turned out to be a writer, and Michael became an artist. Both had published books on their own before their parents prevailed on them to join the family business. Together the sons produced novellas for older children (chapter books for Scholastic Books) about topical issues such as sports, drugs, guns, and social and environmental issues. The family enterprise could not have been planned more intelligently. In the 1990s, the Berenstains were still producing a list of chapter books, written by Leo and Stan and illustrated by Michael.

The Bear family continued to grow in many ways. In 1996, inspired by a visit to their home by Surgeon General C. Everett Koop, they published a book called *The Berenstain Bears and the Sinister Smoke Ring*, about the dangers of smoking. Five states bought and circulated a total of 2.4 million copies. As the twenty-first century began, sales in foreign countries picked up. By the end of 2009, I had licensed fifty Berenstain titles for production in mainland China, many to be published in both Chinese and English text.

But Random House, which had nurtured the Berenstains for forty years, now had other priorities. By the 1990s, it had lost interest in its more traditional lines of books—Richard Scarry, Dr. Seuss, Sesame Street, and the Berenstain Bears among others—in favor of new TV and movie tie-in books. By 2003, the publisher's catalog listed forty-one Nickelodeon book titles.

Even though they were perennial bestsellers, Random House no longer cared about the endearing bears. The Berenstains began receiving letters from parents, complaining that they could no longer find their books at Target, Walmart, Kmart, and Toys "R" Us.

The effect on the Berenstains was devastating. While sales in 1992 were close to two million, ten years later, they had slipped to one-sixth that amount.

Management at Random House was not as exacting as Geisel had been and wanted the Berenstains to write stories that they thought inappropriate for their bears. Worse, perhaps, Random House rejected fifteen of their books for the "Step into Reading" series. Long before this, I had begun to realize that Stan knew more about what children were interested in than Random House.

Aware of Random House's preoccupation with TV glitz, the Berenstains crusaded to put their bears on TV, to help their book sales. Following the advice of a friendly Random House editor, we diligently pursued the idea of an animated television series and eventually made a deal with Nelvana, the Canadian television producer, knowing it had a commitment from PBS, which the friendly editor said could sell more books than Nickelodeon. The Berenstains spent two years and nearly $1,000,000 working on the deal. It was the major project on my desk during that entire time. By 2003, they had a new PBS animated strip show—a show that aired a different episode every day of the week—which received favorable reviews from the *New York Times*, the *New York Daily News*, *TV Guide*, and other publications. Initially it reached 92 percent of the US television market. What bothered the Berenstains and me was that despite the fact that they produced a forty-eight-segment public TV series mostly to stimulate sales of the books, we weren't aware of anything Random House did prior to or during the series to take advantage of the substantial publicity generated by the TV show. The publisher could have linked the programs with the corresponding books. Coincidentally, among the many companies seeking merchandising arrangements with the Berenstains, none were attracted to us by the TV shows; all came forward because they had read the books.

Then, in 2003, there was the painful rejection of their beautiful *The Berenstain Bears Save Christmas*, illustrated by their son Michael. A few weeks later, I sold it to Harper Collins's children's-book department, which bought it with great enthusiasm, paying a larger advance than we had ever received for any book from Random House.

It's tough to leave a company you have been working with that long, but by 2004 Stan and Jan were ready to exit. Stan was furious at how badly he felt Random House had let him down; he and I talked about it, but rather than having me go after them, he wanted to do it personally. Sensing the intensity of his feelings and the depth of the problem, I agreed to let him.

After Random House had rejected the Christmas book and I had sold it to Harper Collins, I had begun to negotiate in secret for the Berenstains to move their entire operation to Harper Collins. While Random House was overcommitted and under pressure, Harper Collins had money and plenty of time to think and plan. And there was this in our favor: Historically, Harper Collins's children's-books division had carried the company financially. It was a very strong department, and it had been so for years.

Everything had to be done with the utmost secrecy. If the deal had fallen through and it became public knowledge, it could have harmed the Berenstains' relationship with Random House, making it impossible and messing up what we hoped would be a smooth departure. I couldn't even tell anyone *in my agency*. The moment you tell someone—anyone—you've lost control. Despite the neglect the Berenstains endured, their books were still big sellers for Random House. I doubted the publisher would want to lose them.

Random House had taken the position that they only wanted to publish 8x8s that had seasonal or holiday themes for marketing purposes. As a result they turned down (or put off considering) *The Berenstain Bears Lose a Friend* and *The Berenstain Bears and the Bad Influence*, both of which we later sold to and were published by Harper Collins. Also, Stan and Michael developed a presentation for a version of the hardcover picture book *The Berenstain Bears' Big Bedtime Book*, which was turned down by Random House and later published by Harper Collins in a highly altered form.

My negotiations with Harper Collins would take eight months.

I began by going to meet Kate Jackson in her office at Harper Collins. Kate was a senior vice-president of the company, associate publisher and editor in chief at Harper Collins Children's Books, and a young mother. When I told her the Berenstains wanted to move to Harper Collins, I could see the smile and twinkle in her eye. From that meeting on, all negotiation was done by e-mail. It was an interesting negotiation: She wanted us and we wanted her, so it was only a matter of working out the details and keeping it under wraps. Stan had carefully worked out a long-range publishing program based on his knowledge of what books sold and what Harper Collins did well, and midway through the negotiations, I asked Kate:

"Wouldn't you like to know how much money we're going to ask for?"

"Why not?" she responded, adding, "That would be a good idea."

I could tell by the tone of the interchange that money probably would not be a problem; we were negotiating what we had expected to be a long-term relationship.

I worked closely with Stan on this. If we talked about ten board books, we'd discuss how much we wanted for each. He was astute, having figured out what was a strong but not unreasonable advance for each book.

Stan's estimate, and then our total asking price, was in the millions, but the unit percentages were reasonable, and Kate and Harper Collins agreed totally to our asking price: $3,150,000.

Stan had respect for the people he had been working with at Random House, and when we reached an agreement with Harper Collins, he insisted on personally telling the Random House editors we were leaving. That turned out to be a strong, detailed eight-page letter written by Stan, with advice from his attorney.

In the letter, Stan blamed Random House for the decline in sales, which he wrote, "represent a massive failure on the part of Random House to deliver our books to our audience."

Stan pointedly said that in the Random House children's-book catalog section on Mass Market Promotions, hundreds of books were listed. And he wrote: *There is not a single Berenstain Bears book among them!*"

In words that resembled a legal brief, he wrote: "The fact that Random House is failing to ship our books to where most of our audience shops is extremely damaging to us and our property, The Berenstain Bears."

Sounding much like their mentor, Ted Geisel, the Berenstains found fault with titles that had been changed. After someone at Random House complained, *The Berenstain Bears and Too Much Stuff* was changed to *The Berenstain Bears Think of Those in Need*. The original title, Stan wrote, "was a powerful title that *everybody* could identify with. It has the kind of immediate universal appeal that *Messy Room* has." Writing as the expert that he was, Stan concluded, "The title that replaced it has severely crippled the book."

Stan wrote that worse than having their Christmas book rejected was the "harsh, dismissive manner of the rejection . . . rather than the rejection itself." Random House had told them that expensive Christmas books don't sell. Stan said that the *New York Times* bestseller list last Christmas proved that axiom wrong. Random House had further advised the authors that they shouldn't reach, but should stick with low-priced paperbacks. Stan wrote that Random House "rather cruelly . . . rubbed our noses in the dismal sales" of a Berenstain Bears Christmas tree book, failing to mention that it was a reissue of one that had sold over 200,000 copies.

Stan recounted all the disappointments the couple had endured and said that all that was left was for the publisher and the authors to "agree to disagree," and for the Berenstains to return all relevant advances.

"For all the above reasons, we believe that Random House has failed in carrying out its responsibilities to us," they wrote. They said they would deliver the three spring titles they had agreed to do and would "return the advances on all undelivered books."

That was the first and only time I have had authors with that length of continuity fire their publisher. Their letter was the clearest method of departing. Random House never challenged Stan's assertions.

At the end of our secret negotiations, I was at a literary cocktail party when I saw Jane Friedman, the boss of bosses at Harper Collins, who took me aside to tell me how excited she was to get the Berenstains. I had closed the deal only twenty minutes earlier. If anyone else at Harper Collins knew, I saw no such signs. They had kept our secret.

Later, when I spoke to Kate Jackson, she said that the reason the negotiation had gone so smoothly was that Jane herself had kept in close touch with her through the whole process.

Ironically, after we left Random House and the TV series started appearing, even though Random House made no promotional efforts, their sales of Berenstain Bears books went up.

Nearly half a century after we began our collaboration, the family and I continue to sell their work vigorously. My longtime client and friend Stan Berenstain died in 2005 at the age of eighty-two. After that, their son Michael assumed the major operational role. He and Jan produced the books, and son Leo handled the financial affairs and kept the records.

There was hardly a hitch in the transition.

Michael had created a series of Living Lights books, which Zonderkidz, the Christian children's-book publishers, were selling very well. I had closed a deal with Fox Walden Films for a live-action/animated feature film scheduled to open in 2012. Already in 2010, I completed a deal with Starz, a major worldwide distributor of the animated videos the Berenstains did for NBC (1979–1983) and CBS (1985–1987).

By the end of 2011, the Berenstain Bear books had sold nearly 150 titles to Chinese publishers, and 280 million copies in the United States and Canada alone. But I regretted that Stan had not survived long enough to see the feature film, something he had wished for and worked during the last ten years of his life.

## CHAPTER 12

# The Women in My Life

Being a literary agent in the US, at least the way I practice it, is a labor-intensive occupation. Office hours are only a small part of it. Reading manuscripts into the night is a common occurrence. You have to love books, or writers, or both, so much that you put them ahead of almost everything else in your life—including marriage. Had I realized that from the beginning, I might have warned my numerous wives (or made different choices), and I've had many chances . . . I've been married four times.

While still in Paris in 1952, I married a Frenchwoman, Denise "Dodie" Yencesse, who had applied to work for Dick Jones and me at *Weekend* a few years before. She had been an artist for the well-known couturier Jacques Heim, and we thought that qualified her to be our art director so we hired her. Dodie was very attractive in the French way, with her long, brown hair worn slightly down from her oval face. (She went through elaborate processes, it seemed to me, each time she washed it.) She always presented herself well, and like many Parisian women she had a sense of style. She was lively and enjoyed good conversation.

In those days, I was often attracted to well-spoken, good-looking

Denise "Dodie" Yencesse was a sculptor and a designer for the coutu-
rier Jacques Heim in Paris, before I hired her to be the art director of an
English-language magazine called *Weekend*, which my friend Richard
Evan "Dick" Jones and I published in Europe just after World War II.
Dodie's father was a protégé of artist Aristide Maillol. She was an excel-
lent art director for us, and she later became my wife.

women, and that was the case with Dodie. I have matured a bit since
but still have many positive memories of her.

It was a short but interesting courtship. I remember one evening
when I visited Dodie at her parents' apartment at 108 rue du Bac and
both were out for the evening—purposely, I thought. And just as I was
leaving, they returned to see Dodie trying to force me to kiss Katuchka,
the family cat. During the German occupation of Paris, when the Yencesse family fled to the South of France, Katuchka was with them; she
was a genuine part of the family, and Dodie loved her. But I had been
raised on dogs, and somehow had a negative attitude toward cats in
general. But with Cécile and Hubert standing there watching us, and
Dodie threatening to end our relationship if I didn't kiss Katuchka
good night, I kissed the cat and went out into the night and to my own

apartment across town. Was I irritated? Not at all. Rather, I admired Dodie's loyalty, and I had learned something more about her.

The daughter of a well-known French sculptor, she knew something of the creative life. By the time we left Paris, she had introduced me to a number of interesting Parisians in the art, business, and science worlds; I was fascinated. But by the time I brought her to New York—the first time she had been in the US—I began to realize she had little interest in what interested me, including American literature and tennis, my major lifetime sport. I was flattered that this young Parisian girl was interested in me—a boy from Iowa; I didn't realize her lack of interest in what interested me would be that important. In fact, an incident at Roland Garros in the French national championships (open tennis had not yet been invented), where I was playing against the captain of the Israeli Davis Cup team, was symbolic of our disconnect. I had been leading my opponent in the match until I pulled a muscle in my lower back. I kept on playing, like a trouper, but less well, of course. Seeing that I might lose, Dodie rose from her seat in the stands and walked out of the court area. Anyone involved in sports would have noticed the slight difference in my movements and understood what was happening to me on the court, but Dodie didn't. She just didn't want to watch me lose, which I suppose was a natural reaction of a non-sports wife. The sports-knowledgeable wives or girlfriends stay through everything.

Once we were settled in Manhattan, it became clear that her major concern was not us, but the relationship between her father and mother back in Paris. As their only child, she felt she was the principal element that held their marriage together. Although she never said so, I think she felt guilty for leaving them. I knew her mother had a distinguished Parisian lover, a Chevalier de la Légion d'Honneur—a title awarded by the French government for excellence in the civilian or military areas—who treated her mother, Cécile, very well. He set her up in the women's clothing-design business, and in fact, was the man who, in lieu of Dodie's father who was less involved and didn't speak English, conducted the man-to-man pre-marriage talk to make sure I'd be good to his mistress's young daughter. The interview took place at the Hôtel de Crillon, the ornate, palatial landmark, built by Louis

XV in 1758, on the Place de la Concorde. By that time, I knew Henri Bouvier rather well, and had drinks often in the bar, so it wasn't that special—just another day in Paris. After we were married, Dodie made an effort and learned something about the arcane world of tennis.

In Manhattan, though Dodie enrolled immediately in the Art Students League on West Fifty-Seventh Street and eventually studied with a few well-known sculptors including William Zorach, she was interested in seeing almost anything typically New York. So I took her—at her request—to a Yankees game. As we were sitting down deep behind home plate, I started giving her a superficial description of the game: names of the players, positions, and what they did. She had no immediate reaction, but as the game started and moved along to the bottom half of the third inning, she turned to me, and I could see I was about to hear her reaction to American baseball. "Sterling," she said, "it's like ballet. The batter hits to the right and everyone runs to the right. He hits to the left and everyone runs to the left. And the pitcher with his windup motion is like a ballet figure." It was an interesting comment— the French view of US baseball in the early fifties. She was trying to understand American pastimes and to find common ground.

Once I had started the agency, Dodie's attitudes about money emerged. I didn't have much of it, but we had enough to support the two of us. I never knew the cause of her concern, but it would become the beginning of a rift in our marriage. We lived simply, in a moderately elegant one room, plus kitchen and terrace apartment on Gramercy Park. And Dodie was employed by the Galéries Lafayette, the grand Paris department store, which hired her to tour New York City stores looking for new retail items that might be marketable in Paris, or which they could copy. I always thought she had an interesting job. If you like shopping, and she seemed to, it could be very satisfying.

Despite our both working, Dodie's income stayed with her. And that led to a few embarrassing and revealing moments in our relationship. This was before credit cards, and I didn't always carry enough money in my pockets. One evening, I took Dodie and Al Hirshberg, the Boston sportswriter, to a French restaurant in the East Forties, just west of First Avenue. Before the bill came, I realized I did not have enough cash with me to pay, so I turned to Dodie and with Al listening, asked her politely if she could lend me the money until we got home. She said no, and she was adamant. I was privately irritated, but never showed it. I was embarrassed more for her than for myself. So, in the middle of dinner, I got up, took a cab down to my apartment at Gramercy Park, scooped up the money, returned to the restaurant, apologized to Dodie and to Al, and paid the bill. Nothing more was ever said about it. It turned out to be a difference we could never resolve.

A little more than a year later, the same situation occurred, only this time the repercussions, which couldn't have been predicted, would be longer lasting. I was having lunch with a prospective client at Michael's, a friendly restaurant only two doors down from my office on Forty-Eighth Street off Fifth Avenue, and in the course of the lunch, I once again realized I didn't have enough cash to pay for myself and my guest. While trying to figure out what to do, I remembered that Dodie was lunching at Chanteclair, a French restaurant on Forty-Ninth Street between Madison and Fifth Avenues. I excused myself as if I were going to the men's room and dashed around the corner to her restaurant. Dodie was with another Frenchwoman, whom she had just met through mutual friends. I explained my circumstances, but again, Dodie calmly and firmly, and slightly angrily, said no. I did not give up, although it wasn't until her companion offered to lend me the money that Dodie finally complied.

The other Frenchwoman eventually became my second wife.

After the divorce, October 31, 1955, accomplished by Dodie's flying to Mexico and initiating the action (which is the way it was done in those days to avoid the complex and costly aspects of a New York divorce), Dodie returned to Paris and subsequently married an Italian engineer who lived and worked in Paris. Her parents remained together but in the French manner: Cécile's lover was still Cécile's lover.

I was not in touch with Dodie again until 1995, when an American woman friend of mine who lived in Paris and whom I had indirectly introduced to Dodie when she wanted to find a studio for herself, arranged a party for her French friends to which Dodie and her husband and I were invited. She knew I would like to see Dodie again; we had had seven years of shared experiences, after all. I was fond of her and had come to realize that despite our differences, she was really a good person, and I was looking forward to seeing her again. It was purposely scheduled for the time I was in London on a publishing/ Wimbledon trip and could hop over to Paris easily. It was a remarkable evening. When Dodie and her husband arrived, she introduced me to him and then joined me sitting on a couch in the center of the room, where we spent the entire evening discussing what each of us had done in the intervening forty years. I think we had matured a good deal. While we spoke, the North African Frenchman with whom I was staying kept Dodie's husband occupied. She told me about her daughter and her sculpting and how it had progressed since her days at the Art Students League in New York, that her parents were still married, and that her mother still kept her lover. It was a happy evening, no feelings of regret from either of us. I was moved by how much of my life she knew about, from one source or another. She cared. And I did, too: She is a very decent and honorable woman. That night at my friend's apartment, I could hardly sleep. I was emotionally shaken by seeing Dodie again and bringing all the long-ago events back into my consciousness.

We have kept in touch, and in 2000, when I took my thirty-five-year-old daughter Rebecca to France, I arranged for her to meet Dodie. By this time, Dodie's husband, father, and mother had all died, and Dodie was living in a simple but attractive home in a pleasant suburb of Paris. Long after lunch, when we were leaving, Dodie walked us to the gate and, in parting, said, "Rebecca, you are welcome back any time, with or without your father."

Danièle St. Paul was the other woman at the table at Chanteclair. She phoned me after hearing on the France/NYC grapevine that Dodie and I were divorcing. I was pleased to hear from her, and I wanted to thank her again for persuading Dodie to pay that day.

She was not only attractive, with curly black hair, and slightly flirtatious, she was also intelligent. Like Dodie she was lively, but unlike Dodie she was more giving of herself, and I suspected quite sensual, which turned out to be true. She dressed well and, surprisingly, seemed very taken with me. She was, I believe, the first Jewish woman I had dated. I wasn't very conscious of the distinction. I would learn that Danièle's family name had been Leven, but when the Germans invaded France in WWII, Danièle's mother escaped with the children into the mountains, and to further protect them, changed the family name to St. Paul.

One might wonder why, if my first French marriage was fraught with cultural differences, I would marry another Frenchwoman. I pondered that briefly at the time, but realized the difference: I had brought Dodie from Paris to the United States, where she had never been. Danièle was in New York of her own accord. And she came from a much more sophisticated international background. Her Uncle Gustav was the president of Perrier and a purchaser of major paintings on the world market. Her Uncle Raymond had a seat on the Paris Bourse. I wouldn't have to help her adjust. In fact, she and her family would help me. Both Dodie and Danièle spoke fluent English, which was good and bad; they weren't interested in helping me with my French. While in New York, Danièle was staying with Monique Uzielli, a charming woman who had been married to Danièle's Uncle Raymond at one time. At Danièle's request, Monique, the baroness de Gunzburg, invited me to her home on Ninety-Second Street in Manhattan (with her husband Giorgio) for an elegant cocktail party. She was a superb hostess, introducing me one-by-one to every guest, none of whom I had known before, and in each conversation, adding substantive information about the other person that she knew would ignite a conversation. It always worked. I noticed, too, that she treated every guest the same way. I had never before, in Paris or New York, seen a cocktail party run so well. It didn't hurt that Giorgio, who had a seat on the New York Stock Exchange, was also a tennis buff and former captain—nonplaying he would always add—of the Italian Davis Cup Team, and he had his own court on a modest, well-cared-for, and attractive bayside estate nearby on Long Island. I was a far better tennis player. Later, he would take Danièle and me there with his family on the weekends.

Of course I wasn't marrying either Monique or Giorgio, nor was I marrying into their lifestyle, but I have to admit, it was easier to fall in love in such a seductive environment. I enjoyed those weekends and realized immediately that I played an unusual role in that crowd. My tennis skills were well above those of any guest there, and Giorgio would brag about me to his friends and try to have better players there to play me.

I enjoyed and was amused by the Uzielli lifestyle, but was I dazzled? Not at all. Tennis had social connotations in those days before the pros and money came to play. That was not why I played, of course, but it existed. Before the Uzielli period, I had played in and often won tournaments in Wiesbaden, Garmisch-Partenkirchen, and Davos, Switzerland, where the hotel had started playing an American tune each evening as I walked into the dining room after winning a match. I'd played in the French National indoor and outdoor tournaments, was on the premier équipe at the Racing Club, had the privilege of playing at Roland Garros whenever I wished, and had been invited by the Casino at Monte Carlo to play in the first major outdoor tournament of the year, which they sponsored. I had also played with or against at least four players who had won world or national titles. You meet a great many people and see a great many interesting sights that way. I'd also been to at least two of the spring cocktail parties in a large, elegant apartment facing the Seine where they served only champagne and ice cream—the latter for the children and the former French tennis star of years ago, Jean Borotra, who never drinks.

Danièle and I were married in October 1955 in Burlington, Iowa, in the Unitarian church my parents had founded. Long after I left Burlington, they organized a group of like-minded friends and took over a building that had originally been a large garage on an elegant old estate in a close-to-downtown residential district. It was the only wedding of mine that my parents were able to attend, and I was pleased. That's one reason we married in Burlington. Danièle's parents were divorced, but her lovely mother and one of Danièle's brothers flew over from Paris to attend, so I felt it appropriate to set it up so they could meet my parents.

Danièle didn't need to work for financial reasons, but she was full of energy, as we used to say in Iowa. She needed to work to keep herself out of trouble. She wanted to work in my agency, I remember, and to bring French writers to me, but she didn't know the Parisian literary scene very well and despite the energy I gave trying to help her, she was not interested at that time of her life in hard work, and it didn't pan out.

After we had been married three or four years, her Uncle Gustav—the art collector—came to New York for about a month. He must have seen that Danièle, as bright and full of energy as she was, needed some commitment to occupy herself, so he proposed we set up an art gallery to exhibit works by young French artists. It was a clever idea; Gustav knew the Parisian agents who represented young French artists whose work was already selling well in other parts of the US. The plan was that Danièle would be in the gallery daily and really run it, but Gustav wanted me to drop by every noon, stepping out from the agency and literary lunches to see that all was going well.

In preparation, Gustav and I spent many noontimes walking the streets of midtown and the Upper East Side looking for a location for our gallery. A few days before he was to return to Paris, we found one between Seventy-Eighth and Seventy-Ninth Streets on Madison Avenue in the center of an art-gallery district, in a building that already had two galleries in the upper floors. We were trying to secure the ground floor. The night we met with the building's owner/manager to try to close the deal—Gustav was willing to put up the guarantee for the rent of five years—in the middle of the negotiation, Danièle volunteered that she was not willing to take the responsibility for her Uncle Gustav's investment. I was stunned. Both Gustav and I had invested a good deal of time and thought to set it up. That ended the dream of an art gallery, which, I guess, was not her dream after all. Danièle's withdrawal did not make sense to me, but I couldn't get a further explanation from her.

I quickly came to realize that I did not have the time Danièle needed from a husband, particularly as she had no career of her own to pursue. My business came first.

If she was bored, Danièle was finding other, less acceptable—to me—outlets. She began spending more time in France, which bothered me considerably. Also, I started to feel she was not faithful to me—in France or New York—and that she had only married me because she thought it would be chic to have an American husband and carry that fact with her through life. I regretted the way things were going and wasn't happy. I phoned her in Paris one day and told her I was divorcing her. I can still hear the crack in her voice. But she didn't try very hard to dissuade me; I think she knew that neither one of us was happy with the other any longer.

Shortly after the divorce was completed, Danièle, who had returned to Paris for good, became the chief editor of the very successful French magazine *Marie Claire*. As far as I know, her entire prior literary experience before that was with my agency in New York. But then, she had great connections.

I never saw Danièle again, but from time to time, I'd hear about her. If she had found such an important job in the US, perhaps our marriage would have lasted longer, but perhaps not. I felt differently about her departure than I did about Dodie's. I was already beginning to think Danièle had used me for her own purposes. In those days, in a certain social strata in Paris, it was impressive to have had an American husband.

When I met the woman who would become my third wife, in 1959, she was known as Cindy Degener. At Radcliffe she had been Cindy Sweeney. Her father was Patrick Sweeney, and when she was born she was named by her parents either Claire Cynthia Sweeney or Cynthia Claire Sweeney. Whichever it was, Patrick Sweeney got it mixed up on the way to the records office in New Bedford, Massachusetts, so it was recorded incorrectly. Patrick Sweeney was generally an imaginative, effective, intelligent man who founded and was president of the Continental Screw Company. I think the excitement of having a daughter—their first child—distracted him.

By the time I met her, Cindy was well established in the talent-representation business in New York. She and Ron Wilford, who later became chairman and CEO of Columbia Artists Management, ran a small talent-representation company that, among other accomplishments, brought the great French mime Marcel Marceau to the US for the first time.

But in 1956, as she and Wilford split up, Cindy was hired by Music Corporation of America (MCA), headed by Lew Wasserman, the great talent agent, to work with Kay Brown and Audrey Wood, two top playwright agents who, between them, represented William Inge, Tennessee Williams, and Arthur Miller, among others.

Cindy Lord (Claire "Cindy" Degener), a graduate of Radcliffe and the Music Corporation of America—and mother of our daughter, Rebecca—joined the agency in 1961.

I had been thinking seriously about opening an agency in Paris. To make it work, I knew I would need a strong supporting agent in New York. John Cushman, an agent with whom I was acquainted, knew his friend Cindy was leaving MCA, so he introduced us. At the time, I was still legally married to Danièle and Cindy was ending her marriage to Arnold Degener. But a number of events happened in a short period of time: As a result of my continuing research, and in view of my faltering marriage, I realized I was in no position to start or even work in an agency in Paris. Meanwhile, Cindy signed a three-year contract with Curtis Brown Ltd., a New York branch of the prominent and well-established London literary agency.

With Danièle spending so much time in Paris, I started the divorce paperwork. Cindy's divorce had gone through, and even though our potential business deal never happened, we were spending time together. I was strongly attracted to her Irish beauty, her charm, intelligence, and wit. We became good friends, and on weekends I joined Cindy at her parents' family farm in Westport, Massachusetts, just outside of New Bedford. All the time we were discovering more and more areas of compatibility and were getting closer and closer. In the middle of her three-year contract with Curtis Brown, we married. We seemed to have a great many personal values in common, including decency, concern for others, loyalty, respect for elders, a strong work ethic, good sense of humor, and the ability to be self-effacing. I met many of her friends from the theater, the literary world, her days at Radcliffe and Harvard, and many other interesting people. For the first time, I was marrying someone in my milieu.

We had been married almost four years when, in April 1963, Cindy's father died. Two years later, she gave birth to our only child, Rebecca. I suspected the two events were related. This may sound a little silly, but in the early years Cindy's father treated her like a boy, and I think she may have felt she needed to wait until he was gone to have a child, though we never talked about it.

In the early years, we were extremely close. Cindy had been noticeably overweight when we first met, and still was, despite many efforts to change after Rebecca's birth. So we began a serious diet. I say "we" because whether we were dining at a restaurant or dining at home, we ate identically and together. Even though I have always been lean, I ate what she ate as a gesture of support. We were eating quickly, not lingering over the meal. This reduced temptation. It worked; Cindy lost twenty pounds in a few months and felt much better about herself. I seem to remember neither losing nor gaining weight. I must have nibbled between meals.

Since we were working for competing agencies, we had to be extremely discreet about business talk, and we were.

My agency was growing rapidly, and I was beginning to realize I needed help in the dramatic area—film, theater, television, radio. So, as Cindy's Curtis Brown contract was coming to an end, I had been thinking about whether it would be good for her, for the marriage, for raising a child—if we ever had one—and for my business if she came aboard. After much thought, I felt it might work, and I told her that if she wanted to come to the Sterling Lord Agency—and only if she really wanted to—I would be delighted to have her. In 1961, she joined my agency. On May 23, 1965, our daughter, Rebecca, was born. Within a few days, I could see parts of Rebecca's face reflecting

Cindy's, and other parts mine. Of course she was beautiful and animated—what father could say otherwise? Her birth was the beginning of the longest-lasting personal relationship of my life.

A week before Rebecca was born, a woman who became very important in our lives, arrived from Sweden. Since Cindy and I were both working, we decided to hire a baby nurse. The Swedish-Finnish woman, Anni Jansson, had helped raise the children of a friend of ours very masterfully in Greenwich Village, and before that she had raised the children of the Swedish Ambassador to Washington, DC. So we felt we had a gem—and we did. She arrived to live with us in our rather spacious apartment.

As Rebecca grew, I spent various kinds of times with her. She and I would put large pillows on the floor of our hallway just outside her room and the adjacent nurse's room, jumping over them, simulating a hurdle race.

Later, when she reached the age of eleven, we took a bus trip along the Pacific Coast—Los Angeles to San Francisco. It was an interesting trip. Rebecca was the only child aboard. Our first major stop after lunch in Santa Barbara was William Randolph Hearst's grandiose castle, San Simeon, and we spent more than one hour traipsing through the various buildings. As we re-gathered in the parking lot waiting to board and continue up the coast to Carmel, Rebecca spotted one of the other passengers, an architect from Cleveland, Ohio. Rebecca was curious as to what he thought of San Simeon after the tour. He responded immediately and surprised us all: "It will never last," he said, and then proceeded to identify major walls composed of a substance that would be destroyed after sixty years. So much for authority, but Rebecca was amused.

That night we stayed in Carmel, just a couple blocks from Clint Eastwood's home, which failed to impress Rebecca.

A few years later, we were in the show-horse business. Rebecca started by riding on the Almy farm in Westport, Massachusetts, during the summer, then going up to Bedford, New York, and then traveling to various shows or competitions in the Northeast. There seemed to be one every weekend. In the beginning, Rebecca was too young to drive, so I would get up at dawn to take her. I had no experience in the show-horse business and had no idea how to budget it for my daughter, so what I did was ask one of the mothers—there were more mothers than fathers—how she budgeted this for her daughter. Well, she had no idea. We were all clueless. But I enjoyed watching Rebecca compete.

As Rebecca grew up, Cindy and I edged farther apart, and Rebecca began having emotional eating problems—specifically, anorexia. I had to hospitalize her the day before she was to graduate from Town School.

Cindy and I divorced, and as Rebecca gradually (after four hospitals) started coming back and getting stronger, so did Cindy. Both profited by overcoming adversity. Cindy worked diligently to establish a new and separate life without parents or daughter or husband and began writing and reading. Rebecca has grown into a caring human being. She was able, over time, to transform her difficulties into compassion and a profound gift for healing herself and others. She works as an acupuncture physician and medical intuitive at a practice that she owns and runs. She loves and is loved and has the sense of self and joy that I always wanted for her.

My first three marriages failed—although I am on very friendly terms with two of the three, Cindy and Dodie—but my fourth marriage was a mistake. I was giving in many ways and getting nothing back. I thought we shared an interest in writing and publishing, and I thought we were in love; I was half right. When it ended, I promised my friends I'd never marry again—and I haven't.

In the course of building my agency in the sixties and seventies, I leaned heavily toward the hiring of women for key roles. The nature of agency work includes what I would call "mothering," and women generally are much better at that. Also, the first area in publishing open to women was work in a literary agency.

I was well aware of the growth of the women's movement (in fact, I represented Gloria Steinem until *Ms.* magazine appeared), and the increasing appearance of women in important positions in book and magazine publishing. All this had no direct effect on my hiring, although it may have increased the availability of capable women in the marketplace. I was looking for talented people with the kind of energy it takes to attract writers and sell books, who were also literary.

I can think of only one instance when the women's movement had a direct effect on me: One of the three women mentioned in this chapter used to attend luncheons of women in publishing and related fields, and she would return from such a luncheon and ask that afternoon to meet with me. The subject of our meetings was essentially her revelations on what women in comparable positions were asked to do and how much they were paid. She described what the rest of the working world was like, as discovered in her luncheon, followed by a suggestion that she should get a raise. She was very good and contributed substantially to the agency, so I gave it to her—each time.

Over the decades of building my agency, these three women made substantial contributions quite apart from the income they produced or the writers they attracted. No men in my employ made anywhere near these contributions. The contributions of these three were essential to the growth of the agency over its first fifty years.

My third wife, Cindy, who joined my agency in 1961, was an imaginative agent and an excellent negotiator. I wanted her to join the agency, but I didn't want anyone to misunderstand and label it a "mom-and-pop shop"; I had broader ambitions. I was the sole owner of the business, and she was the first agent with agency experience whom I hired.

In 1961, when she joined me, Cindy brought with her an assistant, Deborah Rogers, a delightful and savvy British woman, as well as writer Terry Southern (*Candy*, 1958, *The Magic Christian*, 1959); Tony Walton, the set designer (the only one we ever represented), at the time married to Julie Andrews; A. R. "Pete" Gurney, the playwright; and the musical comedy team of Lee Pockriss and Anne Croswell (*Ernest in Love*, 1960).

Although I had been working as an agent for ten years, there were still many things I didn't know about the business: I had never worked in another agency. Cindy provided much of the structure that was essential to our business. She not only had good agency knowledge, she knew about record-keeping and operating procedures that I knew nothing about—all of which became more valuable as the agency grew.

Cindy also added considerable depth to the office, noticeably improving our film, television, and theatrical strength and range of expertise, and increasing the exposure and impact of the agency. She took us to a new level.

She could be forceful and persuasive. Her first venture at our office in her first year involved programmed texts, textbooks based on the principles of programmed learning, providing small steps for students to learn at their own pace. Cindy represented three young writers who had been approached by Harcourt, Brace and Company to write these programs. After preliminary negotiations, Harcourt drew up contracts and submitted them to us. At the time, textbook authors tended to negotiate—or non-negotiate—their own deals, but Cindy had great range, and these authors knew it. Even today (2012) there are few agents working in the textbook field.

When Cindy appeared in the offices of Harcourt with the draft contracts in hand, the resistance of textbook publishers to the arrival of agents became obvious. She carefully and thoughtfully listed the clauses she wanted altered or eliminated before asking our clients to sign. The publishing executives listened attentively, but silently. At the end of her recitation, the ranking editor calmly announced that despite Cindy's demands, they wouldn't alter one word of their basic contract. With the sharp tongue of the Irish, she answered in a firm voice, "Gentlemen, you are denying my clients their constitutional rights!" The men blanched, and changes were made.

Another time, as I walked by her office, I heard her listening to a screaming Hollywood producer with whom she was negotiating a film deal. Cindy was not a screamer. After the screaming stopped, I heard her say, "Sam, why don't we wait to finish the negotiating until some day when you are feeling better." That stopped him.

Before Cindy retired in the late seventies, she had not only put three plays by our clients on the boards, she had also completed extraordinary feature-film sales. She sold Jack Kerouac's *On the Road* to GJL Productions at Warner Bros., fronting for Francis Ford Coppola's American Zoetrope. Despite the excitement about Jack and *On the Road* in the literary world, no one else in Hollywood would touch it. Coppola tried valiantly over the years to get a screenplay written, but one after another writer failed to satisfy him. (Inevitably he would show almost every one of them to his friend and my client—just a block or so away—Lawrence Ferlinghetti.) Finally, after years of effort, *The Motorcycle Diaries*, the film based on the early adventures of Che Guevara, was released, and we all realized that the director, Walter Salles, and screenwriter, Jose Rivera, of that film should be doing *On the Road*, and they were hired.

Cindy also sold Jimmy Breslin's *The Gang That Couldn't Shoot Straight* to producers Robert Chartoff and Irwin Winkler, an energetic and talented pair who later produced all the Rocky movies, before the manuscript was even finished. It was released in 1971 and starred Jerry Orbach.

In the early seventies, the agency was continuing to grow and I had some good people working for me, but I needed a good assistant/office manager. Fortunately for me, I met Patricia Berens, the second-most-important woman to my agency's growth. She had been executive secretary to Clifton Daniel, managing editor of the *New York Times*, and had left there to return to graduate school to work on a PhD on the history of the Reformation, as she intended to teach at the college level. She eventually took a leave of absence from graduate school, and never went back.

She helped enormously. Without coaching from me, she automatically knew exactly what tasks every employee should be performing. She transformed the talented individuals working for me into a cohesive unit, and it showed promptly in the agency's gross.

In Pat's early years at the *New York Times*, the role of secretary was restricted to the old-fashioned limitations of typist and stenographer. But after female employees brought a class-action suit, the paper's executives found greater use for at least some of their female workers. Pat began sitting in news conferences with Clifton Daniel, where she spoke up with questions and comments. She helped him write and edit the many speeches he gave around the country, mostly about freedom of the press. Despite the lawsuit, she also became a good friend of Margaret Truman Daniel, Clifton's wife.

At Sterling Lord she immediately and quietly began to take charge. I had never had anyone who raised the standards of performance so effectively; I didn't have to tell her what to do—she knew better than I. First she fired our receptionist, who occasionally came to work unkempt, with dirty hair and fingernails, a gaping hem, and a terrible voice. She had dressed up for the job interview, but I didn't remember why we had hired her. From then on, we always hired well-educated, well-spoken young men and women.

We had an intelligent but lazy mail clerk who took his time processing bound books to be sent overseas for foreign sales. Pat quickly fixed the problem, and our foreign sales increased immediately. She helped me set up an overnight banking system so that we were drawing interest each night. But most important, she took care of the clients who couldn't reach me instantly on the phone, an enormous time-saver for me, and she did it all usually without my asking. She was also experienced and mature enough so that I felt comfortable discussing any agency-related problem with her.

One morning in October 1972, Pat stepped into my office and announced, "Sterling, I want you to meet someone I have been interviewing." She never said that if it wasn't really important.

That's how I met Philippa "Flip" Brophy. The interview, as I recall, lasted about thirty seconds. (Patricia Berens had done the nitty-gritty screening.) Flip's intelligence, quick reaction time, energy, attentiveness, and clear way of expressing herself were apparent. What clinched it was her work history, which included a stint as a Fuller Brush salesperson. Anyone who could succeed in cold door-to-door sales had to be good. And she had the written word in her DNA. Her father, Arnold, who died when she was thirteen, was a well-known and highly regarded *Newsday* writer. I wanted her. We offered her the job as receptionist/switchboard operator on the spot.

Viking Press had offered Flip a job in sales at the same time, but she chose us because she thought the agency would be less demanding, offer less of a career, and be easier for her to leave, as she was planning to go in a couple of years to graduate school in psychology. Little did she know . . .

Flip is the only person in my long run in the agency who grew step-by-step from the bottom to the top. That kind of experience is very valuable in any company, but very rare today. Ultimately, she became the third significant woman in the growth of my agency, but it didn't happen immediately.

In her first years, Flip was an extremely problematic employee. At one point, I was furious because I thought she had done something disloyal to the agency, but Pat changed my mind. We both felt she could be a valuable employee, and eventually a very successful agent if she would just settle down and go to work. Pat's strong feminist feelings persuaded her to give Flip a great deal of support. I began by seating Flip next to a wonderful old-fashioned secretary named Ceil Aboff, who had been a secretary for the president of Macmillan Publishing Company. After her retirement, I was able to get her on a part-time basis. She knew office routine like the inside of her pocket (as the French say). She knew the correct way to do everything secretarial. Flip stayed on that job less than a year before becoming my secretary, although she didn't stay solely my secretary for long. With coaching by Pat Berens, Flip was soon helping sell foreign rights and magazine rights for some of my nonfiction clients, such as Joe McGinniss (*The Selling of the President*), Jimmy Breslin (the front-page columnist), and David Wise (Washington bureau chief of the *New York Herald Tribune* at the time—the youngest in the paper's history). Eventually, I believe, Flip decided the agency was a career she wanted, and it was smooth sailing from that moment on.

I subsequently made her my assistant. She also squeezed in a private life. Before the birth of her first child she worked right through to the end of the last week of her pregnancy. On Friday evening, she went home, and the next day she gave birth to baby Zachary. When she had to take time off after the birth, Pat Berens and I valued her so highly that we did everything we could to help her—and her clients—until she had recovered sufficiently to work full-time.

In 1979, after she returned from maternity leave for her second son, Alexander, I pointed out to her that she had children A to Z, and I assumed that was her signal to us that there would be no more children. She smiled but said nothing. Time proved me right. This time she returned to work no longer as my assistant, but as a full-time agent.

Early in the 1980s, I realized I was tired of running the business—

not tired of being an agent at all, but I wanted a situation where I didn't even know the names of the outside accountants. I also realized the ideal solution was to bring in an agent whose age was somewhere between mine—I was approaching seventy—and the younger agents on staff, who were in their early forties.

I confided in my friend Michael Sissons, the British agent I had been representing for twelve years, and he suggested his friend Peter Matson, who had his own agency in New York City. The merger was consummated in 1987, and we started working together early the following year, with Peter taking on the management of the agency.

Flip was effective at every job she did at the agency during those days, though for much of that time she was guided by Pat Berens. During the eighties, she became more and more successful as an acquiring agent. In the following decade, she represented three national bestselling books: *What It Takes* by Richard Ben Cramer (1992), the chronicle of the 1988 presidential race; *The Nightingale's Song* by Robert Timberg (1995), the story of five Vietnam vets and graduates of the US Naval Academy including John McCain, John Poindexter, Bud McFarlane, Jim Webb, and Oliver North; and *The Color of Water* by James McBride (1996), the loving tale of the author and his mother, a Polish immigrant and Orthodox Jew, who raised her biracial children in the fifties, when mixed marriages were very much stigmatized.

Flip also started representing Senator John McCain.

In 2005, she became the largest stockholder in the agency (as stockholding was readjusted to allow for successors), as well as president of Sterling Lord Literistic—and my boss. The former Fuller Brush salesperson was now running the agency.

My staff selection over the years left a strong, successful, functioning foundation for Peter Matson (he sold John Irving's blockbuster, *The World According to Garp,* as well as Dee Brown's classic, *Bury My Heart at Wounded Knee*), and for Flip Brophy to build on, but along the way, I trained six other agents now successfully functioning independently or in other agencies. Deborah Rogers, who came to me with Cindy, is a recognized agent in London at Rogers, Coleridge & White.

New York–based Lynn Nesbit (whom I met at the Radcliffe Publishing Program the summer I spoke there) and Stuart Krichevsky (who started in my mailroom as an NYU intern, and by the time he graduated knew the agency backward and forward) are each recognized as being extremely effective, as is Joan Brandt in Atlanta and Don Cutler (whom I rescued from his job as religious editor at *Harper's*) in the Boston area. All started at the Sterling Lord Agency, which in 1987 became Sterling Lord Literistic, Inc. (Literistic was the name of Peter's agency when we merged.)

## CHAPTER 13

# The Ken Kesey I Knew

If the fifties and sixties belonged to Jack Kerouac, the sixties and seventies belonged to Ken Kesey—their ages, personalities, and writing styles were so different, but there was room for both. They were both iconoclastic thinkers whose writing and philosophy inspired passionate devotion in their readers. I was interested in both as individuals as well as writers. And both were my clients.

Before I ever met Kesey, Tom Guinzburg, president of Viking Press, called me one day to see if my client Jack Kerouac would read and write a blurb for the jacket of *One Flew Over the Cuckoo's Nest*, Kesey's first novel, which Tom had bought for Viking but had not yet published. Publishers are always looking for well-known writers to give them positive comments they can use on the jacket or in a press release for a book they are about to publish. It can be particularly helpful if readers feel there is a creative relationship between the two writers. I had no idea whether or not Jack would help—some writers do not like to blurb another writer's work at all. But I did not think Jack would be offended if asked. In fact, I thought he might even be flattered that his publisher had thought of him for this task. I told Tom to send me the manuscript. I read it before sending it on to Jack, and I knew then that I wanted

Photo courtesy of Ken Kesey

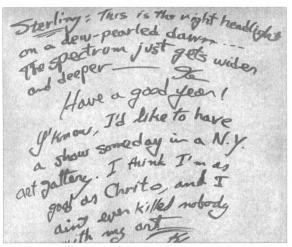

Photo courtesy of Ken Kesey

A gift from the New Further. Ken Kesey was looking over the New Further one day, in a nostalgic moment, and noticed on close inspection the interesting details painted on some parts of the bus. He subsequently borrowed a 35 mm camera and took a series of photos of these parts. The photographs turned out beautifully, so Ken, according to Faye Kesey McMurtry, sent a different photo to each of the various people he associated with the bus. I was the only non–Merry Prankster to receive a photo, as far as we've been able to tell. Kesey considered the photographs a gift from the bus, and I received it and cherished it as such, as I knew how much it meant to him.

to work with Kesey. (Incidentally, Jack did not write the blurb; he felt uncomfortable doing it, and I respected that.)

I was immediately captivated by the content and Kesey's writing. I made a courtesy call to Tom Guinzburg to tell him I'd like to represent Kesey, if he didn't have an agent—he didn't—and then got in touch with Kesey. He was delighted and we started working together. A year later, he and his wife Faye were baffled by the logistics of various aspects of publishing *One Flew Over the Cuckoo's Nest*, including foreign rights, discounts, and other routine maneuvers. I volunteered to be their agent on that book and said I'd do it for 5 percent. Not having represented them from the start, I didn't think it was justifiable to insist on what was the going rate of 10 percent. I planned to do everything I would normally do for a client, but I hadn't done the initial deal with Viking.

A few years later, I was riveted by the play of *Cuckoo's Nest* at the Broadway opening. It was a bold, creative story of what happens in a mental institution and a very daring subject for the time. Ken had just delivered to me his second novel, *Sometimes a Great Notion*, and had come to New York for the opening of the play based on *Cuckoo's Nest* starring Kirk Douglas, with British actress Joan Tetzel playing Nurse Ratched.

When I met Ken Kesey in 1963, he was twenty-eight and with his piercing blue eyes and warm smile, he reminded me of Paul Newman—with less hair. He was five foot ten and trim, and he had signature bushy sideburns that he topped with a woolen bill cap. He seemed to be enjoying everything he did. And he shook hands with a firm grip.

Before I had started working with Kesey, his life trajectory had forever changed. Following his graduation from the University of Oregon in 1957, while on a Woodrow Wilson Fellowship at Stanford University, where he was studying creative writing with Wallace Stegner, he volunteered in an unorthodox CIA-funded study on the effects of psychedelic drugs, a subject on which he became a lifelong expert.

For the opening of the play, Kesey arrived in Manhattan with his family and friends, and I soon realized that despite his many varied interests and peripatetic life, family was a major part of who he was. In addition to Ken and his wife Faye, there was his older brother Chuck and his sister-in-law Sue, and Grandmother Smith, the mother of Ken's mother, Geneva, who did not come. With them was George Walker, a close friend and writer from the Eugene area.

Most of them had flown into New York, though George Walker drove from Oregon in his 1958 Chevrolet station wagon, painted bright orange with a prominent slogan on the side: "Dizzy Gillespie for United States President." The group was joined by New Yorker Sandy Lehmann-Haupt. Sandy was the brother of Chris Lehmann-Haupt— the *New York Times* reviewer who later on reviewed *Sometimes a Great Notion* for the *Times*.

The night before the play opened, we were gathered in my high-in-the-sky apartment on Central Park West, and although the view of the city looking south toward the Empire State Building and all the office buildings between was spectacular, the Kesey contingent, who had that day visited the Museum of Natural History and the site of the upcoming World's Fair, which would open the following year in Flushing Meadows, was totally absorbed with one another. I had just finished reading the manuscript of *Sometimes a Great Notion* and was impressed and moved. I had never been to Oregon, but Ken's writing gave me a vivid picture of that part of the country.

"Ken," I said, "I think you've written a novel that will become an American classic!"

"Thanks very much," he said immediately, "but I don't think you're right. The story is too complicated."

He turned out to be more right than I was. In a subsequent reread-ing, I realized that although the story bears all the markings of an epic American tragedy, the obscuring, rotating first-person narrative (often blurring between one character's perspective and that of the next) reinforces the ways in which this veers, stylistically and categori-cally, away from the premise of the Great American Novel: No single character or situation serves as emblematic of the novel's contempo-rary period; there is neither a clear hero nor a villain. But the ways in which it speaks to the East/West Coast divide, to nature versus civili-zation, and to "rugged individualism" versus communitarianism were very much in keeping with the spirit of the times.

Opening night at the Cort Theatre on November 13, 1963, was memorable. It was a packed house. Dale Wasserman's dramatization was superb. The subject of a mental institution was not yet accepted fare by all patrons. It was a riveting performance, but at the end of Act I about 20 percent of the audience walked out. Those of us who remained were spellbound.

A few days after opening night, the Kesey group left town, Ken accompanying George Walker and Sandy Lehmann-Haupt in Walker's orange-painted station wagon back across America. It turned out to be a poignant trip. While they were driving through western Pennsylvania, the car radio announced President Kennedy's assassination.

Everyone in the car was shocked and angry. Kesey spoke first: "The pricks, the goddamned pricks." Kesey continued, "I don't know who did this, but I know they are the enemy."

In a subsequent letter to his friend, Ken Babbs, who was still out of the country with the US Marines, Kesey explained the enemy was a force trying to drive a stake through the heart of the American spirit; to divide the country into warring factions, to make it impossible for anything positive to happen, to destroy any chance of cooperation in Congress, to keep power in the hands of those who saw the whole system as a way of feathering their own nests. People were here to be used, to be exploited; the natural resources of the land were to be harvested without concern for the future. For a short while, in the aftermath of Kennedy's death, something happened that the enemy never expected. Instead of setting the warring factions at each other's throats, the assassination united the country in a common emotion of grief. We were one in our sorrow.

Kesey's notion of America was that we are a big family, with all the arguments and tussles and bickering, but down deep, when the shit hits the fan, the family comes together and faces the threat or disaster as one.

After his two books were published and Kesey moved into the next chapters of his life, he often said, when anyone asked him what he was doing, "Our job is nothing less than saving the world." And "The only true currency is that of the spirit."

During this trip back to Oregon, they began forming their think-

This is the legendary busload of Merry Pranksters with Ken Kesey, heading east on a hot, lonely Texas highway towards New York. It is 1964 and they eventually arrived safely and took over the city.

In 1996, Ken Babbs (left), Ken Kesey, and I are standing in front of the New Further, successor to the original Further, on Kesey's farm outside Eugene, Oregon. Babbs was one of Kesey's closest friends, and wrote a novel, *Who Shot the Water Buffalo?*, after Kesey died. At the time this was taken, the original Further had been formally retired and was rusting in peace in the woods about 100 yards away.

ing for what would become the Merry Pranksters bus trip to New York the following year to see the World's Fair.

Although New York City, the hub of book publishing, was slow to recognize it, the sixties were rapidly becoming Kesey's decade. Not only were his first two novels published in the sixties, but Kesey's bus, Further, appeared in New York City in 1964, with a group calling themselves the Merry Pranksters. It was a varied fun-loving group of Kesey and his friends and their friends. Neal Cassady, the wiry, muscular inspiration for Dean Moriarty—the character in Jack Kerouac's *On the Road*—drove the bus across the country.

There were roughly sixteen to twenty men and women on the trip, all of whom were given nicknames relating to what they wore—or didn't wear—or their individual actions. Kesey wore a red, white, and blue bandana around his head, so he was Captain Flag. Others were the Intrepid Traveler (Ken Babbs), Hardly Visible, Camera Man, Stark Naked, Gretchen Fetchen, Zonker, Hassler, Highly Charged, Dismount (Sandy Lehmann-Haupt would leave the bus at almost every stop to run into a convenience store for some candy), Generally Famished (Jane Burton, a Stanford philosophy major who was always hungry), Sometimes Missing, Brother Charlie (Ken's brother Chuck who ran the family creamery), and Betsy Flag (Faye Kesey).

When the bus reached Manhattan (they all referred to it as Madhattan), Kesey phoned me right away.

"How was it?" I asked, not knowing what to expect.

In a classic Kesey response, he said, "Sterling, when we hit Manhattan, the city just rolled over on its back and purred." It was his way of saying the city had welcomed him, the bus, and the Pranksters.

I had never met Neal Cassady before Further arrived in New York City, and I wouldn't say I got to know him well even then—he didn't sit still a great deal on a trip like this. I was told he shaved every morning with a dry razor, which seemed somehow appropriate. He had done two years in San Quentin on a minor drug charge, and when he got out, he had gone to Perry Lane, Kesey's hangout at Stanford. They had been friends ever since. Some of the Pranksters told me he was an "all-time great talker who could go on for hours nonstop without repeating himself"—not talking nonsense, "he had a brilliant mind and could recite whole paragraphs of Proust."

Five years later, Tom Wolfe's *Electric Kool-Aid Acid Test* was published and sold many more copies than either of Kesey's novels at that time. Kesey the man was rapidly becoming more of a legend than Kesey the author. Over the years, people who knew how close Kesey and I were asked me if I wasn't bothered by that publicity, which distracted him from his writing, and why I didn't do something about it. As I've said elsewhere in this book, I was not his life agent. In addition, I respected Ken a great deal and admired so many efforts he made in his life, and I wouldn't have dreamed of trying to redirect him.

Despite the fact that Kesey's designated bus driver was Kerouac's friend Neil Cassady, Kerouac and Kesey met only once, in Manhattan in June 1964, at the end of the Merry Pranksters' cross-country trip.

Kesey and the Merry Pranksters were staying in the temporarily vacant Manhattan apartment owned by a cousin of group member Chloe Scott. It was a forty-year-old apartment building on Madison Avenue between Eighty-Ninth and Ninetieth Streets. Further was parked in front of the Ninetieth Street Pharmacy on the other side of Madison Avenue for about a week.

I had told Kerouac that Kesey was going to be in town and would be in touch with him. Neil Cassady contacted Allen Ginsberg, and the two of them, along with Peter Orlovsky, Allen's partner, and Peter's brother Julius, who was one day out of a fourteen-year stay in a mental institution, drove out to Long Island to pick Kerouac up and bring him into Manhattan.

Kesey, Ken Babbs, and other of the Pranksters were anxious to meet Jack, as they had been deeply influenced by reading *On the Road*.

Jack was twelve years older than Kesey and Babbs, and there was a marked difference in their energies and interests. Jack had been living in a house with his mother in Northport, although he still had to deal from time to time with the public adulation inspired by the 1957 publication of *On the Road*. His led a relatively passive life.

Kesey and the Pranksters, on the other hand, were on an extended high that peaked in New York. According to Ken Babbs, every place they had stopped on the bus trip, they got out their musical instruments, donned their regalia, turned on the cameras and tape recorders, and broke into "spontaneous combustion musical and verbal make-believe shenanigans." The Pranksters were still doing a version of this in the New York City apartment.

This was the atmosphere into which Kerouac walked. Unlike the intrepid Pranksters, Jack sat quietly on the side, "slightly aloof," as Ken Babbs told me. They draped a small American flag over Jack's shoulders, but he took it off, folded it, and placed it on the arm of the couch.

There was absolutely no serious or colorful discussion between Kesey and Kerouac. Jack was never loud, nor critical, nor indignant. He seemed tired, but he was patient with the Pranksters' antics. It soon became apparent that the Kesey lifestyle was not his bag. An hour after he arrived, he left. He was uncomfortable with Kesey's overwhelming display of exuberance.

The Kerouac-Kesey encounter carried a message: Ken Kesey was not a part of the Beat Generation. Thanks to the CIA, Kesey was the spark plug or focal point of the Psychedelic Revolution, which spawned the hippies. Kesey brought LSD to people's awareness, and he and the Merry Pranksters spoke of its mind-expanding, life-enhancing properties, but not with me. Nor did I see ever any of them doing drugs.

Apart from the above, I realized Jack was deeply committed to writing. Kesey was just as deeply committed to living and experiencing the lives of others; for him ,writing was just a part of living.

The Beats and the Pranksters showed us different ways of opting out of society. They were both the personification of countercultural movements. The Beats were trying to change literature, and the Pranksters were trying to change the people and the country. Kesey, in fact, was his own cultural revolution, striving to keep the upbeat, freedom-loving spirit of America alive.

With all that happened to Kesey in the sixties, why wasn't he the darling of the East Coast literary world, as Jack Kerouac had been in the fifties? Kerouac was basically shy when outside his own milieu, and in no way a self-promoter. He lived much of the time in New York or nearby Long Island and, at least during the fifties, was accessible to the radio, television, and magazine people, but he did not seek publicity or present himself well in public. People came to *him*. He was good copy for newspaper reporters, some of whom wanted to publish his work. *On the Road* electrified the literary community and sharply marked the arrival of a new generation.

Ken Kesey was anything but shy. He embraced people; he gave of himself to others. *One Flew Over the Cuckoo's Nest* was the debut of a daring new voice, but in the end, Kesey's profound impact on his generation and those to come was the result of his whole lifestyle—novels, bus trips, acid tests, public performances, and the like. Kesey also didn't seek out the press, and he lived farther from what earlier journalists called "the ballyhoo belt"—New York City. He always believed—and later in his life stated—that "fame gets in the way of creativity."

I remember asking him toward the end of his 1963 visit to New York City what he planned to write next. His answer was that he planned to do a little living next.

Kesey had an open mind, but once he had made his mind up, he stuck to his decisions. For example, when people think of *One Flew Over the Cuckoo's Nest*, many think of Jack Nicholson's outstanding performance in the film. Kesey never saw the film. He purposely never saw it. Shortly before it was released, he and Faye met with a studio lawyer to clarify the potential financial earnings from the film. The lawyer totally offended both Ken and Faye and, at one point, became so irate with Ken that he yelled at him: "When the movie comes out, you will be the first in line to see it." Ken glared back at him and swore to himself he would never see the film.

When I was with Ken in New York City a few months before he died, I asked him again if he had seen it. He still hadn't and had no desire to do so. We were sitting in the Royale Theatre with David Stanford, Ken's editor and longtime friend, and a reporter from the *New York Times* who was doing a story about Ken, and we were watching a revival of *One Flew Over the Cuckoo's Nest* by the Steppenwolf Theatre Company which had come in from Chicago. I could tell that Ken was extremely interested but not very enthusiastic about the performance, so I asked him, "Ken, what's the best theatrical performance of *Cuckoo's Nest* you have ever seen?" Without a moment's hesitation, he said, "Sacramento High School." I was really surprised. And then he added, "They caught the ambiance better than anyone before or since."

I didn't see Kesey in his natural habitat until 1996, when I spent four days with him and Faye in their barn/house. Ken was busy editing film, but he took time off three afternoons to drive me through the countryside. Each day the area he showed me was more beautiful than the day before.

At the end of the second day's trip, I went out into the pasture with Ken and Faye to feed the cows. Ken drove the small tractor that pulled a low-slung hay wagon. Faye and I had been tossing off bales of hay to the cows as Ken slowly circled them. I stuck my pitchfork in what turned out to be the last bale of hay—but that was not enough to hold me. I fell off the wagon to the ground, Ken stopped the tractor, and Faye jumped down and helped me up, suggesting aspirin and a hot bath, neither of which I took. It wasn't that serious, I decided—only embarrassing.

"It's the first time I've ever seen you when you weren't in total control," Ken told me at breakfast the next morning.

We were sitting at the great round table in the Kesey kitchen, near the picture window that looked out over the nearby pond and the cow pasture.

"Look," I said to Ken and Faye, pointing to the place I had fallen the night before, "the cows are all gathered around the spot where I fell, as if to commemorate it." I heard years later that Ken had told the story, with minor embellishments, many times over the ensuing years.

At the end of my stay, Ken pulled Further out of its garage to drive me to the airport. He had collected a few of the Pranksters, who rode on the top of the bus, and Ken Babbs came from over the hill to drive it. Kesey sat inside to control the music. I felt honored. The music didn't work—something was broken—but we took off. Faye got out the family car to follow us (I assumed she and Ken wanted a fallback position in case the bus broke down), but it was a colorful and elegant way to end my visit.

When Ken died on November 10, 2001, at the age of sixty-six in a hospital in Eugene, Oregon, I felt I had lost a friend who was a special and fascinating man. I had last seen Ken in May, when we went to the new Broadway revival of *One Flew Over the Cuckoo's Nest*; the Steppenwolf Theatre Company production starring Gary Sinise. Ken stayed overnight with me. He was already showing some of the effects of the liver cancer that would kill him. David Stanford, his longtime friend and editor at Viking, later told me that I had seen Ken during one of his good periods. He had just stopped taking Interferon after several months on the medication, which had been very hard on him. Even so, he was a pleasure to be with.

Ken had surgery back in Eugene in late October. One day Babbs called to tell me the doctor was letting Kesey out. At first we thought he was being discharged, but it turned out to be just for the afternoon, so Ken could visit with family and see the farm once more. Toward the end of the second week the news was ominous. When I talked to David at his home in upstate New York on Thursday, November 8, he had already booked a flight to Eugene for the next day.

On Saturday morning I called David's wife Therese, who told me Ken had died in the hospital around 4:30 a.m., when family and friends, sitting in a nearby room, had dozed off.

I immediately called Ken's wife, Faye—was it all right to come? Arriving in Eugene at 8:50 p.m. that same day, I was met by Faye and David. Faye rode with me as David guided me to my motel in Eugene. In her quiet voice, she told me that the hospital had taken extremely good care of Ken. She and David came into my room with me and stayed for a brief chat, a very courteous gesture on that fateful day.

The next morning, I drove out to the farm and walked around the grounds. I looked into the bus barn, and there stood the huge International Harvester Further, in which Ken had driven me to the airport in 1996. In the field behind the house, I saw the low-slung hay wagon, the one I had fallen off. I walked around and got up on it just to relive that incident, to see how far I had really fallen. It wasn't far. The story had profited from the distance halo: The farther away in time or geographical distance, the more a story is likely to grow.

The strength and size of the Kesey family soon became apparent. Shortly after noon, family members and neighbors started coming by, bringing a great variety of food. A buffet lunch continued through the afternoon, served and managed by the women. Faye and Ken's daugh-

ter, Shannon Smith; her husband, Jay, and his parents, Elaine and Irby;
Ken's son, Zane, and his wife, Stephanie; his daughter Sunshine and her
mother, Mountain Girl; his mother Geneva and her husband, Ed Jolley;
his brother Chuck, his wife, Sue; their son, Kit, and daughter, Sheryl,
and her husband, Bill; and many others were there, as were Ken and
Eileen Babbs. There was a wonderful feeling of warmth and goodwill.

There were no tears, no sad faces. I think it was the way Ken would
have wanted it: a quiet celebration of his life.

On Tuesday, I drove out with a group of friends and relatives to
Chuck and Sue Kesey's Springfield Creamery, near the airport. (The
same creamery was saved financially years ago by the Grateful Dead.)
George Braddock, a family friend, had constructed a beautiful white
wooden coffin. Outside there was a large stainless-steel vat filled with
water, into which Ken's son, Zane, poured many colors of oil paint.
Together we carefully dipped the coffin into the vat. The whole pro-
ceeding had a feeling of ritual solemnity despite the customary Prankster bonhomie. The coffin and its lid emerged psychedelically marbled
with beautiful pastel colors.

The next day the Kesey women started cutting and sewing together
colorful lengths of silk Ken had bought in China to make the lining
for the casket.

The service was held Wednesday, November 14. That Monday and
Tuesday had been what Oregonians regarded as typical winter days,
overcast and gloomy, with intermittent rain. Wednesday started the
same way, but midway through the morning, the sun broke through. By
noon, when the service was scheduled to begin, the McDonald Theatre
in downtown Eugene was tightly packed. A former movie house where
Ken had appeared on stage in the early days, it seats 750 people. Sunday
night Ken Babbs had a dream in which Kesey appeared and said, "What
do you mean the McDonald can't accommodate the crowd? Put loud-
speakers in the street!" And that's what they did, to accommodate a total
attendance of 1,000 persons, as reported by the newspapers the next day.

The family had planned the ceremony carefully. David Stanford
had designed the program and printed it the night before. Earlier
that week, when David asked me if I wanted to speak at the service,
I had declined. Overwhelmed by the dignity and strong presence of

the Kesey family, I thought I might be intruding. But David knew the scene and the family. He convinced me that my being part of the service was the right thing to do.

I called my remarks "The Writer and the Man." I was thinking of the phone call I had made on Sunday morning to my daughter, Rebecca, who was living in St. Petersburg, Florida. She had first met Ken when she was five years old, had seen him again when she was twelve; then about ten years before he died, she was with me when I saw Ken in Toronto. She had just heard of Ken's death an hour before I called, and was very sad.

"Dad," she said over the phone, "whenever I was with Ken Kesey, I felt safe and loved. It was as if his heart was reaching out to touch my heart." Earlier in the week at the farm I had told that story to one of the Kesey men and his response was "But isn't that the way we all felt!" So that's the way I concluded my speech.

At the end of the service, the eight pallbearers climbed onstage, shouldered the multicolored coffin, and carried it through the crowd out onto Willamette Street, where Further was parked, and loaded it onto the rear platform of the bus. Kesey fans crowded around the bus before it chugged off on its way to the farm.

Ken had wanted to be buried on a low rise that offered a beautiful long view down the valley in either direction. The spot he chose was beside the grave of his son Jed, who had died in 1984 when the University of Oregon wrestling team's bus went over a cliff en route to a match.

The day after Ken's death, his family and friends had started digging the grave. It wasn't until I was down in the hole, shovel in my hand, that I realized what an extraordinary thing this was: that Ken's remains would stay, hopefully forever, on the land he loved, next to his son, in a grave dug by family and extended family. A member of the family told me that Ken had wanted to ensure that the land would stay in the family forever. Since that was not possible legally, this was the next-best move.

By Tuesday, a white tent large enough to cover the grave as well as fifty or sixty folding chairs was in place. That was the destination of Further, which carried the coffin there the following day. The burial service was for family only, but by the time I reached the farm in my rental car, the hayfield in front of the home was crowded with cars, and the driveway was full. The Kesey women and family friends were serving a buffet lunch in the living room/kitchen. Soon, people started wandering out to the gravesite, where Ken's casket was on a metal support base at the head of the grave. Later, as the sun was setting and everyone was under the tent, there was an informal service. Half a dozen people spoke, and then we filed past the open coffin to see Ken one last time in his purplish red beret.

Once the casket was lowered into the ground, many of the men, women, and children took turns shoveling dirt into the grave, covering the coffin, while others filed by to pay their respects to Faye. David and I participated in the shoveling. By the time darkness began to fall, the grave was completely filled, and Ken had been laid to rest. The headstone bearing the engraved words "Sparks Fly Upward" was yet to be put in place, but the sparks were surely already flying.

A year later, I returned to Eugene for the unveiling of a life-size bronze statue by Eugene sculptor Pete Helzer. It now stands in the very center of Eugene, just a block away from the McDonald Theatre. Ken is sitting on one end of a bench (a marble slab), reading a book to three children sitting at the other end—his grandchildren, Kate, Caleb, and Jordan. Between them and Kesey is an open space where anyone who wants to be part of the group can come and sit.

# CHAPTER 14

# A Writer's Triple Crown

Bill Nack is probably the only writer in the history of American book publishing to have one book—albeit an extremely good book—published by three unrelated companies during his lifetime. But then there was only one Secretariat, and probably no other figure in any sport who was both as dominant and well known, and Bill was far and away the best writer to tell the story of the fastest thoroughbred horse in modern history.

Bill had been involved with horses and literature almost all his life.

By the time I met him in 1973 in the clubhouse at Belmont Park, the legendary track in New York, Secretariat had already won the first two races in the Triple Crown. I had been invited to Belmont by my friend and client, Mike McGrady, the well-known columnist and reporter for *Newsday*, who brought along his friend, a fellow *Newsday* writer. As we met, Mike said, "Bill, I'd like you to meet your future agent, Sterling Lord. He's the best there is."

That was the innocent beginning of a long and fruitful relationship.

Before he wrote about horse racing, Bill had been a political and environmental reporter, writing stories about Long Island duck sludge and the effects of untreated wastewater on the Blue Point oyster. That all changed when he exhibited his encyclopedic knowledge of race-horses at a raucous end-of-the-year *Newsday* party in December 1971. "Egged" on by his eggnog-fueled coworkers, he climbed up on a desk and recited the names of all the horses who had won the Kentucky Derby from 1875 to the present—all ninety-seven of them, or as he put it, "from Aristides, the little chestnut who won the inaugural running, right through to Cannonero II, the big bay from Caracas who had won it just seven months before." When Bill stepped down, to loud applause, he was approached by editor in chief David Laventhol, a closet horseplayer, who asked if he wanted to cover horse racing for the paper. Laventhol's only condition was that the reporter write him a letter applying for the job and telling him why he wanted it. Laventhol planned to post it to head off questions from the staff as to why Bill was making such a dramatic change in his career at *Newsday*. Bill remembers only one sentence of that letter: "After covering politicians for the last four years, I'd love the chance to cover the whole horse."

Bill's prodigious memory served him well. As a youngster in Chicago, he discovered it didn't take him long to memorize any writing he liked. He memorized works by Tennyson, Robert Frost, Yeats, and Nabokov, among others. One summer, as a college student selling hot dogs out of a small van between the first and eighteenth tees of a golf course in Wheeling, Illinois, and reading *The Great Gatsby*, he was so enchanted by the language that he memorized whole parts of the book, and for many years recited the entire first page in English and Spanish.

Bill's interest in thoroughbred racing started early. As a boy he accompanied his father, a $2 bettor, to the track, and soon became fascinated by the thoroughbred world, later working as a hot walker and a groom. And he began memorizing the Kentucky Derby winners.

Despite his early immersion in the thoroughbred-racing world, Bill had never imagined himself—even after a period as sportswriter at the University of Illinois paper, *Daily Illini*—as a turf writer.

Bill's timing and location were impeccable. *Newsday*'s editorial offices in Garden City, New York, are not far from Belmont Park. Bill became the paper's turf writer in 1972, a few weeks after Secretariat left his Virginia birthplace at Meadow Farms to arrive at the Meadow Stable at Belmont Park.

Meadow Stable owned Riva Ridge, the three-year-old 1972 Kentucky Derby winner, a horse Bill was following. On June 5, just a few days before the Belmont Stakes, Bill was hanging around barn 5, checking on Riva, when Jimmy Gaffney, an exercise rider told him, "Come with me for a minute. I want to show you something."

The two men marched up to stall 7, passing Riva Ridge along the way. Jimmy swept a hand grandly toward the stall and said, "Take a look at this two-year-old colt. What do ya think?"

As Bill described it, the colt inside stall 7 "was a beauty, a bright golden chestnut with three white feet, a white star on his forehead, and a thin white blaze that began at the star and traced down almost to his nose." Bill remembers saying to Jimmy, "He's gorgeous. Looks like a show horse. Can he run?"

Jimmy grinned mischievously. "Someday this colt will make 'em all forget Riva Ridge."

That horse was Secretariat.

When Jimmy told him, "He's by Bold Ruler out of Somethingroyal," that was all Bill had to hear. A student of thoroughbred pedigrees, he understood Secretariat was carrying the bluest blood imaginable in a racehorse. Bold Ruler was America's leading sire, an extremely fast racehorse himself, who was producing some of the fastest animals on the American turf. Somethingroyal was a magnificent broodmare who had already produced multiple stakes winners, including the best horse of his generation, Sir Gaylord, who broke down on the eve of the Kentucky Derby that he had been favored to win. Somethingroyal was a daughter of the great sire Princequillo, a source of great stamina in his offspring. So Secretariat had abundant speed in his pedigree, from Bold Ruler, and abundant stamina in his Somethingroyal/Princequillo blood.

"Keep an eye out for this colt," said Jimmy. "I gallop him every day and he can run. He'll be making his first start any time now."

From that point on, Bill followed Secretariat.

If it hadn't been for Bill's friendship with my client Mike McGrady, the perfect pairing of gifted writer and phenomenal thoroughbred might not have occurred. Bill considered Mike his mentor and the families of the two journalists were close. And Mike believed Bill should become an author.

Mike McGrady was no ordinary journalist. He was a featured columnist at the then-prosperous Long Island newspaper and a man with interesting ideas. He created the book *Naked Came the Stranger*, a sensational bestseller about a married woman seeking revenge on her cheating husband by having a parade of affairs, written by twenty-four journalists (nineteen male and five female) but published under one female pseudonym. He also wrote *The Kitchen Sink Papers*, his personal story of what happened when he and his wife Corinne traded places: He stayed home and took care of their children while she went to work at her own company, a designer and manufacturer of plastic objects. The simple stand-up plastic cookbook holder was one of her ideas. He had by that time left *Newsday*, and their new life was beginning to take form. And while a househusband is a common enough occurrence in the twenty-first century, when Mike wrote the book in 1975, he was moving into uncharted domesticity.

For some time, Mike had been urging Bill to write a book, although neither had a subject in mind. But one day in 1973, after Secretariat had made his first start of the year and won the Bay Shore Stakes, Mike asked about "that horse Secretariat you have been writing about." Bill told him the horse could win the Triple Crown, and then said, "I have enough notebooks filled with stuff on Secretariat to write a book."

Mike blurted out what was obvious only in retrospect: "That's it. Secretariat is your book."

Without wasting time, two weeks later, Mike introduced his friend to Arthur Fields, the editor-publisher at E. P. Dutton. The publisher had never heard of Secretariat, nor did he know about the Triple Crown, but he perked up when Bill told him that Secretariat had just been syndicated for $6,080,000 as a breeding stallion, and that men with aristocratic names like Paul Mellon and Alfred Gwynne Vanderbilt had forked over $190,000 for a single breeding share in the horse, allowing them the right to breed one mare a year to him for as long as he was a stud horse. The involvement of such rich and powerful men hooked Arthur. At the end of their talk, Arthur said, "All right. If this horse wins the Triple Crown, I'll publish your book."

On June 9, 1973, Secretariat won the Belmont Stakes and set a world record. Secretariat followed that with another triple win, appearing on the cover of *Time*, *Newsweek*, and *Sports Illustrated*—all on June 11, 1973. The editor called Bill and admitted laughingly, "Six weeks ago, you came into my office talking about a horse I'd never heard of and about a Triple Crown I knew nothing about. Now that horse is the talk of the nation!"

Arthur Fields was an excellent, experienced, hands-on editor who had his own line of books—his own imprint—at the well-known publisher E. P. Dutton, a company I had known since my childhood as the publisher of A. A. Milne's *Winnie the Pooh*. Arthur immediately phoned me seeking to put Bill Nack under contract. It was signed on June 18, 1973, and it couldn't have been a better match.

Arthur lived and worked in a wheelchair. A foot soldier in the Army, he had been shot in the back on the day before World War II ended. An aggressive editor and publisher, Arthur stayed in close touch with Bill throughout his writing the Secretariat book. Bill worked twelve hours a day, seven days a week, for weeks on end, writing or reporting. This was his first book, and he was nervous about his own ability to do it. He would write the first draft on a typewriter, take it home, and edit it in pencil, dictating it over the phone to Virginia Chepak, the professional typist at *Newsday*, who would return the typed manuscript to Bill the next day. That was it until it went to Arthur Fields's working editor at Dutton, the novelist Laurie Colwin, a fine editor. Bill gained twenty-five pounds during the writing, which he lost soon after returning to his usual reporting pace.

One day, as she realized he was working long hours and excessively hard, Bill's wife Mary called Arthur without Bill's knowledge and told him she was concerned that her husband was working so hard that he might damage his health. Despite a tight deadline Arthur called Bill immediately and suggested he take a week off. Bill resisted, but Arthur would not back down. After his week off, Bill worked even harder: "The end was far ahead of me but by then I knew exactly where I was going and how I was going to get there." The last five months of writing the book went faster and faster, Bill would write "like I was skiing down a long hill, and five months after that break, with a few last-minute reporting interruptions along the way, I was finally at the bottom of the slope." When Bill was in the final stages of the manuscript, Arthur assured him he would never have to go back to a salaried job; Arthur had enough good book ideas to keep Bill busy for years.

But he never had a chance to tell Bill what they were. While reading Bill's final manuscript, Arthur collapsed and died. He was forty-eight years old.

Secretariat started the Triple Crown in 1973, of course, by winning the Kentucky Derby. He broke last, but soon pulled ahead of Sham, whom he beat by 2½ lengths in 1:59:40, a record that still stands in 2011.

Two weeks later, in the Preakness Stakes, he broke last, but beat Sham again by 2½ lengths with a record time of 1:54:40, a record that lasted until 1991.

One of the most exciting and memorable sections of the book is Bill's account of Secretariat's winning of the Belmont Stakes, the third race of the Triple Crown—by 31 lengths, an unheard-of margin in a major thoroughbred race.

Secretariat had just tied the world record for nine furlongs. He is running now as if in contempt of the clock. Those watching him are only beginning to fathom the magnitude of the effort. He is moving beyond the standard by which the running horse has been traditionally judged, not tiring, not leg weary, not backing up a stroke, dimensionless in scope, and all the time [Ron] Turcotte [the jockey] asking nothing of him. The crowds continue to erupt. Looking, Turcotte sees the hands shoot up in the grandstand, the thousands on their feet, hundreds lining the rail of the homestretch with the programs waving and the hands clapping and the legs jumping.

He is still galloping to the beat of twelve. Aglide, he turns for home in full flight. He opens twenty-one lengths. He increases that to twenty-two. He is running easily. Nor is the form deteriorating. There remains the pendulumlike stride of the forelegs and the drive of the hindlegs, the pumping of the shoulders and the neck, the rise and dip of the head. He makes sense of all the mystical pageant rites of blood through which he has evolved as distillate, a climactic act in a triumph of the breed, one horse combining all the noblest qualities of his species and ancestry.

He sweeps into the stretch through a tenth furlong in $0:12^4/_5$, the slowest eighth yet, and Turcotte is still holding him together—his black boots pressed against the upper back, moving with the rocky motion of the legs, his hands feeling the mane blown back against the fingers and the knuckles pressed white against the rubber-thick reins. The teletimer flashes 1:59 for the mile and a quarter, two-fifths faster than his Derby, faster than the Belmont ten-furlong record by a full second.

He is twenty-three lengths in front. He lengthens that to twenty-four. And then to twenty-five, the record victory margin held by Count Fleet since 1943.

He is not backing up yet.

Once again he picks up the tempo in the upper stretch, racing the eleventh furlong in $0:12^1/_5$, as fast as he has run the opening 220 yards of the race. That furlong gives him a mile and three-eighths in $2:11^1/_5$, three seconds faster than Man o' War's world record set in the Belmont Stakes fifty-three years before. Obliterating Count Fleet's record, Secretariat opens twenty-six lengths. He widens that to twenty-seven and twenty-eight. He comes to the eighth pole in midstretch, and the whole of Belmont Park is roaring full-throatedly. The television camera sweeps the stands and hands are shooting in the air. No one can remember anything quite like it, not even the oldest veteran. No one applauds during the running of a race, but now the crowds in the box seats and grandstand are standing as one and clapping as Secretariat races alone through the homestretch. They've come to see a coronation, America's ninth Triple Crown winner, but many are beginning to realize they are witnessing the greatest single performance in the history of the sport. Veteran horsemen are incredulous. Eyes have turned to and from the teletimer and the horse in disbelief, looking for some signs of stress and seeing nothing but the methodical rock of the form and the reach and the snap of the forelegs. For a moment in midstretch, as the sounds envelop him, even Turcotte is caught off guard by the scope of the accomplishment. Passing the eighth pole, he looks to the left at the infield tote and the teletimer, and the first number he sees is 1:09$^4$/$_5$ for the first three-quarters. He sees these numbers but they fail to register. So he looks ahead again. Then they register and he looks back again, in a delayed double take.

By now he has passed the sixteenth pole, with only seventy-five yards to run, and the crowd senses the record, too. Turcotte looks at the teletimer blinking excitedly and sees 2:19, 2:20. The record is 2:26$^3$/$_5$. The colt has a chance to break the record in all three classics—an unprecedented feat. So, keeping his whip uncocked, Turcotte pumps his arm and hand-rides Secretariat through the final yards. Sham fades back to last, and Twice a Prince and My Gallant are head and head battling for the place—Cordero and Baeza are riding all out to the wire—but Secretariat continues widening on them.

To twenty-nine lengths.

Turcotte scrubs and pushes on Secretariat and he lengthens the margin to thirty lengths. The wire looms. The teletimer flashes crazily. All eyes are on it and on the horse. Many horsemen have seen Turcotte looking at the timer and now they're looking at it, too. He is racing the clock, his only competitor, and he is beating it badly as he rushes the red horse through the final yards. At the end, the colt dives for the wire. The teletimer blinks the last time and then it stops, as though it had been caught in midair—2:24.

*Big Red of Meadow Stable* was published in 1975, but Arthur's death had been costly. With him gone, no one had the same commitment, emotional involvement, and enthusiasm. The hardcover sales were under 12,000 copies. That little extra push that made the sales, promotion, and rights people take the extra step that means sales, was lacking. This is a phenomenon that happens in publishing almost every time a book's sponsor—editor or publisher—dies, leaves, or is fired before the book is published.

Once *Big Red* was out of print, we retrieved all rights from Dutton and sold the same book to Da Capo Press, a small, respected house in Boston, giving them the right to use "Secretariat" in the title. Bill signed the contract with them in 1987, when they first published it. They later republished it in 2002 with a new introduction. That contract expired in 2009, and I then sold the publishing rights to Hyperion Books: same book with a new preface and the potential for a new life. I went to Hyperion because, in the meantime, we had sold film rights to *Secretariat* to Disney, and I knew the book would benefit most by being published by a Disney-owned company, which Hyperion was.

In the fall of 2005, Bill had received a call out of the blue from Disney screenwriter Mike Rich, who told Bill his 1990 *Sports Illustrated* story, "Pure Heart," about the life and death of Secretariat, was Rich's favorite *Sports Illustrated* story and he wanted to turn it into a movie. He had written the screenplay of the movie *Miracle*, about the US hockey team that beat the Soviet Union in the 1980 Olympics, and another successful sports movie called *The Rookie*, about a baseball player. Years before that, he had broken into screenwriting when he wrote the original screenplay of the movie *Finding Forrester*, starring Sean Connery. He wanted to interview Bill and then present the idea of a movie about Secretariat to Disney executive Dick Cook. Mike told Bill there was enough there, in "Pure Heart," to make it a good movie. He was confident that the Disney executive, a fan of Secretariat's, would agree.

A few months later, Bill received an e-mail from Mike saying Dick wanted to go ahead with the project but with one significant difference: He wanted a heroine, not a hero—which would have been Bill. Bill immediately gave Mike his blessing. He had never been quite sure he wanted his life told on the big screen. And he believed the story of Penny Chenery Tweedy—the woman who succeeded her father in running Meadow Farm, where Secretariat was raised, and left her family in Denver to return to Virginia to take over—would work. And that led to basing the film on the book, rather than the magazine article. Disney still wanted Bill involved as a consultant, so he called Jody Hotchkiss, who works with me on film rights, who sold Disney the rights to Bill's biography, *Secretariat*, and made him a consultant on the film.

When the movie was released in the US on October 10, 2010, it was the third-highest-grossing film in the US. With the success of the movie, Bill's book finally reached the level of acceptance that both he and I thought it deserved. By the spring of 2011, Hyperion had sold more than 135,000 copies, and it had been on the *New York Times* bestseller list for nine weeks.

Each year, the racing industry honors its thoroughbred champions, including the Horse of the Year, by conferring upon them Eclipse Awards, so named in honor of Eclipse, a British racing and breeding sensation of the eighteenth century. The industry also confers Eclipse Awards upon the nation's outstanding jockey, owner, trainer, breeder, and journalists. Bill has won the Eclipse Award seven times, more than any other individual except Jerry Bailey, the superb jockey, now retired. He has also been given the A. J. Liebling Award for excellence in boxing writing by the Boxing Writers Association of America and the Alfred G. Vanderbilt Award for lifetime achievement in racing by Thoroughbred Charities of America. Bill has appeared numerous times in *The Best American Sports Writing* annual anthologies and his story "Pure Heart" was picked by David Halberstam for inclusion in his anthology, *The Best American Sports Writing of the Century.*

In 2010, Bill was inducted into the inaugural class of the Turf Writers' Hall of Fame.

Despite his success at the track, Bill's interest and talents are not limited to thoroughbred racing. As his longtime friend Roger Ebert has written, Bill "was and is a great American prose stylist . . . At a reading for his book *My Turf*, about the death of Secretariat, he made a woman cry. Then he read another story, about a filly breaking down and being destroyed on the track, and there wasn't a dry eye in the house."

Few people know Bill and his talent with words better than his movie-critic friend Roger. The two have been close friends since 1962, when they worked together on the *Daily Illini*, and Bill succeeded Roger as top editor. But over the years Bill and Roger have talked together, read books together, argued politics together, and in recent years, even vacationed together with their wives, though it took some convincing for Roger to persuade his friend who thought "he didn't need no stinking spa."

Ebert convinced the spa, Rancho La Puerta in Tecate, Mexico, to schedule an evening titled "A Concert in Words, with William Nack." Ebert says it was a somewhat dicey proposition: "That's exactly what you want at 8 p.m. after you took the morning mountain walk and busted your ass in the gym all day, right? Some guy standing up there readin' po-ems."

Bill recited from memory for an hour. Ebert reports, "The campers demanded an encore. He recited for another thirty minutes. Then he got a standing ovation, and they marched on the concierge to demand a second performance. He read the next afternoon for another hour."

It was the remarkable Secretariat's good fortune to be matched with a writer as poetic as Bill Nack.

When Secretariat's racing days were over in 1973, he was flown back to Kentucky in preparation for his retirement duties. It was November 12, and as the plane carrying Secretariat and Bill descended toward the Blue Grass Airport at Lexington, a voice from the control tower came in over the plane's radio: "There's more people out here to meet Secretariat than there was to greet the governor." Pilot Dan Neff responded quickly, "Well, he's won more races than the governor."

Sixteen years later, Secretariat came down with laminitis, a life-threatening hoof disease. On October 4, 1989, the decision was made to put him down, and a concentrated barbiturate was injected into his jugular vein. He was gone in forty-five seconds. A little later that day, a professor of veterinary science at the University of Kentucky prepared the autopsy. All the horse's vital organs were normal in size, except the heart, which was almost twice the size of an average horse's heart. As the doctor revealed, "I think it told us why he was able to do what he did."

In my world, to beat the magnificent Man o' War's fifty-three-year-old record (he won Belmont in 2:14:20 in 1919, but it was only a $1^{3}/_{8}$-mile race then, not 1½ miles), was the equivalent of beating Roger Federer or Rafael Nadal 6–0, 6–0, 6–0.

As Ebert said in his review of the film *Secretariat*, "I remember Bill telling me in the 1970s about a racehorse he admired with great passion. I thought it was curious that Nack, who could recite long passages from

Fitzgerald and Eliot by heart, had been lured away from literature by a racehorse. Now I understand. He found literature in a racehorse."

Photo by Jon Wise

Bill Nack received a set of four horseshoes, two of which you see above, from Secretariat's exercise rider, Jimmy Gaffney, in June 1973, shortly after Secretariat won the Triple Crown on June 9. As Bill says, "Jimmy collected many sets of Secretariat's racing plates, as they are called, because he used to hold the colt's lead shank while the farrier removed the old shoes and put on the new. Someone had to be there to hold the colt while the farrier worked on his feet. Jimmy told me that he took those shoes off Secretariat after he won the Bay Shore Stakes in them on March 17, 1973. This was his first race as a three-year-old on his way to the Triple Crown. He won the Bay Shore in the mud at Aqueduct. When Jimmy gave me the shoes, they still had the mud in them that he had picked up on the racetrack. I did not polish the shoes, as many shoe collectors do, and I did not remove the mud caked in the grooves of the shoe. I wanted to keep the shoes as real as possible." One shoe is a back shoe and the other a front shoe. Since the movie *Secretariat* came out, Bill has been told two shoes could easily bring $25,000, but he would never sell them. He treasures them. Jimmy gave them to Bill as a gift, and with them he also gave Bill a signed paper declaring their authenticity. A few years later, Bill happened to see Secretariat's farrier at Belmont Park, and told him he had four of the colt's shoes. Bill told him they had little felt pads on their tips. The farrier smiled. "Those are Secretariat's," he said. The colt struck the ground very hard and he had put the felt there to act as cushions.

## CHAPTER 15

# Changing with the Times

When I was thirty-three years old and my agency was two, I had my first potential major film project, the autobiography of fighter/actor Rocky Graziano, which had been written by my client Rowland Barber and was to be published by Simon and Schuster. This was in 1954 and I had had no prior experience at any level with the movie business. Publishing friends, including one of the editors at Simon and Schuster, told me I should enlist the help of an experienced co-agent in Beverly Hills. They recommended H. N. Swanson. Swanie—everyone called him that—was the very best at selling books and magazine stories to film as well as selling screenplays. His client list included F. Scott Fitzgerald, Raymond Chandler, Pearl Buck, and William Faulkner. And while Rocky Graziano didn't fit on the same shelf with such literary giants, his was an up-from-the-gutter-to-respectability-and-personal-triumph story that offered a dramatic role for a good male actor.

Knowing that Swanie's client roster gave him instant access to any studio or producer in Hollywood, I went with him—splitting the 10 percent agent's fee fifty-fifty.

Even before he phoned to talk strategy, Swanie, who was twenty years my senior, did an excellent job of spreading the word and messengering galleys to interested studios.

A few weeks later, in one remarkable phone call, he told me there were ten studios or producers ready to bid.

The film sale of almost any nonfiction book requires releases from all subjects to be depicted in the film except for public figures. That was particularly true in Rocky's case since so many of his interactions were with identifiable people. So even though we did not have to pay for any of the twenty-three releases, because everyone welcomed their being depicted and identified in a feature film, Swanie suggested we put an odd price on the book, which would imply we had paid. He suggested $195,000. "Swanie," I said, "I agree with your approach to the price, but not with your figure. It's too low."

I don't know where I summoned the nerve to outdo the king of the industry, but I said, "I think we can get $230,000, and that's what I want to ask."

A few days later, within an hour of receiving the telegram with Swanie's and my price demand, Metro-Goldwyn-Mayer agreed to pay $230,000.

It became an MGM vehicle that launched the talented young actor Paul Newman, who played Rocky.

I took no particular joy in topping Swanie, but I derived great pleasure in collecting another $35,000 for my clients. What prompted me to price it at $230,000? I believed in my clients, their book, *Somebody Up There Likes Me,* and in myself. Maybe at that age I appeared brash, but mostly I trusted my instincts, sensing we could make a better deal. I would not be intimidated by Swanie or millionaire Hollywood producers.

That taught me no one is infallible, not top dogs, heads of companies, or respected experts. The business of the arts, I was discovering, was full of and often based on subjective decisions and personal enthusiasm. Knowing that allowed me to exploit situations, take strong stances in negotiations, and demand better deals for my clients.

Months later, when I finally met Swanie for lunch in Beverly Hills, I was struck by his presence. He had the patina of a prominent Hollywood figure and that taught me something, too: how someone presented himself—his clothes, his demeanor, his manner—was part of the marketing and selling of the story.

Swanie seemed to be all business with me, leaving the charm for others. He came from a smaller town in Iowa than I did, and had graduated from Grinnell College, as I had, yet he wasn't interested in talking about either. That was fine with me because I was keen to learn more about the film business.

Except for *Fear Strikes Out*, the Jimmy Piersall story, written by Al Hirshberg, I didn't use Swanie after that—I was attracted to agents who also represented directors, screenwriters, or even producers, so they could present a complete or semi-complete package to the studios—but often during weekdays I would return to my office in New York after lunch to find that Swanie had called. The first two times that happened, I returned his calls but never reached him, nor did he return my return calls. Swanie had a reputation for being so tight with money, it was rumored he locked all the office phones every night when he left. Since he always called me person-to-person, his calls to me cost him nothing, and yet they served a purpose. They were his way of reminding me he would like to do more with me.

The Swanie/Graziano episode would set the pattern for my growth in the business. There are no schools for becoming an agent, or at least there were none then. I would learn through experience and observation.

My love of story and books was instilled in me as a child. My father had learned bookbinding long before I was born, and bookcases of leather-bound books with gold inlay covered one entire wall in our living room. When I was fourteen, Dad taught me to bind a book myself. All the bookbinding equipment was stored on the Ping-Pong table. Both my parents were interested in books, and we (my two younger brothers and I) were read to in the evenings. As I started to read some of the books Dad had bound, and thumbed through the gilt-edged pages, and heard my father talk about binding a book, it elevated the book in my mind. All that bookbinding and gold inlay made the book more elegant, more valuable, and more important as an object. It also emphasized the value my father and mother placed on the written word.

I was interested in more than just reading, and I started writing—primarily journalism—in grade school and continued through college.

As the local high-school stringer for the *Des Moines Register* sports department, I began to develop a good story sense early on. By the time I graduated college, I had met half a dozen well-established journalists through my father and friends, and I began to think I wanted to be one of them. As I grew, I began to realize there were countless men and women journalists and other nonfiction writers who wrote better than I did. Without planning it or thinking about it, I believe, I moved into agency work because it enabled me to work with these dramatically better-than-I writers. It also came to me that my chances of earning a living were better in the agency.

During my early years in New York, I was not in constant touch with my parents or my hometown, but in the beginning of my career, when faced with certain kinds of problems, I would ask myself how they would handle them in Burlington. I never wished I was back home, but I never forgot where I came from or, as a result, who I was and where I was going.

Most of my agency schooling was on the job, from more experienced agents, editors, or producers than I, but also from people in my own company. As mentioned earlier, Cindy Degener and Patricia Berens both had rich work experience before joining my agency, and both helped educate me. You can't necessarily make real growth work if you hire primarily or exclusively on that basis, but if you hire someone with extra experience who is willing to pass along his or her knowledge, it can be better than having a PhD yourself.

I picked up helpful ideas wherever I found them. For instance, I gleaned a useful observation from Jerome Hellman, an excellent agent when I met him who wanted me to join his agency, and who later became a feature film producer and director, with the movies *Midnight Cowboy, Coming Home, Promises in the Dark*, and *The Mosquito Coast* to his credit. He told me the most important part of a business meeting often occurs after it's over. When it's breaking up, and you are gathering your papers, often the person you have been interviewing will drop his or her guard, revealing what's really on his or her mind.

I learned the importance of remaining silent from Harold Matson, the agent in American publishing I most admired. Harold, who worked until the age of eighty-nine, was a superb negotiator for such heavyweight clients as Evelyn Waugh, C. S. Forester, Flannery O'Connor, Arthur Koestler, and Malcolm Lowry. A former employee of his told me how he was able to coax a movie producer to double his offer for a book he was representing simply by remaining silent after the producer made his initial offer: In the pin-drop silence that followed, the movie producer doubled his original offer of $100,000.

Over the decades, I think it's fair to say, I earned a reputation for having a group of bestselling authors and for being an astute negotiator.

During a conversation about tennis over lunch with my client Mike Murphy, one of the founders of Esalen and author of *Golf in the Kingdom* (in print since 1972), Murphy saw a direct relationship between my competitive spirit in my agency work and my over eight decades on the tennis court. "As you were telling those stories," he said to me, "I could see that your dealing with the great variety of experience both on the court and off prepared you well for the great variety of deals and situations you pull off in your agency." He was referring to deals like the one I secured for Jack Kerouac to read from *On the Road* at a Village nightspot (unusual in those days), or the commercial Jimmy Breslin did for Piels Beer despite the strong objection of Jim Bellows, his editor at the *New York Herald Tribune*. And then there was the two-author textbook contract that kept one author from knowing the other author's advance; that contract also delayed the repayment of the advance from the flow of royalties to each author, so that they could count on royalty income for a number of years.

Beyond this kind of preparation, I attribute part of my success to doing my homework. Before negotiating with a publisher, I would try to learn what was important to the person I was hoping to persuade to buy—what were his or her interests and concerns at the moment? Ironically, the most dramatic example in my career had nothing to do with books, but with selling a house on Martha's Vineyard. A friend had paid $860,000 for the home and its land six or seven years before and, wanting to move to a smaller and more convenient location, was ready to sell. I volunteered to sell it for her—at no commission. When a broker on the island told me he had a potential buyer, I did some research and found the buyer was not only wealthy, but his forty-nine-year-old wife had vowed she would own a house on the Vineyard— reachable only by boat and plane—before she was fifty. Knowing how much she wanted to become part of the vacation-and-beach colony, I was able to make the sale for $5,000,000, a sum that at the time was so unusual that the sale was known all over the island twenty minutes after the private deal was done.

As for my work at the agency, you could say I was driven or that my work became my life. I hardly noticed—though my wives did—that my work permeated every aspect of my life. I enjoyed representing authors, and as my own boss, I never limited myself to an eight-hour day.

My motivations were simple: I was interested in good ideas and good writing and in learning from the people I dealt with and improving the lives of my authors.

In the course of my agency life, there were those who set personal standards for me, and Bill Haber was one of them. I first met Bill at lunch in New York's Regency Hotel in the early summer of 1977. He had called from California a few days before, asking to meet; having heard of his excellent reputation, I said yes.

Bill was one of the founders of a then-new agency in Beverly Hills called Creative Artists Agency. It was rapidly getting the reputation of being a very hot shop, and Bill was being talked about as the most effective television agent in what we Easterners still called Hollywood. He represented Aaron Spelling (probably the most prolific and successful television producer in the US), among others, which put Bill in the center of a great deal of action and success.

Bill and Aaron wanted very much to get involved with a book I was about to offer for a major television series, Doris Kearns Goodwin's *The Fitzgeralds and the Kennedys*. I was envisioning a deal of twelve one-hour installments, which was at the top of the market in those days. I had, at that point in my career, reached a certain plateau, and I was looking for ways to expand.

As I remember it, Bill offered to co-represent the entire package with me—book and producer. When I told him the share I'd want, he

This small marching band had just delivered the check for the first deal I did with Bill Haber, CAA's chief television agent. They are playing "We're in the Money" in my office. This delivery was a complete surprise to me, but it turns out my secretary, who took the photo, had been secretly alerted. It beats regular mail delivery for drama.

gulped, but we kept on talking. Two or three weeks later, CAA had to drop out of that deal due to a conflict of interest. But from the beginning, Bill had been persuading me to use him as a co-agent on other literary projects I represented. In those days, the television networks, stimulated by the enormous success of the eight-part ABC series *Roots*, based on Alex Haley's novel, often bought rights to bestselling commercial fiction, to adapt as miniseries with four or six one-hour episodes. I told Bill I really didn't represent that kind of commercial writer, and that I doubted I had anything that would interest him. Bill never forgot that statement of mine. It became the basis of a personal—unspoken—joke between us.

I did show some books to Bill, and about a month later, we did our first deal together. When I received my first network check from Bill, it arrived unannounced but not unheralded. One morning, as I was busy on the phone, I heard noise—music—in the outer office. It was a four-piece marching band playing, "We're in the Money." The band was in uniform, and our receptionist, who had probably been briefed by

Haber's office, let them march right into my personal office. They presented me with a huge gift basket, and played on as I pored through its contents. In colorful wrapping there were many books about money, scores of fake bills, and one real twenty-dollar bill. At the bottom of the basket was a check for that first sale.

My secretary had secretly brought her camera to work that morning, having been alerted by Bill's secretary. Bill was in show business, after all, and he had staged the entire performance very carefully. I hadn't quite recovered from that initial show when, about six months later, Bill staged another one, choreographed around the second check from CAA. This time a string quartet, dressed in tuxedos, gained entrance to our lobby. (We had moved in the meantime to offices with a large lobby.) We occupied the entire twenty-second floor, so there was no question who the concert was for. This quartet brought a similar gift basket. By that time, my agency had grown and some of the new employees, not knowing what was going on, closed their doors to shut out the noise. But the veteran agency members went to the lobby, as delighted and amused as I was. It was Bill's very subtle way of saying he was right, despite my original claim that I didn't have the kind of literary properties he was looking for.

Bill not only had a dramatic sense of humor, but he was also the most perceptive agent I have worked with on either coast. If he was selling my material and he also represented the purchaser, he knew the terms and the price had to be impeccable. In that area, Bill let me set the prices. It was pretty hard *not* to do business with him.

My relationship with Bill was a professional one that also became personal. I had other relationships that worked the other way around— the personal became professional—and those could also become increasingly exciting and rewarding.

Mike Burke first took me to a Yankees baseball game in the mid-seventies. It was a series the Yankees were playing late in the season against the Kansas City Royals, and it turned out to be a day that was very fortuitous for me. Mike had been president of the New York Yankees, but by 1973 he had moved over to become president of Madison Square Garden. I had season tickets to the Knicks basketball games at the Garden, but my seats were so far above the court that I couldn't see as well as

I wanted to, and they weren't elegant enough to use for business friends I wanted to please. So that day, I had been trying to get the proper office at the Garden to help me transfer to better seats, and if that wasn't possible, I would just dump them. When Mike, whom I had met through my client Willie Morris, editor in chief of *Harper's* magazine, called me out of the blue and asked me if I'd like to go to a Yankees game with him that night, I said yes, of course. Then I explained my Garden situation to him, and he said, "Before you get rid of them, can you give me an hour? I'll call you back." I said yes again. In that hour, I later discovered, he contacted a powerful and high-profile man on Wall Street for whom he had been saving good seats, to see if the man was really able to use them. The answer was no. So when Mike called me back, he was able to give me two seats to the Knicks games—aisle seats in the third row, eight feet from the Knicks bench on one hand and eight feet from Woody Allen on the other. He also extended an invitation to use Suite 200, the executive hospitality suite, any and every evening before games, for dinner or drinks, on the house. It was like a gift from heaven. And, yes, he was picking me up in his sports car to take me to the game that night. We got through the evening okay, and that was the beginning of a closer relationship with Mike, for whom I quickly developed great respect. A few years later, we did a wonderful autobiographical book, *Outrageous Good Fortune*, published in 1984. *Kirkus Reviews* said of it:

> Brains, charm, pizazz: Burke has it all, and he knows it—but he's just modest and vulnerable enough that the reader is still on his side after nearly 500 pages of his "outrageous good fortune." A jack of all trades, Burke has mastered practically all of them: athlete (star offensive and defensive back at Penn), soldier (he parachuted behind Nazi lines and fought with the French Resistance), spy (CIA agent in postwar Europe), showman (general manager of Ringling Brothers Barnum and Bailey Circus), media executive (16 years near the top of CBS), sports mogul (president first of the Yankees, then of Madison Square Garden), friend of the famous from Ernest Hemingway to Reggie Jackson), sexy socialite, bon vivant, and now autobiographer.

Mike Burke and I are trying to keep warm and dry, and the gentleman on the left, with the Rangers umbrella, is standing by in case he can be of help. Our seats that night were right behind the Yankees' dugout, fitting for the former Yankees president. Most of the Yankees recognized Mike and said their warm hellos. Photo by Louis Requena from the Mike Burke Family Collection.

The book brought Mike back in touch with some friends he hadn't seen in a long time and pleased him enormously.

Gordon Parks was another example of a relationship that deeply affected me. Gordon was a remarkable, multitalented man and a pleasure to be with. I think we met sometime in the sixties on a tennis court in Bridgehampton, but in one of our last sessions in Gordon's apartment, neither of us could remember how or when our friendship began.

Gordon Parks is the only writer I have represented who wrote four autobiographies. He also directed feature films (*Shaft* was one), wrote serious music, and was a photographer for *Life* magazine and other publications. His books, though interesting from a historical and biographical point of view, didn't produce much income. Yet when, in the last few years of his life, he asked me to come over to his apartment to give him my opinion of his current work, I went without hesitation. I knew it was not a wise investment of my time, but I admired Gordon and he didn't call on me unless he really needed help. In this instance, he wanted me to help in the physical layout of the pages of his latest book, which combined poetry and photographs. (The work was published in 2005 as *Eyes with Winged Thoughts*.) Gordon had been through many tough times in his life. He was seven-eighths African American and one-eighth Native American, and grew up on a small farm in Kansas. He turned out to be a talented, thoughtful man with a beautiful spirt, which I greatly admired. Of course I would help him when he needed it.

When I arrived at his apartment, where he lived alone, he immediately asked me if I wanted a drink. I declined, but then he suggested tea and went into the kitchen and brought us out two elegant cups, covered with oriental art and containing freshly brewed tea, and that's how the serious work began.

Gordon Parks was the renaissance man of our culture in the twentieth and early twenty-first centuries. The picture above, *Blue Dove*, represents the new photography he was doing in the 1990s and early 2000s. I bought it from him four or five years before his death in 2006. Similar Gordon Parks work was published in his book *Glimpses Toward Infinity* (1996).

Jack Kerouac was a distinctive personality, but much more retiring and less socially comfortable than Gordon Parks. When Jack was forty-three years old—it was 1965—he came into the office unannounced and handed me a piece of lined paper six or seven inches long, on which he had written words that named me as the exclusive executor of his literary estate. We had never discussed his will, and for all I knew, he would live for many more years. I couldn't have known that he would die in 1969.

It was a poignant and emotionally charged moment. In the days following, I kept wondering what had prompted him to prepare that document. It seemed unusual to me that a man seeming to be in his prime was writing his will. I didn't think he expected to die soon. I assumed it was based on something he had read or that some other writer had suggested. But I never asked and never found out. I was surprised that he had thought to establish an executor at his relatively early age and honored that he chose me. Perhaps it was because, while there were many seeking his attention and friendship, he didn't necessarily trust that others would have his best interests in mind after he was gone, and I would.

Other clients rewarded me, often unknowingly, with their friendship.

When Dick Francis, whose work I have described in a previous chapter, arrived in New York City each September, en route from England to his home in Fort Lauderdale, and later Grand Cayman, it was a cause for celebration, including a publisher's dinner, book signings, and a separate and private dinner for me with Dick and his wife, Mary. In addition to the Dick Francis books selling well for Putnam each year, Dick and Mary were attractive and delightful people.

I made a point of visiting him as often as I could, whether it was in the Berkshire Downs, Fort Lauderdale, or Grand Cayman.

In the summer of 1984, while I was meeting with writers and publishers in London, I experienced one of my greatest pleasures as a guest of Dick and Mary. They escorted me to the Royal Ascot Racecourse, where we sat in the Royal Enclosure, the exclusive location designed for the royal family and a few hundred others with proper credentials.

Dick had guided me on what I needed to do to qualify for admission to the Royal Enclosure. I was to start by applying to the American ambassador to the court of St. James for approval. The ambassador's office, in turn, told me I needed a recommendation from a prominent American. Through one helpful friend, I received what I needed from New York Governor Mario Cuomo, who wrote as follows in a letter dated April 20, 1984, addressed to Ms. Evelyn J. Cox in the ambassador's office at the US embassy in London:

I have known Sterling Lord for a long time. He is an extraordinary individual. As head of one of the most distinguished literary agencies in the world, he has been a pioneer in broadening the concept of representation for authors, playwrights, and writers. He has also single-handedly encouraged the careers of unknown writers, and advanced the notion of the intellectual arts throughout the United Sates. He is one of the foremost members of our American literary community.

It was almost embarrassing.

Dick Francis and I are dressed for the races. We are standing in the Royal Enclosure Parking Lot prior to the start of races at Royal Ascot. I am holding a program from the prior day's racing to further identify where we are—in case anyone asked.

In his later years, Dick Francis lived in warm climates year-round, in response to his wife, Mary's, health problems. Here we are sitting about ten feet from the large glass window of his Grand Cayman apartment (to my left) and fifteen feet from the ocean on Dick's right. Behind us is part of the mile-long beach Dick walked every morning—followed by a short ocean dip before breakfast and writing.

I had come a long way from Burlington, Iowa.

The Royal Enclosure at Ascot was a canvas of men in gray and black top hats and what the British call morning coats, and women in floral silk and linen with wide-brim hats that balanced like Frisbees on their heads. The Queen Mother and Princess Diana, I noticed immediately, were the royal family favorites of the crowd. One only had to see the crowd's reaction as they walked around during the intervals: respectful and admiring. No one approached either of them as they walked through the grounds and they did not approach anyone—with one exception: The Queen Mother went up to Dick Francis. They were old friends, and Dick had once been her steeplechase jockey.

One week later, I took Dick and Mary to my turf, Wimbledon, for lunch at the NBC hospitality tent, which was where all the people you wanted to see were gathered. I had access through my friend Patricia Bradshaw, whose late husband had been the head of RCA, which owned NBC. The tennis players Ted Schroeder and Gene Mako were there one year, as well as the great sports agent Mark McCormack, and many newscasters and television executives. On the way to the buffet table we stopped to talk to Lori Budge, wife of the great American tennis champion Don Budge, who, as my client, had written *Budge on Tennis* with Frank Deford. I knew Lori was a Dick Francis fan. Don was not there yet, but twenty minutes later as Mary, Dick, and I were eating at the far side of the tent, Dick noticed Don Budge had arrived, and he asked me if I would take him to meet Don. "Of course," I replied.

I was able to introduce two of my favorite clients to each other. It was a delightful moment for all of us. And while I did not yet know this, another client-to-be was an important part of the story. I later found out that the effusive letter from Governor Cuomo had been written by his staff member Stephen Schlesinger. I admired his writing well enough to ask him to be my client, and he was pleased to accept. He subsequently wrote a fascinating book about the founding of the United Nations called *Act of Creation* (2003).

Although I was immersed in literature and the art of the book, and enjoyed the personal and professional rewards that came with being an agent, I recognized that the literary agency, like other businesses, has its peaks and its valleys. Perseverance helps. While I am better known by the bestsellers I helped launch, I did not always have an easy time convincing publishers of the value of the manuscripts I was selling.

Three times in the sixties, it took me twenty or more submissions to sell a book. David Markson's *The Ballad of Dingus Magee*, as mentioned in Chapter 9 of this book, was one. The other two have asked me not to identify them in this capacity, I'm sorry to say. In each case I believed in the book, so the mound of rejections didn't discourage me. I kept telling myself that I was smarter than many editors. I may not have been smarter, but I had to believe that I was—and I had to really believe in the book—to keep on going. My success in finding a publisher for each of these three books was a cause for rejoicing. Which leads me to another truism for survival: Whether it is a major triumph or a serious disaster, I would take only ten minutes to moan or to celebrate before moving on to the next client or the next deal. And on those very rare days when nothing works, I would spend a few minutes thinking of who in publishing, film, or related business I enjoy talking to, who gives me a lift, then dream up a legitimate question to ask them so it didn't sound like my call was what it really was—therapeutic. If I found the right person and had the right question, it always worked for me.

As time went on and the demands of my clients mounted, I grew old enough to begin to think about my physical and mental self and realized a number of things were important. I decided a balanced life was essential: work hard, exercise regularly, and support a social life that was at least partially non-business-related. I couldn't always achieve and sustain that balance, but it worked when I could and the knowledge of that balance was very sustaining. Later, in the late seventies, I realized that all my primary energy was going toward serving my clients, and I was still not giving myself unadulterated pleasure— not even ten or fifteen minutes a day. I conceived the idea of buying, at the start of every week, a single red rose and putting it in a glass vase on my desk. Such a simple idea! But it worked. More than just being enjoyable to look at, the rose reminded me that there was nothing wrong with devoting energy to my own pleasure.

As I began representing authors in the early fifties, two of my publishing friends told me how important personal health was—you couldn't afford to be sick. Particularly if you were a sole practitioner, you had to be on the job, available to your authors every day. I wasn't too concerned, as I had thought I lived a healthy life and had for years. I exercised—seventy-eight years eventually of competitive tennis— consumed very little alcohol, took no drugs, and hadn't smoked since I was in my thirties (and then I never inhaled). But as I reached my early eighties, some of my parts started to wear out. True, I had been hit by a runaway car, apparently stolen, driven by a man without a license, as I was leaving Madison Square Garden after a New York Knicks game, breaking both bones in my lower right leg. I got to a hospital right away, thanks to the St. Clare's Hospital ambulance service, and the next morning I remember taking a call from Judge Sirica—his book *To Set the Record Straight* was about to be published—as I was lying in bed at the hospital, waiting for the doctor to check me. Two days later, I had a telegram from the well-known tennis commentator Bud Collins, challenging me to a tennis match. (He had obviously already heard about my accident.) Great joke! I'd beaten him convincingly the only time we'd played previously—traveling with the top players of the world does not necessarily make you a really good player. I thought about what my life would be like if I couldn't play tennis again. But I was back at work within two weeks of leaving the hospital, thanks to a car service, crutches, and a wheelchair, and I was playing tennis a few months after that.

But in December 2003, when I went out to play tennis (I had been playing three times a week), I saw the ball double—three months and four ophthalmologist later, I was told I had macular degeneration, an eye disease I had never even heard of. Since then, I have seen a specialist in treating this condition, Dr. Richard Rosen (his uncle was once president of the New York Yankees), twice every six weeks. Macular degeneration—I have the "wet," very serious version—stopped my tennis completely after seventy-eight years of competitive play. I had played with or against, at one time or another, two different world champions: Helen Wills Moody, who had won women's singles at Wimbledon eight times—at the time we played together, it was only four years after she had won her last Wimbledon—and Don Budge, the first player to win all four major tournaments that comprise the Grand Slam of world tennis in the same year.

But my new condition didn't stop my agency work. The first thing I did after learning I had it was buy a very effective reading machine, which focuses a strong light on the book or manuscript and has a simple magnification device to make reading easier. By 2011, I had bought four of them—one for my office, home office, office in Florida, and another when the first machine started failing after ten years of use.

Is the machine as helpful as having 20/20 vision? Not quite, but how many adults who read regularly have 20/20 vision? With the machine I can read almost as easily as before, though my eyes tire sooner. When that happens, I stop and do something else for ten minutes, which gives my eyes renewed energy. I often have an assistant or other staff member do a first reading of a manuscript from a writer I haven't represented before, and in other special cases. I try to be very selective in choosing anyone to pre-read: They have to be very good. I do that a lot more than I used to, but it is very helpful to my work schedule. Also, in my recent years I have been more selective in taking on new clients, though I continue to acquire new writers. My finding is that any agent who doesn't take on new clients is probably on the way out of business.

While there is only so much you can control in your life—business or personal—I was fortunate to have had impeccable business timing. My agency's life coincided with the birth, life, and death of the Golden Age of publishing. For the first time, large sums of money were available. Back in the fifties, almost all publishing houses—Random House, Simon and Schuster, Doubleday, Farrar Straus, Viking, and most smaller houses—were owned and operated by the founders.

When I began, I knew quite a few publishers personally, but I never heard any of them talk profit-and-loss or the bottom line. They always talked about the quality of the books they published or their pride in their authors, many of whom had become their personal friends.

Then came the single-book deals that drew $1,000,000 advances. My first was Erica Jong's *Fanny*, which I sold to Holt (hardcover) and New American Library (mass market) together for $1,200,000 in April 1978.

As of this writing, in 2012, the money is still there for big books, but much of the fun and antics are no longer possible in the twenty-first century, as publishing has come to resemble less the selling of paintings or other creative work and more that of carpets or refrigerators. Books are no longer bought by publishers on the basis of one editor's commitment. The editor and sometimes even the publisher have to check with other editors, advertising, sales, promotion, or a higher authority, or all of the above. It is "committee publishing." In the twenty-first century, I've discovered only two houses that can buy without checking with all the other departments: Knopf and Farrar, Straus. The on-site principal owner of a publishing house has long since been replaced by the executive-for-hire—someone who knows more about business than he or she knows about the quality of a book.

Starting in the last decade of the twentieth century, I felt it was a new and different ball game. Editors were no longer able to make the same leaps of faith on submitted material that they had before: Earlier in the twentieth century, I could secure contracts for certain known authors for nonfiction books on the basis of an eight- or nine-page summary or outline. Now, it has to be thirty or forty pages from the same writer for me to get him or her a $300,000 or $400,000 advance. Often editors are more interested in promotability than content. In 2002, I called an eager young woman editor at Simon and Schuster to describe a book I wanted to sell her. Before I could finish describing it, she interrupted: "What's the platform?" which translates into *Is the author a well-known television or film personality or a well-known public speaker, or otherwise nationally known?* Naturally, I didn't bother to send the proposal to her. In addition, there is a lack of flexibility in negotiating the terms of a contract: Sometimes, since we are dealing with creative people, a slight difference in time of delivery or payment can make a major difference to the author and is not as easy as it used to be to achieve in many cases. I can solve some of these problems by personally advancing money to the author, but that shouldn't have to happen.

In the nineties, I suspected that one major publisher had instructed editors—in an effort to make them more helpful to the bottom line—that if a manuscript under contract when delivered needed substantial editorial work—no matter how important the author—they should dump it rather than spend all the time to work with the author to fix it. I was never able to substantiate this, but it happened enough times to make me believe it was true.

Another publisher, in the early years of the twenty-first century, instructed editors not to buy any book unless they were absolutely sure it could sell 20,000 copies or more, which of course eliminates one of the most interesting and exciting aspects of book publishing.

As the economy of the country and the publishing industry changed, a different kind of person was attracted to book publishing and the agency business.

I was representing writers because I liked good writing—everything from Charles Dickens (whom I didn't represent) and Howard Fast, author of *Spartacus* and dozens of other dramatic historical novels (whom I did represent), to the superb journalists Jimmy Breslin, the columnist who magnified the voice of the underdog; Frank Deford, generally regarded as the best sportswriter in the US, and a television and radio personality; Bill Nack, the leading turf writer in the late twentieth and early twenty-first centuries; and Jeff Greenfield, the fine writer and distinguished political commentator. And once in the agency business, I realized many of the writers were outliers, anti-establishment, and larger-than-life characters.

I never represented Ron Fimrite, the excellent *Sports Illustrated* writer, who died in 2010. In fact, I never met him, but in his obituary, the *New York Times* wrote, "he contributed to what many describe as the magazine's literary heyday when it featured reporters like Frank Deford, Dan Jenkins, and Bill Nack"—all of them my clients.

When I was getting ready to open the agency in the early fifties, I was advised by the superb magazine editor Ken Purdy, who had been my boss at *True*, that I was rather too young and inexperienced to attract writers: The top agents were all much older than I. Undaunted, I started my agency, and the rest you've just read in this book. Now, however, as I reach the stage when I am older than any active agent currently working or who was active in recent memory, I get the feeling that some editors think I might not know as much as the younger agents in the business. Times have changed, but many aspects remain the same. I did have a bestselling feature film and a book that sold 150,000 copies (despite being published twice before) at the age of ninety years.

As the world has changed around me, my goal as an agent has remained the same: to help the writer advance his or her career, rather than to increase my personal income. If I did the former successfully and chose my clients well, I assumed the latter—personal income—would follow, and it has.

The most rewarding aspect of being an agent has been the representation of authors whose books have changed our culture. Kerouac's *On the Road* influenced many young people of his generation and every generation since, as well as many older readers. His wild adventures and his words, which seemed to meander rather than stay within the lines, presaged the era of the beatniks, and now, more than sixty years after its initial publication, the book is still taught in high schools and colleges across the country. When writer, artist, and professor Ed Adler was assigning *On the Road* to his New York University college students in the last days of the twentieth century, he warned them that reading it might change their lives—and for many it did.

Ken Kesey's *One Flew Over the Cuckoo's Nest* was a defining force for the generation that came after Kerouac. His antics broke through barriers of public reticence and normality, ushering in the era of psychedelics and preparing the stage for the hippie movement. *The Invisible Government* by David Wise and Tom Ross was the first publication that disclosed the clandestine and often-sinister role of the Central Intelligence Agency in American foreign policy and opened up the intelligence community's activities to the press and the general public. I also represented Erica Jong, whose bestselling books tossed away the cloak of female sexual desire. And Bob McNamara's *In Retrospect* was an honest and frank inside account of his thinking and actions and those of the Johnson White House during the Vietnam War.

Photo by Carl Glassman

These were the days when publishing parties were very common. Elaine Koster (on the left), editor in chief of the New American Library, hosted, and Erica Jong, who had just become my client, was the honoree of the party. Philippa Brophy, then my secretary, is on the right. New American Library published *Fear of Flying* in paperback in a big way after Holt did the hardcover edition.

And probably the most significant of the books I helped launch was Judge John Sirica's *To Set the Record Straight*, his account of the Watergate trial, over which he presided, and President Richard Nixon's failed attempt to control the Watergate tapes. The trial was called the most important criminal case in US history. I quietly took great pride in my association with all these authors and their historically important books.

In my long career I have witnessed many new publishing ideas, from Harry Evans, former editor of the London *Sunday Times*, who created a team of top-notch British journalists to write quick high-profile topical nonfiction books, to the Instant Books of Oscar Dystel, then-president of Bantam Books. Oscar published *The Warren Report* and, among others, a book by my clients Senators Ted Kennedy and Mark Hatfield. It was called *Freeze! How You Can Help Prevent Nuclear War*. It started with a call to me from Kennedy's chief of staff, Bob Shrum. He told me to get a publisher who would have it on sale in a matter of weeks. I thought of Oscar Dystel immediately and made the deal. The book was written, edited, printed, and on newsstands throughout the US thirty days after I received Shrum's call.

The one innovation that has blown the industry apart and is destined to endure is, of course, the electronic book, which may have contributed to the shuttering of bookstores nationwide as readers have flocked to the Kindle, iPad, Nook, and other devices.

By 2012, I had sold electronic rights to more than 125 titles and, additionally, had granted publishers the rights to more than 110 titles. The time had come.

As the electronic-publishing world becomes more prominent, I have often been asked if I believe the book as we now know it—the physical book—will last, will be with us in the years to come. My answer is always "yes," but that is not the right question to ask. Readers are always interested in storytelling, and they have been for centuries, since the days when tales were carved on stone tablets or, later, when legends were scrawled on the inside walls of caves. Storytelling will be with us forever although the form through which it is transmitted to us may change. Electronic transmission has become more promising than any other new form. It is invading the territory of mass-market paperback books and even, to a certain extent, the area of hardcover books.

But hardcover books still have certain appealing aspects—their tactile qualities and their occasional role as a signifier of intellectual interest—and electronic books don't compete in those areas. If you see a person carrying a hard copy of a book, it says something about that person, which I think the book carrier is conscious of. There is no electronic equivalent. There may soon be variations of the present electronic form in all areas. But the hardcover book or its equivalent will remain.

As my father would have asked me, what have I learned from my long experience? What wisdom can I impart? Sometimes it's the unanticipated moments that clarify and offer a larger meaning.

That happened for me on a sunny day in late spring of 2009, when I was hailing a cab at Lafayette Street and Bleecker in Manhattan, half a block from my office, to take me uptown to a luncheon appointment. The first empty taxi saw me, stopped, and I hopped into the backseat. The cabbie was a Middle Eastern man in his late thirties or early forties, and unlike so many cab drivers these days, he was not talking on his cell phone for the duration of the trip. As we headed up Park Avenue South, which at midday is like traversing quicksand on rollerblades, we engaged in conversation. We were about up to Fortieth Street when, emboldened by our conversation, the driver said to me, "Excuse me, sir, but may I ask you a question? This may sound like naïve, but I'm relatively new to the city. How do you get rich in New York?"

Since the years I lived in Paris, I have personally dressed in a manner influenced by the men of that city, and that often gives a grander impression to people who meet me. Why else would he have thought I would have the answer?

"What you should do as early in life as you can is find an occupation or line of work in a field that really interests you. If you get involved and become committed and stay with it, you can live a long time and enjoy it, and have a rich life," I said.

He was talking about money and I about personal reward, but he seemed to understand.

After stepping out of the taxi, I realized I had given him a two-sentence synopsis of my life.

For seven decades, my work has sustained me emotionally and spiritually. It carried me through four divorces and periodic difficulties in business. It enabled me to work with and be at ease with men and women of talent, influence, and status.

I'm now, as I write this, ninety-two years old and still in business, five-plus days a week. I long ago came to the conclusion that if you stop learning, you might as well give up. I am still learning . . .

# Acknowledgments

Since the last book I wrote was only around 10,000 words long and about tennis, a sport I played for more than seventy years, I needed help to complete the 90,000-word book you just read.

The authors I wrote about here, if alive at the time, were extremely helpful with details I might have forgotten or never known. David Wise, Peter Gent, Bill Nack, Frank Deford, Ralph G. Martin, Jan and Mike Berenstain, David Markson, Fred Graham, Chris Wren, Jack Shepherd, Faye Kesey, and Ken Babbs (regarding Kesey) were of enormous help and, in each case, have read and okayed the final version of what I wrote about them.

Jack Sirica of *Newsday* checked the accuracy of what I wrote about his father, the late Judge John Sirica.

Sam Gelfman confirmed some of the details of the meeting in which Arthur Krim interviewed me to be LBJ's agent, and Krim later showed him my letter of rejection.

Blake Morrison, then of *USA Today* and later of Reuters, did research for me in areas I had no access to.

Susan Pogash solved the title problem early on when she suggested *Lord of Publishing*.

Alexandra Page Clark was my emotional support, and she furnished space in her spacious Manhattan apartment for me to work from 2006 until the end of this writing, and flew in from Florida to celebrate Open Road's acceptance of the manuscript. She was also the one who suggested I make arrangements with my client Carol Pogash (sister of Susan) to give me comments and suggestions on each chapter as I went along. I was having trouble writing about myself, and the third time Alexandra suggested Carol might help, I conceded, sent her the rough draft I had completed, and then three days later she sent me an eight-page, single-spaced letter of comments—general and specific—and I knew this was the answer for me. I would send her each chapter as I completed it, and then wait for her comments before revising. She stayed with me until the end.

My three secret and well-known editors, all of whom read the entire manuscript at my request, before I showed it to my agent or publisher, and all of whom were enthusiastic about it and made suggestions: Ralph Graves, former managing editor of *Life*, and the editor in chief of all Time-Life magazines; Al Silverman, former head of Book-of-the-Month Club and once-editor in chief of *Sport* magazine; Bob Loomis, recently retired from Random House and generally regarded—by me and others—as the very best book editor in US publishing. Thanks, thanks, thanks.

None of the above could have happened so smoothly if it were not for a very intelligent, well-organized, conscientious young woman from a farm in eastern Nebraska. Mary Krienke's memory, typing and writing skills, interest in good reading and good writing, and superior ability as a reader made the writing of the book, for me, a dramatically easier job. Some moments it was hard to tell whether she was my assistant, or I was hers.

And last, because they couldn't start their magic until all the persons above had finished theirs, the consistently efficient, talented, and professional people at Open Road Media, publisher of this book: Jane Friedman, Tina Pohlman, Nicole Passage, Stephanie Gorton, and the others of their remarkable staff.

—Sterling Lord

"Kerouac and Me" originally appeared in *Publishers Weekly* in 2007, and the chapter regarding Ken Kesey originally appeared in the *American Scholar*, the Phi Beta Kappa magazine, in 2011.

Excerpt from *In Retrospect* by Robert S. McNamara, copyright © 1995 by Robert S. McNamara. Used by permission of Crown Publishers, a division of Random House, Inc.

cover design by Mumtaz Mustafa

ISBN 978-1-4532-7071-4

Published in 2013 by Open Road Integrated Media
180 Varick Street
New York, NY 10014
www.openroadmedia.com

(ı)

OPEN ROAD

INTEGRATED MEDIA

**Open Road Integrated Media** is a digital publisher and multimedia content company. Open Road creates connections between authors and their audiences by marketing its ebooks through a new proprietary online platform, which uses premium video content and social media.

CPSIA information can be obtained at www.ICGtesting.com
Printed in the USA
BVOW010921030113

309372BV00006B/9/P